OY DIVISION emerged in the mid-seventies
t the start of a two-decades-long Manchester scene
hat was to become much mythologised. It was a city
still labouring in the wake of the ruins of war, and
something of this spirit made its way into the DNA of
he band. Over the course of two albums, a handful
of other seminal releases and some legendary gigs,
oy Division became the most successful and exciting
underground band of their generation. Then, on the
brink of a tour to America, Ian Curtis took his own life.

n THIS SEARING LIGHT, THE SUN AND
EVERYTHING ELSE, Jon Savage has assembled
three decades' worth of interviews with the principal
players in the Joy Division story: Bernard Sumner,
Peter Hook, Stephen Morris, Deborah Curtis, Peter
Saville, Tony Wilson, Paul Morley, Alan Hempsall,
Lesley Gilbert, Terry Mason, Annik Honoré and many
more. It is the story of how a band resurrected a city,
how they came together in circumstances that were
both accidental and extraordinary, and how young men
armed with electric guitars and good taste in literature
can galvanise a generation of fans, artists and musicians
with four chords and three-and-a-half minutes of
music. And it is the story of how illness and inner
demons can rob the world of a shamanic lead singer
and visionary lyricist.

THIS SEARING L
EVERYTHING ELS
Division in an intimate an   ted
by the lodestar of British n   iting, Jon Savage.

THIS SEARING LIGHT, THE SUN
AND
EVERYTHING ELSE

THIS SEARING LIGHT, THE SUN
AND
EVERYTHING ELSE

·JOY DIVISION·
THE ORAL HISTORY

JON SAVAGE

ff

FABER & FABER

First published in the UK in 2019
by Faber & Faber Ltd
Bloomsbury House
74–77 Great Russell Street
London WC1B 3DA

First published in the USA in 2019

Typeset by Faber & Faber Ltd
Printed in the UK by CPI Group (UK) Ltd, Croydon CRO 4YY

A CIP record for this book
is available from the British Library

ISBN 978–0–571–34537–3

FSC
www.fsc.org
MIX
Paper from
responsible sources
FSC® C020471

2 4 6 8 10 9 7 5 3 1

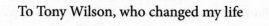

To Tony Wilson, who changed my life

Contents

DRAMATIS PERSONAE   IX

INTRODUCTION   XI

1 THE CITIES SPEAK   1

2 1966 – 76   11

3 JUNE 1976 – JUNE 1977   33

4 JULY 1977 – APRIL 1978   61

5 MAY – JUNE 1978   82

6 JUNE – DECEMBER 1978   102

7 OCTOBER 1978 – MAY 1979   127

8 JUNE – SEPTEMBER 1979   160

9 OCTOBER – NOVEMBER 1979   192

10 NOVEMBER 1979 – FEBRUARY 1980   216

11 FEBRUARY – MARCH 1980   254

12 APRIL – MAY 1980   275

13 MAY 1980   300

A Note on Sources   321

Acknowledgements   323

DRAMATIS PERSONAE

In order of appearance, as they were then:

Bernard Sumner: Joy Division
Peter Hook: Joy Division
Stephen Morris: Joy Division
Deborah Curtis: wife of Ian Curtis; witness
Tony Wilson: presenter, Granada Television; Factory co-founder
C. P. Lee: Alberto y Lost Trios Paranoias
Peter Saville: Factory co-founder and art director
Paul Morley: writer, *New Musical Express*
Liz Naylor: writer, 'No City Fun'
Terry Mason: Joy Division road manager
Iain Gray: witness
Ian Curtis: Joy Division
Mark Reeder: Factory Deutschland
Michael Butterworth: bookseller
Martin Hannett: producer and director, Factory Records
Pete Shelley: Buzzcocks
Alan Hempsall: Crispy Ambulance
Richard Boon: Buzzcocks manager
Kevin Cummins: photographer
Jeremy Kerr: A Certain Ratio
Bob Dickinson: writer, *New Manchester Review*
Richard Searling: Grapevine Records, Wigan Casino DJ

Rob Gretton: Joy Division manager; Factory co-founder
Lesley Gilbert: partner of Rob Gretton; witness
Richard Kirk: Cabaret Voltaire
Malcolm Whitehead: film-maker, Joy Division
Jon Wozencroft: witness
Lindsay Reade: wife of Tony Wilson; witness
Jill Furmanovsky: photographer
Dave Simpson: witness
Mary Harron: writer, *Melody Maker*
Annik Honoré: witness
Gillian Gilbert: partner of Stephen Morris; witness
Anton Corbijn: photographer
Daniel Meadows: photographer
Dylan Jones: witness

INTRODUCTION

Bernard Sumner: I felt that even though we were expecting this music to come out of thin air, we never, any of us, were interested in the money it might make us. We just wanted to make something that was beautiful to listen to and stirred our emotions. We weren't interested in a career, or any of that. We never planned one single day.

Peter Hook: Ian was the instigator. We used to call him the Spotter. Ian would be sat there, and he'd say, 'That sounds good, let's get some guitar to go with that.' You couldn't tell what sounded good, but he could, because he was just listening. That made it much quicker, writing songs. Someone was always listening. I can't explain it, it was pure luck. There's no rhyme or reason for it. We never honestly considered it, it just came out.

Stephen Morris: He was pretty private about what he wrote. I think he talked to Bernard a bit about some of the songs. He was totally different to how he appeared onstage. He was timid, until he'd had two or three Breakers, malt liquor. He'd liven up a bit. The first time I saw Ian being Ian onstage, I couldn't believe it. The transformation to this frantic windmill.

Deborah Curtis: He was so ambitious. He wanted to write a novel, he wanted to write songs. It all seemed to come very easily to him. With Joy Division it all just came together for him.

Tony Wilson: I still don't know where Joy Division came from.

1

THE CITIES SPEAK

Factory landscape, Greater Manchester, October 1977 (Jon Savage)

Tony Wilson: I think that psychogeography and the concept of the city was at the centre of situationism in the fifties in France, and the degraded city was part of Joy Division's life: Macclesfield boys, Salford boys, and there is the city – Manchester. The idea of the city is a theme that runs through this whole thing, Manchester being the archetypal modern city.

C. P. Lee: They used to say that what Manchester thinks today, London does tomorrow, and in the nineteenth century this was an amazing place for innovation. Salford, which isn't part of Manchester but sits side by side, had the first street lighting, the first trams. All these things came out of Manchester: municipal housing, the first public lending library – all of these great, fantastic innovations that we assume are twentieth century emerged in the nineteenth century.

But at the same time there is a tension inherent within all of this, and the tension evolves around the great unwashed, the working classes. They're there as a mob. Now some of the movers and shakers within Manchester want to work with them and want to make things better, want to move the city on, but there are other people who regard them as very, very dangerous, so you get these tensions.

So you've an area like Angel Meadows, so called because the dead were buried in such shallow ground that when it rained, it washed away the topsoil and the bones would stick out. Areas where policemen would only go round in twos. In the thirties my father was a policeman and went round there with another officer. It was three in the morning and people were sat outside, and my dad said, 'Why are they sat there?' And he said they stay there and get as drunk as possible for as long as possible, so that when they go to bed they sleep, despite the bed bugs.

You have a city which exists in great innovation, with wealth which has been generated by Cottonopolis, generated by the future, visions of the future. Things like the Ship Canal, which is fantastic. The sea is thirty miles away at Liverpool, but Manchester doesn't sit there and take it. It says, 'We'll bring t'sea to the city,' and they build the Ship Canal, and it comes here and it's fantastic.

There are docks in Salford. It becomes known as the Barbary Coast and it's full of dusky Lascars, it's full of Italianates, it's full of Mediterraneans and Spaniards who swan around with earrings and neck scarves, and it's fantastic. There are men with monkeys on their shoulders. The docks bring in everything to Manchester, and it becomes a fantastically opulent melting pot of different influences and different styles, but at the same time, underneath it is an underbelly of the working classes, who haven't exactly got a slice of the cake.

In the early years of the nineteenth century you have a massive political movement which starts developing in the north-west of England, and it's the Chartists and it's the free-traders, and what they basically want is what we have now, which is universal suffrage. They have a massive demonstration in 1819 at St Peter's Field in Manchester, and what do you do when people want the vote? You send in the cavalry, and the cavalry and the yeomanry went in and massacred the crowds that were there. Hundreds were injured, fifteen dead, probably more.

This was celebrated by the erection through public subscription of the Manchester Free Trade Hall, which becomes a gigantic epicentre of psychogeographical energy. Every major artist and musician of the twentieth century appeared in the Free Trade Hall. It was the site of political debate. When trade unions went on strike they had their meetings there, Louis Armstrong played there, Bob Dylan was booed and heckled in the Free Trade Hall in 1966, the Sex Pistols played there in 1976, and in 1996 the Dalai Lama did his last blessing to the people of Manchester in there.

It was built on a field drenched in the blood of the dead, and that's what makes Manchester unique, because you have this fantastic dichotomy between the haves and the have-nots, the rich and the poor, the thinkers and the non-thinkers, and it's a tension and it's an energy which has made it the vital and important place that it is today.

Tony Wilson: Two words were redolent of the northern cities of Britain, and in particular Manchester. One was the word 'slum' – I always hear Laurence Olivier in my ear for Granada, saying, 'You're a slum slug,' in one of those Pinter plays. Slums were dirty working-class housing. And the other word is 'unemployment'. Those are the two words – the 'S' word and the 'U' word – and then you add the word 'dirt'. It was a dirty, dirty old town, and I think we had to struggle to remember that this had been the historic centre of the modern world, that we invented the Industrial Revolution in this town; that even though we did, we also invented these conditions.

I've only recently got round to reading Elizabeth Gaskell and the novel *Mary Barton*, and essentially communism came about because Marx and Engels just looked at this utter shite that was the first industrial city.

The great triumph of Manchester in the mid-nineteenth century was that the first great industrial city had fallen apart after the American Civil War, and delightfully from a Mancunian point of view: that's because we sided with our non-business partners. Our business partners were the plantation owners, but every time that the South and Richmond tried to get recognition for the Confederacy, it was stopped by the Manchester workers rioting, and Westminster would pull back from recognising the South. That's why we have a Lincoln Square in Manchester.

Most people in Manchester don't know why we have a Lincoln Square, because no one can really read the inscription, but President Lincoln wrote a letter to the working people of Manchester, saying that in all our struggles to overcome this evil, one of the most significant forces helping us has been you, the people of Manchester. The one difference is that you have done it against your own best interests. Because far from finding ourselves with our business partners, the plantation owners, we felt we had more in common with the black slaves, which is probably very true.

Anyway, that left us fucked, and also by that point in time the major economic factor in business had become shipping, freightage. There's a wonderful statistic from around 1870: to get a tonne of coal from New York to Liverpool cost six and fourpence; to get the same tonne of coal from Liverpool to Manchester would then cost eight and sixpence, so basically, not having a port, we were fucked, and in true Mancunian spirit a bunch of Mancunians in some hotel one night said, 'Right, we're going to build the port of Manchester.'

So we went ahead and dug a canal from the bottom of the Mersey bay into Manchester, and it didn't work because all the modern factories were on the Mersey at the Liverpool end and there was no reason to come down the Ship Canal. But then someone said, 'Why don't we build somewhere that's specifically for modern factories?' And we then built the world's first industrial estate, which is Trafford Park, and that made the Ship Canal work. That's why my parents' shop was half a mile from the entrance to the port of Manchester in Salford.

Bernard Sumner: You were always looking for beauty because it was such an ugly place, whether again on a subconscious level. I mean, I don't think I saw a tree till I was about nine. I was surrounded by factories and nothing that was pretty, nothing. So it gave you an amazing yearning for things that were beautiful, because you were in a semi-sensory-deprivation situation because you were brought up in this brutal landscape, but then when you did see something or hear something that was beautiful, you would go, 'Ooh, new experience,' and really appreciate it.

I remember being on my scooter when I was a scooter boy and driving up on the moors, and not being able to believe all these open spaces. It gave me the freedom to move around, just going up on the moors in the middle of winter, taking the day off school, there was all snow everywhere, going up there and just looking and thinking, 'Amazingly beautiful.' And that has stuck with me till today.

The hills are the escape from it, from the horrible, industrial, dead landscape of Salford and most of Manchester; the sheer contrast between the moors and the industrial filth that surrounded us in the sixties. I remember someone telling me on the way home from school that Salford was considered the biggest slum in Europe, and I couldn't believe it, because it was where I lived. I read that living in Salford was the equivalent of smoking seventy cigarettes a day.

Tony Wilson: Salford and Manchester are virtually the same place. In a helicopter you'd have to come very low to make out the River Irwell that separates the two great cities, and yet there used to be this real conflict, in that typically, if people in America say, 'Oh, you come from Manchester?' people like me say, 'No, I don't, I come from Salford.' – 'The same thing.' – 'No, it's not.' Salford had its own sense of pride; it was a city eight hundred years before Manchester was a city. It felt like the working-class city on the edge of the urban centre of Manchester.

I think one of the strange things about the whole process, when you look at the regeneration of this great city region, which is now the way we call it, one of the moments comes in the mid-eighties, when suddenly people like me would go, 'I come from Manchester,' and that's when the word 'Manchester' came to represent the project, a project to rebuild this drastically cut-down, dirty, filthy, derelict estate that was Manchester and Salford.

Bernard Sumner: I was actually raised in Salford, in Lower Broughton, a place called Alfred Street, number 11, with my grandparents and my mother. It was actually good. I'm supposed to say, 'Oh God, it was awful, it was a grim, dreadful place. It was just factories everywhere.' We had a chemical factory at one end of our street and a family of local thugs at the other end, but it made life interesting.

There was a lot of funny characters living round there, and loads of pubs, right near the River Irwell, so there was a lot of midges in the summer, I remember. But you could walk everywhere. My primary school was about five minutes' walk away, but it didn't stop me being late every single day. I used to get in terrible trouble because I was late, and the teachers used to go, 'But you only live five minutes away, how is that possible?'

It was a good laugh really. Could be violent. I got chased by a gang with spears one day, that was quite frightening. I've been chased by a gang with sabres, seen women fighting in the street, people getting beaten up with iron bars, but I'd move back there any day. At least it's not guns. It was rough – I know it's a cliché – but there was a fantastic sense of community.

I guess what happened in the sixties was that someone at the council decided that the chemical factory and my street and my area wasn't very healthy, and something had to go, and unfortunately it was my neighbourhood that went. What then happened was my mother married when I was eleven, so we then moved out of my grandparents' house and moved just across the River Irwell to a place called Greengate.

It was a tower block, which I thought was fantastic. I thought, 'This is like moving to New York: it's got central heating, we've got a bath and we've got an airing cupboard for drying out all your towels.' So I just thought, 'This is it, it's like Buckingham Palace.' I loved the tower blocks. I loved the way Manchester was being remodelled. To me, they were changing it into New York, and that equalled excitement and the Future.

The first thing I did was sit in the airing cupboard and put the heating on full and pretend it was a sauna. I thought, 'Great, it's a sauna, it's a palace.' I was wrong about that. It was a horrible place to live, just because primarily you lost that community spirit that we had on the other side of the river. Everyone knew everyone; on a nice summer's day everyone would sit outside and talk to each other. You lost all that. It was like living in a prison for that reason. You had the home comforts, but it was an isolating experience.

Peter Hook: I was born in Ordsall, in Salford, and I was raised there for most of my life, apart from a brief three-year stint when I lived in Jamaica for some strange reason. Salford's special and Manchester isn't. I'm not proud of it, Salford has a very stubborn and very aggressive reputation, whereas Manchester's just Manchester. It's always been a struggle living in Salford. It's very, very poor, very downtrodden, very industrial.

It's interesting when Bernard says that *Unknown Pleasures* came from that, which I suppose it did. I don't think consciously Bernard and I were struggling to get out of it. I think we were quite happy with our lot, to be honest. But I suppose subconsciously it would have a big effect on you.

Stephen Morris: When I was growing up we used to come to Manchester and go back again. I remember the first time in

Manchester, seeing all these end-to-end terraced houses, and then the next time you went there was just a pile of rubble, then the next time you went there was all this building work. Then, by the time you were in your teens, it was this big concrete fortress, quite futuristic at the time. The College of Music was there, and Oxford Road was futuristic in the seventies. There were grim bits, but compared to Macclesfield it was the bright lights.

Peter Saville: The geography of Manchester is quite particular. The city seems to radiate outwards in bands. Hardly anybody lived in the centre of Manchester, and from that point of view it's unlike London or even Liverpool or more historic cities like Bristol. The residential areas of Manchester developed beyond the immediate city centre, and during the course of the nineteenth and certainly during the twentieth century the desirable residential areas moved further and further out.

It's a relatively modest-sized city, so you can live out on the edges of Greater Manchester but commute in and out of the city in twenty or forty-five minutes, depending on the time of day. I lived out in south Manchester, on the borders of Cheshire, in the stockbroker belt. And while I was at art college I had this daily journey into the centre of the city. I didn't really appreciate what it showed to me at the time, it was something that I just absorbed subconsciously.

I didn't really notice until I lived in central London and then realised the actually much more uniform social and geographic engagement when you live in the centre of a large city like London. Having been away from Manchester for a few years, I realised that that journey from the edges of the city in was taking me every day through a cross-section of the social profile of the UK. You witness many types of life and work and activity and ways of living in that half-hour journey in and out of Manchester: you see semi-rural farmland and you see suburbia, and you see tough inner-city areas where life is a lot more difficult and a demanding experience for people, and then you come into the business, professional, retail city centre.

I think it's actually quite a healthy experience. Things are not hidden from you, the spectrum of life is there. Where I grew up afforded me a certain kind of romantic vision of the city, of an industrial city – or at least by that stage a post-industrial city. I found the factories and the warehouses exciting. I wasn't having to eke out an existence among them. They were a sort of sculpture park for me.

Paul Morley: You didn't have to walk far out of the city centre for it to just fall apart and become nothing. It was bombed and had never really been repaired. You didn't really ever feel it would be built up and turned into anything. You felt that would be it for ever.

Liz Naylor: Nobody lived there, there was nothing there. It was a post-industrial city, it was empty. I loved walking round there. I can feel how it felt in 1978. I can walk down Tib Street, which is now the Northern Quarter, but to me it is for ever 1978. And also I can really picture the old Eighth Day in All Saints, and now it's very different from the small shop it was.

It was just a really amazing way of experiencing the city for me as a young woman. I was always on my own as well. It wasn't like I was truanting with a gang of kids; it was a very solitary experiencing of the city and I wasn't frightened of it. I was very much in love with its decay, because of course it completely matched my depression. I wasn't badly behaved; I was just enormously depressed and suicidal, so wandering around Manchester in the late seventies was absolutely perfect. It was the thing I wanted to do.

It was like the collision between pre-war Manchester and the post-war razing of all that and the building of new slums, so the two slums were existing side by side. It was like a bomb site, north Manchester, it was terrifying. I used to have to walk into town, so I'd walk up Oldham Road and Rochdale Road, which at that point were really grim places. It was full of abandoned buildings with no windows and bomb sites. The war was there again.

The city at that time was just overrun by the dispossessed, and I felt extremely dispossessed and disempowered. And it's the most at home I've ever felt living anywhere. Joy Division felt very close to me. They were my first band. I think they were a band that really appealed to outsiders, you know, and girls. I might not have felt like a girl but I was a girl and I was quite vulnerable, and they really connected with me. My thing about Joy Division is they're an ambient band almost: you don't see them function as a band, it's just the noise around where you are.

2

1966 – 76

All Saints, Manchester, October 1977 (Jon Savage)

Bernard Sumner: I was really into music. When I was sixteen my mother said, 'What do you want for Christmas?' I said, 'A guitar.' She bought this Gibson SG copy, and then when I got it I didn't know what to do with it because you've really got to play with other people. So I left it there for years gathering dust in the corner of the room, and it really bugged me, because I don't like wasting. I wanted to see what potential it had, so that's why I wanted to form a band. I liked music, I didn't want to waste the present, I wanted to see what I could do with it. It was in the corner of the room and it kept nagging at me, 'Use me, use me.'

C. P. Lee: Up until 1966 there were over two hundred beat clubs in the Manchester area, and it was a very happening city. Even after 1966 the amount of beat clubs that turned themselves into cabaret premises was massive, and Bernard Manning once said that it was a licence to print money to open a club in Manchester. It was definitely an epicentre: coach parties used to come from as far away as Nottingham because they knew that the night life was cheap, thrilling and fantastic.

In the sixties the city centre was in a sense given over to hedonism. There were lots and lots of empty factory spaces, lots and lots of empty mill spaces, so there were an increasing number of hotels that were cheap and available, there were direct road and rail routes which made it cheap and easy to access, and there was a willing segment of the population who were prepared to provide entertainment, and so music in Manchester has always been integral to the city's life.

From the nineteenth century onwards, you'd have hurdy-gurdy bands, street bands, every pub had music of one form or another. This is pre-jukebox, so live music was de rigueur in lots of places in Manchester. Then, in the sixties, the beat boom fed into the cabaret club, then into the disco boom. For live musicians, though, it got quite difficult by the end of the decade. There was one specific chief constable, a dour Scotsman called McKay, who decided to crush the beat clubs, and the closure of live-music venues meant that earning a living got more and more difficult.

Tony Wilson: Manchester had always been a club city, and we'd had a wonderful club in the sixties called the Twisted Wheel, where people would take purple hearts and speed and see Eric Clapton and the great blues people for the first time. So there was a history and a tradition of culture, but basically this was in defiance of the economic downturn.

C. P. Lee: The crackdown in the sixties on youth led to a dearth of live music. Put that hand in hand with the beginning of the rise in unemployment and a feeling that teenagers had been blanked out of all these opportunities. There was a greyness that we might associate with the eradication of red-brick terraced housing and its replacement by concrete gulags, a feeling of hopelessness that was matched by the aspirations of the time. You needed little more than a colour TV and a tight pair of shoes to have achieved success, but people wanted more than that.

Teenagers were being fed a dreadful diet of garbage within popular music. It had become a leviathan, a great bewildered beast that shrugged its shoulders and off dropped Genesis or off dropped the Electric Light Orchestra, groups that grew too big for their own boots, groups that had pantechnicons that delivered the carpets that they would put the drum kits on so they could play the stadiums. That was the disenfranchisement of the young. Kids want to be part of rock music: they don't just want to be observers, they want to be participants.

Bernard Sumner: I managed to pass my eleven-plus, went to Salford Grammar. I was sat in the back of the class for every lesson, because I wasn't really bright enough to be there, I don't think, not academically anyway. I noticed this other guy sat at the back of the class as well called Peter Hook, so we sort of wasted our time together there. I just couldn't see the point of anything they were teaching me. I just thought, 'Well, what's the point of logarithms, how can I use that in my life?'

The first thing that got me interested in music was spaghetti western music, Ennio Morricone. When I was sixteen I went to see *The Good, the Bad and the Ugly*. We didn't have a record player in our house, we just had a radio, and I wasn't really interested in music, but when I saw those images, the way it was filmed with the music, I found it incredibly powerful. It was a revelation.

I remember when Jimi Hendrix died, and I couldn't understand it, it just sounded like noise to me. I remember sitting next to this guy at school. 'Do you like Jimi Hendrix?' He went, 'Yeah.' So I said, 'Well, there's no tune in it, it just sounds like a load of fucking noise.' So he just turned round and said, 'I like it,' and wouldn't expand on it at all. That got me intrigued, so I went out and bought the record, played it about five times and then went, 'Ah, I get it now.'

There was a big culture of music at Salford Grammar School. It was a very exciting time for music. We used to go to a youth club called North Salford Youth Club, which was opposite Lower Broughton Baths, and they used to have two rooms there: the room down below, which was the disco where you played Tamla Motown and Stax and ska; and then upstairs they used to have another room where they used to play the Stones and Led Zeppelin and Free – and Jimi Hendrix.

So there was a real culture of music there, and it was very important to us. Apart from that I don't think we had any identity. The school I went to was really big, and I guess living in Salford you were a bit of a nobody, you didn't have much chance of progressing in the world. You were thought of as factory fodder. Music gave you a sense of identity, and it was a grim place and the winters were very long, so you'd tend to become internalised.

It's not like living in LA, where you can go roller-skating down the beach every day. It was like, 'Oh shit, this is really boring. It's foggy outside, it's raining – what are we going to do? I know, let's go up so-and-so's house. Let's take a load of records and talk about music.' And that developed into, 'Let's start making music.'

Terry Mason: I've known Hooky since I was eight. Bernard I didn't get to know till I was at secondary school, and I met him in the third year because the school had been in two parts: there was Salford Technical High School and Salford Grammar School. Hooky and Bernard went to the grammar school, I went to the Technical High School, and despite making these choices on where we wanted to go, by the third year they threw us all together.

We got more friendly when we were sixteen and we all had scooters. A scooter gang isn't the right sort of terminology, but at that point there was maybe ten of us in our year at school who all had scooters, and we'd meet up with each other after school. Although Hooky and Barney lived in different areas to where I was, they would come fairly close to where I lived. We were just oiks with scooters. There was no parkas, there was no Union Jacks and RAF roundels.

Peter Hook: I met Bernard in Salford Grammar School when we were eleven. We became friends very quickly. Bernard and I weren't part of the bullied and we weren't really part of the bullying, we were in the middle of it all, so it was quite a privileged existence as a child. I started going out about sixteen. The first club we went to was Salford Rugby Club, at the Willows on a Monday, and then progressed to a Tuesday, and a lot of our school friends went there.

It was easier for me to go than for Bernard because I could walk home. He lived in Broughton, so it became my hangout. It was all just seventies rock – Slade, Deep Purple, Hendrix, Groundhogs, Status Quo. We went to see Led Zeppelin at the Hard Rock in Stretford, Deep Purple at the Free Trade Hall, and things like that. Heavy rock. That lasted until we started going out, and we started to get into pop cos we started hearing it. We didn't hear any disco until we went to clubs.

Terry Mason: Well, it was a grammar school, but it didn't do any of us that much good to be honest. Between the three of us we had five O-levels. It wasn't the time when everyone was expected to go to university. There was maybe 120, 150 people in our year, and the number of people going to university from that school would maybe be four.

You were expected just to go off and get some sort of a job. There were no great designs, it wasn't well known for producing doctors. I think it produced quite a number of lathe operators and machinists, but there was no academic excellence about the school. The factory for Salford was Ward & Goldstone, an electrical factory, but it didn't have any appeal for any of us.

Bernard Sumner: I had a pretty wild time at school. I felt that being young was a time to enjoy myself, so I didn't knuckle down at my studies. What I wanted to do was go out chasing after girls, go shoplifting in Manchester, and do the incredibly stupid things that schoolboys do. When I left school I wanted to go to art college. I had a small portfolio of artwork that I'd done at school and went to Bolton College of Art, and I got accepted.

So I went home and told my mother, and she said, 'No.' I said, 'What? I want to go to art college.' She said, 'I can't afford it.' She got an uncle to talk to me, which was very strange because he was a real distant uncle who I didn't really like, because he lived in a big house in Worsley, probably. He said, 'Look, you can't go to art college, you've got to go out and get a job, support yourself.' So I had to shelve that idea and I got a job.

My mother knew a local councillor, and he pulled a few strings and I got a job at Salford Town Hall in the Treasury department, sending out rates demands. Not something you dream of when you're at school. I mean, my worst thing was mathematics at school. I was absolutely appalling at it. They used to give me ten thousand rate demands a day, and I used to have to put them in envelopes, line them up on me hand, and they had a roller that you wet and you'd just put them down, seal all the envelopes, put them in a franking machine and send them off.

Real life came to me as a horrible shock. 'Jesus, wake up, this is what real life is. Unless you wriggle out of this, like a snake, life is gonna be dismal.' I decided I wanted to do something in art. I'd been to see the careers advisor at school, and he said, 'Well, I've got you two jobs: one is a hairdresser' – and I said, 'That's nothing to do with art' – 'and the other is, you know photographs?' I said, 'Yeah.' He said, 'You know the white borders on the photographs?' I said, 'Yeah.' He said, 'Your job is cutting the white borders off so there's no borders on them.' I was like, 'No way, bollocks to that.'

So what I did was I got the Yellow Pages down, and me and my then girlfriend wrote to every advertising agency in Manchester and said, 'Can you give us a job?' I actually got two, and I actually did both jobs at the same time. Don't know how I managed that. One was in an advertising agency doing newspaper work, and the other was in a place that was doing TV commercials and graphics, but both really as messenger boy, sort of tea boy. I did one one week and I did the other the next.

The one that did TV commercials was really good because everyone was pretty cool there. It was in the media, and everyone was really into music. We had a record player where we worked and people used to bring music in, but because they were much older than me they fucking hated my records, they used to whinge on about them. They used to listen to stuff like Van Morrison, and I used to bring in Led Zeppelin: 'Turn it down, turn it down, it's just a bloody noise.' But they were a really good crowd and I enjoyed my time working with those people.

Terry Mason: Basically, after Bowie's first entrance the music world seemed to go very quiet. There was a lot of long-hair music about that had no interest. A lot of people were looking for the next thing. We were all a little bit too young to get the benefit of Bowie. We weren't in a position where we could have been in a band. Mind you, there weren't many people that were capable of doing it anyway at that point.

After that, we went to all sorts of things: Eddie and the Hot Rods, AC/DC – that was a year before the Pistols. We'd seen the Kursaal Flyers, Dr Feelgood . . . We kept going to gigs on the periphery, not the mainstream. Deep Purple would still come through town every two years, but we wouldn't go to stuff like that. We would go to bands that were on at the university, which in itself was a challenge for us because in them days it was students' union card holders only.

Bernard Sumner: I had a scooter and Hooky had a scooter, and we used to go to pop festivals. We used to go to watch groups play at the Free Trade Hall and the university campuses in Manchester, but nine times out of ten they wouldn't let us in because we were scooter boys or skinheads and they didn't like the look of us. We were actually from the town but we didn't have an SU card – I think that was the excuse.

We used to go and see groups, whoever played. Lou Reed at the Free Trade Hall, there was a massive riot at the end of it. The riot was great. But he was great as well, because he was just completely fucked all the time. He didn't do an encore, so some kid – and I saw him because he was quite close to me, he was like a Rod Stewart clone – had a bottle of beer and he threw it, and it was a lucky shot, it went straight through the skin of the bass drum, and then everyone started punching him and it all went up.

We used to go to a club called Pips on Fennel Street, near the back of Manchester Cathedral, and it had different rooms: it had a northern soul room, a room that played David Bowie and Roxy Music, and another room that played soul music. If you went in pairs and had an older mate, you could just about get in there when you were seventeen.

Iain Gray: Mostly Bowie fans would go there. Pips was the one place where I used to see Barney and Hooky. I never saw Ian Curtis there, but I saw those two – you'd get to recognise people. That was the one club you could go to in Manchester. Other than that it was a very grim place, still very Victorian buildings, a lot of bomb sites, decayed buildings, nothing new.

Stephen Morris: Macclesfield used to have a place where bands played called the El Rio, and there was a long standing story of you'd always meet someone in a pub: 'I remember when the Beatles' van broke down in Chestergate, and me and him over there we pushed the van.' But that was dead and gone, so there was no live entertainment, nowhere for groups to play.

I remember there was a café that we used to frequent, Aggie's Caff. It had a jukebox, which was the main thing, and you'd go in and put a record on, and Aggie would come out and say, 'What the bloody hell have you done that for?' Then she'd unplug the machine. And that was Macclesfield to a T really. There wasn't a lot to do apart from drink underage – I was a staunch advocate for it at the time.

If you wanted any form of musical entertainment, you had to come to the big city, which meant getting on a train and getting off at Piccadilly station and going to see bands at the Free Trade Hall in Manchester. You'd made it then, when you could get off the train and you've got your two and sixpence to see Rod Stewart and the Faces, the Kinks, Bowie. Sometimes I'd just go and buy a ticket, and I ended up seeing Gentle Giant that way. That was what you had to do, you had to get out of Macclesfield because there was absolutely nothing, nothing at all.

I attended the King's School in Macclesfield, which Ian Curtis attended. He was a year or two above me. He was a prefect and I was a bad boy – yes, solvent abuse and cough medicine was quite a favourite of mine. When they discovered that the contents of my desk were not the reference books that should have been there but empty bottles of cough medicine and dry-cleaning fluid, I was shown the door post-haste, and Ian, who I must have seen but probably in a fuddled haze failed to recognise, had the job of going round inspecting the other pupils' pupils for signs of dilation, which was apparently the telltale sign of a cough-linctus fiend.

Ian Curtis (interviewed by Paul Rambali, *NME*, 11 August 1979): Everyone's living in their own little world. When I was about fifteen or sixteen at school I used to talk with me mates and we'd say: right. As soon as we leave we'll be down in London, doing something nobody else is doing. Then I used to work in a factory, and I was really happy because I could daydream all day. All I had to do was push this wagon with cotton things in it up and down. But I didn't have to think. I could think about the weekend, imagine what I was going to spend me money on, which LP I was going to buy. You can live in your own little world.

Deborah Curtis: Ian's parents used to live in Hurdsfield, which is towards the hills. Very neat, very clean, and why they asked for a transfer to those flats [at Victoria Park, Macclesfield], I'll never understand. It was ridiculous. His dad's a bit of a dark horse. He was a policeman. I don't think Ian communicated with his parents very well. They don't like to believe anything bad about him.

Stephen Morris: Ian used to work in Rare Records. It does shame me to mention it, but I can remember going in there and seeing if they had the Jobriath record – Jobriath, who was Morrissey's hero – and thinking, 'Oh, I'll come back and get that next week, nobody's going to buy that.' And then the week after, it had gone. I can only assume that Morrissey got that. Certainly, a lot of people in the punk movement hung about in the basement of Rare Records, and Ian was one of them, but I can't remember ever buying a record off him.

Mark Reeder: I met Ian when he was working at Rare Records. They were very elitist in that shop: all beards and long hair, tweed jackets, and they all thought they were something else. I always thought if I ever worked in a record shop, I'd never want to be like them. Totally unhelpful, ignorant of the people coming into the shop. If you made a mistake in the pronunciation of a track, you'd be ridiculed to death.

Ian wasn't like that. He was always trying to sell me reggae records. This was about 1974. Ian was totally into reggae music. Dub. He wasn't there very long – about a year – and he was the youngest one in the shop, and he was the only one you could talk to. We talked about all kinds of stuff, and usually the topics would cross over from music to history and the war. He was fascinated by the war.

I started working at Virgin Records when I was about fourteen. Just part-time initially, and I got paid in records. They needed someone to stock up the records on weekends, while they were all in the shop. Just helping out, and then I ended up working there. It was back in the seventies. Real hippie days: lots of long hair and 'taches and stuff.

There was this seating arrangement, because people kept stealing headphones. They'd either break or they'd be nicked. So somebody came up with this idea where they'd have this seating arrangement at the back, covered in this vomit-green bri-nylon carpet covering, and the loudspeakers were put in the headrests. And people would sit, obviously, next to each other, and it was impossible to hear anything. You could move these speakers, put them next to your ears in the hope that you could not hear the person next to you.

But Virgin was a place where people just liked to hang out really. That's why it stank of incense in there as well, to disguise the smell of marijuana. It was more rock music than disco then. In 1973, they'd just had this massive success with *Tubular Bells*, and then came Tangerine Dream, and they were the kind of records that put Virgin on the map and made the Virgin shop in Manchester special. All the other record shops were a bit elitist.

I was captivated by the idea of electronic music. I remember in 1968 when you had to have a stereo. We'd seen some bloke offering them in the paper, so one Saturday afternoon we went round to this bloke's house to look at this stereo. It was this massive thing stuck in the middle of the room, like a cabinet, a sideboard with loudspeakers at each end and a drinks bit in the middle, and to demonstrate this stereo he put on *Switched on Bach* by Walter Carlos, and I was like, 'What is that?'

Before that, my only exposure to electronic music had been *Doctor Who*. And 'Telstar'. Then, for years and years, I didn't hear anything synthetic at all, until I came to this bloke's house and he put on *Switched on Bach*. Which was like the Brandenburg Concerto played on a synthesizer. I'd been exposed to classical music cos I played violin at school, but this was something completely different, and it was in stereo. From that moment I was captivated by the idea of electronic music.

In The Court of the Crimson King came out when I was about ten, and I was just overawed. It was avant-garde, ambient, and I'd sit in total silence, listening to this record. Looking at the cover, absorbing it all. And that was my background to working in Virgin. When they started releasing the early Tangerine Dream records, German music didn't sound like British music at all. And the weirder it was, the more fascinated I was. The first Kraftwerk albums were like jazz rock, with flutes and stuff, totally unlistenable to for all my mates.

I knew Tony Wilson from very early on. He'd come in at weekends, just before closing time. I was the person designated to unpack the boxes in the morning and then write up all the records and put them into stock. So I knew every single record that was coming into the shop, even more than the people who actually worked there. I'd have to tell them what had come in – they had no idea. They'd just look at the list, and they had no idea if things that they'd ordered had actually come in or not.

Tony would ask me to put a record aside for him so he could have a listen, then I could put it back in stock on the Monday if he didn't want it. He'd come in, and it would be all, 'Darling!' – and that's how I got to know him. I got to know Rob Gretton because he used to come into the shop all the time and just hang around. It's what I would do as well – go into record shops and just hang around there all day, talking about records and about music.

Ian would come into Virgin when he started working in Manchester and just hang around, complaining about things. He said, 'You can smell the drugs in Virgin.' I told him that's why we burn incense to disguise it, but he thought that was the smell of the drugs. He was always joking, very funny, playing tricks and stuff.

Paul Morley: We had head shops like Eight Miles High, the Manchester Free Press and the Mole Express, and the lefty end of things. That was your great salvation at the time – music and the lefty press and the bookshops where alternative culture seemed to be thriving. Down in London obviously there was Compendium, and we had weird little versions of that where you might find some sanity and discover things. Everything was not easily available; you had to search it out and find it.

I worked in this bookshop in Stockport, and the shop sold all the great Pelican blue books, which were my education. I didn't get educated at school, I got educated in this bookshop, and they had a science-fiction section – Harlan Ellison's *Dangerous Visions*, all the J. G. Ballard novels – they would have underground magazines, and weird folk singers from the backwoods of Derbyshire would come in to get their weekly fix of odd alternative culture.

But we made money in the bookshop out of the soft porn and the Mills & Boon, so you had a strange thing where old ladies would totter in every month to get their ten Mills & Boon, and men would come in to get their soft porn, which we had to order off a van that came in every week. Then I would be selling second-hand records. I would go into Manchester, buy bootlegs for £2, bring them back to my bookshop and sell them for £2.50.

You'd get the people coming in to buy war books, all those Sven Hassels. Of course, if you were going to open that kind of independent bookshop in the north-west at that period, you would have lefty tendencies, so you'd be pushing that, but to make your money you would have to sell *Whitehouse* and *Mayfair*, and the dreadful thing is you could bring them back to exchange, so these grubby copies of this soft porn would come back glistening with some suspect substance.

But what was interesting were the creatures that would come in to check out the weird combination of books, which sounds fairly standard now but at the time was unformed and raw: Ballard and Philip K. Dick and Burroughs. William Burroughs was definitely part of it. They were prophets of something that we were about to enter, this commercial entertainment landscape that would become where we are now sat, but at the time it was very odd, and it was a beautiful attachment to your love for weird music. There was no doubt that it was connected. There didn't seem to be any difference between reading Ballard and Dick and Burroughs and listening to Faust and Velvet Underground and Iggy and the Stooges: you were constantly curious to find out strange things that might explain your situation, even though it didn't directly have anything to do with where you were.

And there were characters. There was a guy that used to come into the bookshop called Paul, and he did the first fanzine I'd ever come across. It was called *Penetration* and it was basically obsessed with Hawkwind. He used to come in and he always used to wear all black. He had the whitest skin I'd ever seen, and his girlfriend would always wear white lace, and they used to float in bringing ten copies of *Penetration* every so often. In fact, that's where I first wrote. I wrote a piece about Lenny Bruce for *Penetration*, which Paul pasted up in the wrong order, incidentally. I think it's influenced my writing ever since, because I quite liked it being in the wrong order.

But there were lots of characters like that floating around and, obviously, Ian Curtis. I get the sense wherever he was at the same time – '74, '75 – he was coming across similar sorts of routes, similar source material out of which he could piece together his vision.

Stephen Morris: I'd get the train and go in to Savoy Books – before it was Savoy Books it was called The House on the Borderlands – and we used to have a right laugh at the old blokes looking at the porn. There was science fiction, weird books and over in a corner there'd be naked ladies, and surprisingly enough the science fiction had little appeal for the vast majority of the clientele, who were going over to the naked-lady corner. I'd just be trying to negotiate some sort of discount on a large, expensive book: 'Yeah, have you got Michael Moorcock's new book?'

Ian had *The Atrocity Exhibition* by Ballard, *Naked Lunch*, William Burroughs, and also a collection of Jim Morrison's poems. I seem to remember that you could go to W. H. Smith's and they had a lot of Burroughs and a lot of Ballard, and it was just mixed in with the rest of the stuff.

Michael Butterworth: Bookchain was opened in 1977. It was alternative and youth-culture stuff, both second-hand and new. I must clarify, though, that this was the most famous of our shops and the one everyone remembers, but it is not the shop Ian Curtis first came to. There were two Savoy shops before this one, and David Britton's most vivid memories of Ian are of him coming into the first shop.

All three shops were modelled on two London bookshops of the period: Bram Stokes's shop in Berwick Street, Soho, called Dark They Were, and Golden Eyed – which sold comics, sci-fi, drug-related stuff, posters, etc. – and a chain called Popular Books. David Britton used to visit a branch of the latter in Camden Town when he was living in London in the late sixties. They sold everything from *Private Eye*, girlie books, pin-up stuff and *Penthouse* to film stills, posters and any sort of media ephemera.

These two bookshops inspired David (with his then partner, Charles Partington) to open a bookshop on Port Street, off Newton Street, in Manchester centre. The shop they opened was called The House on the Borderland (after the William Hope Hodgson novel), and they had all this kind of stuff in the window. There was a strong emphasis on alternative culture and American imports. The window looked very exotic, and this is what probably attracted Ian and Steve Morris inside, once they had followed the yellow-brick-road poster trail leading to the shop. The attitude radiating from the shop was, 'Fuck everybody in authority,' and that's what they responded to. The shop played loud rock'n'roll over the speakers, which sounded out into the street years before other shops were doing the same kind of thing. And I mean loud.

They were disparate, alienated young men attracted to like-minded souls. They wanted something offbeat and off the beaten track, and the shop supplied this. They probably saw the shop as being a beacon in the rather bleak Manchester of the early seventies. Ian was interested in counter-culture and science fiction. David remembers them being enthusiasts about Michael Moorcock, whose hard-edged fantasy writing and lifestyle were a great influence, very rock'n'roll.

Ian bought second-hand copies of *New Worlds*, the great sixties literary magazine edited by Moorcock, which was doing something very different, promoting Burroughs and Ballard, and it's possible Ian picked up his interest in these writers from these magazines. In exchange for their help in the shop they were allowed to take whatever books took their fancy. They came in every couple of weeks, sometimes more often. Steve was the most frequent. This close contact came to an end gradually, as Ian and Steve's interest in a band was getting more serious.

Stephen Morris: Once I started going out, my first concert was Hawkwind and Status Quo. I was into psychedelic music really. Apart from Hawkwind, the first two groups that I got into were Frank Zappa and the Mothers of Invention, and the week after that it was the Velvet Underground, and that was it. I liked collecting groups and I remember I liked Alice Cooper until everybody else started liking Alice Cooper, then I decided I didn't really like Alice Cooper that much. That's a bit pretentious really, but that's the way it was.

After that glam happened. Actually, after saying that Macclesfield was a cultural desert, once a year there was a discotheque – there were two discotheques, one at the rugby club, where you could go and dance to the Faces and Jeff Beck and get in a fight, or you could go to Boddington Civic, which was later on, where there was a big glam rock following and you had the Sweet and Bowie and Roxy Music, and so we went from psychedelic to glam rock – again, till everybody started liking it.

I discovered Krautrock about that time, and Can – I was into *Tago Mago*. I should say we were forming a band, me and this other guy from school – Mac, he was called. We were going to form this avant-garde jazz combo called the Sunshine Valley Dance Band. Everyone thinks it was just going to be like a dance band, and Hooky thinks it was jazz, but no, we were going to be avant-garde, and people would book us on the strength of the name and we would shock them with our appalling performances.

It never got off the ground, but through Mac's elder brother I got into Can and then, after Can, Amon Düül and Neu!. I was into the punk rock before punk rock, which was the MC5 and the first Stooges album, which I bought from Kendals in Manchester. Anything that wasn't disco. I later came to regret that opinion, but at the time disco was shit, and so it was anything that was a little bit long-haired but not like the boys in the year above me, who would wear RAF greatcoats and walk about with copies of *Disraeli Gears* or *The Best of Cream*. I wasn't too mad on anything bluesy; it was just anything a bit unusual that was not Eric Clapton.

Paul Morley: You were looking round to see if there was anybody like you. There was nobody like me at school. Eventually we all found each other at a particular show, but for two or three years before that happened we didn't really know where each other was. If you went to a Pink Floyd or David Bowie concert at the Free Trade Hall, you didn't really find anybody else. They were probably there somewhere, but you didn't find them because there was a bigger disguise going on.

At that point – '74, '75 – music fundamentally came to Manchester. We used to think of the local bands as not being right. Even bands that were local, like 10cc or Sad Café, didn't seem to be Manchester. They seemed to be more LA, they were already in Las Vegas. There were a couple of kind of strange heavy metal clubs in Manchester where local bands would play, but you wouldn't take them seriously at all because they just seemed like bands you'd see at school. There was just no way that that music would ever come from Manchester.

C. P. Lee: One of the most wonderful things that happened in Manchester in the early seventies was the fightback against the lack of opportunities for professional musicians. There was the formation of a workers' cooperative called Music Force, and it came about after a meeting that was called by Victor Brox, a Manchester blues player, Tosh Ryan and Bruce Mitchell. The idea was to set up a workers' cooperative. Premises were opened on Oxford Road in Manchester, where groups could rent equipment, hire vans, have their posters designed.

More importantly, there was a guy called Martin Hannett, and Martin was part of the Music Force cooperative. He was a do-everything guy. He used to write for the Music Force newspaper, which was called *Hot Flash*. He also had a great interest in sound mixing and he used to design sound systems, so he would be forever buying new kinds of equipment, new speakers. But at the back of his mind, because he was a musician as well, was the idea that he wanted to produce groups. In 1975, he'd been working with Belt and Braces, who were a radical theatre group.

Martin Hannett: I was running that office. Anyone who was any kind of musician used to come up there eventually, cos they'd need to rent a PA. It was supposed to be a musicians' cooperative. The Band on the Wall started when Steve Morris came back from a lifetime working on the *QE2* and bought the place. I used to go to the Band on the Wall in the sixties, every Friday. There was a band there called the New Religion, who had a foot-operated light show. I think they eventually turned into Stack Waddy. They were good, fast and indifferent to musical values.

Belt and Braces was my second production. First one was a soundtrack for a cartoon some guys at the poly did: *All Kinds of Heroes*. Steve Hopkins came along and said, 'I've got to do this – help!' He wrote out all the dots, and I looked after the way it sounded. I was playing bass with Spiderman King, who could have been Elvis Costello if he wasn't so stupid. Just pre-punk, the biggest thing was Sad Café. There were no labels then, but lots of venues. I was booking the poly, the university, UMIST, The Squat, a little place in Chester, Eric's – I had a little circuit.

Tosh Ryan had always been around. Music Force was where we first worked together – I used to organise his poster business as a way of paying the phone bill. The poster bandits used to rocket around the country at all hours of the day and night, for weeks at a time. They were like the weavers, they used to light their joints with ten-pound notes, the poster men.

Bruce Mitchell came into the office with a good idea once. He said he'd been talking to Tosh: we should get into fly-posting cos there's loads of money in it – 10p a poster. We approached the record companies, we just steamed straight into them, and told them they had to do this particular kind of marketing because the bands like to arrive in a town and see their posters all over the place. It made sense.

Tony Wilson: I had a TV show because Granada, strangely, had always wanted to rival *Top of the Pops*. They didn't like the fact that the BBC had this programme which dominated youth culture and they didn't, so they were always jealous of *Top of the Pops*. In order to get myself on-screen in a studio, I'd taken over Granada's local arts show, called *What's On*, in late '74, early '75. It became a cult show, it was quite cool, and someone on the sixth floor said, 'Why don't we make this into our *Top of the Pops*?'

So they gave me a pilot in the autumn of '75, took one look at it and thought, 'Oh my God, that's not going to rival *Top of the Pops*, but we'll let him do it.' Late-night isn't the word: it was at half eleven on Granada and I think it went out at one o'clock in the morning in London, after Melvyn Bragg talking about the meaning of life for an hour from twelve till one, which with all respects to Melvyn wasn't the best intro to my programme.

At that point – this was November '75 – we devised our programme as a comedy programme. We thought the music wasn't worthy of our real care, which history proves us to be completely correct. And in fact the only music of any value in the autumn of '75 was the new cowboy music coming out of Austin, and I was pretty much in love with Guy Clark and Willie Nelson.

Then in the Christmas of '75 a dear friend of mine called Dennis Browne rang me to say, 'There's this new album you've got to buy, Tony, it's just come out this week.' I went out and bought this wonderful Mapplethorpe black-and-white photograph of a New York poetess, inside which was a piece of plastic called *Horses*, and wow, wow, what is this?

In mid-January I received a battered New York Dolls album cover in a brown package without any vinyl inside it and a covering letter from a Stretford schoolboy called Steven Morrissey, saying, 'Mr Wilson, can you make sure we have more bands like this?' I had no idea who the New York Dolls were, I certainly had no idea who Mr Morrissey was, and certainly no idea even who Malcolm McLaren was at that point in my life.

And then the third thing was a cassette that came through in February from Howard Trafford, saying, 'Mr Wilson, you've got a music show. Here are three tracks by this new group we're bringing to Manchester in early June. I think you're going to love them.' And that, of course, was the Sex Pistols.

Pete Shelley: I'd met Howard at the beginning of 1975. I was doing electronics at Bolton Institute of Technology, and I was living at home in Leigh, which is about eight miles from Bolton and about thirteen miles from Manchester. I used to have various bands. We used to put on our own gigs. It set us in good stead for later on. Then, as the year went on, I got more and more disillusioned with doing electronics. I couldn't see myself being an electronics wizard.

I dropped out from college, and the next year I started doing this part-time course. It was round about that time that I saw the advert on the college noticeboard about this guy, Howard Trafford, who wanted to find out whether or not anybody wanted to do a version of 'Sister Ray' by the Velvet Underground. I'd actually got a copy of 'Sister Ray' and I knew how the chords went, so I thought, 'Well, this is the kind of music that I like.' I wasn't doing anything with my own band, so I thought, 'I'll give them a ring,' and that's how I met up with Howard.

A bit later, I was going down to London for a meeting of the part-time students' national committee. It was a Thursday, and the *NME* came out on Thursdays, and Howard and I met in the coffee bar, and he had a copy of the *NME*. He remembers me flicking through it and pointing out there was this review for this band who'd played at the Marquee called Sex Pistols, and it said that they did a Stooges song. So I pointed it out to Howard, and there was a little bit at the end that said, 'We're not into music, we're into chaos,' which Howard particularly liked.

And it so happens that that weekend he was asked by a person who lived in the house he was living in if he could pick up the car from being serviced, and was told that he could have the car over the weekend – 'Just pay for petrol if you need to use it.' So Howard knew I had to go down to London that weekend and he had a car, so the plan was concocted: we could then go into London and try and see if we could find a gig of this band called Sex Pistols.

We arrived at about four o'clock in the morning at Richard Boon's house in Reading, and in the morning we thought, 'Right, let's see if we can find out where this band's playing.' We thought, 'Well, the best way to do it is to buy a copy of *Time Out*,' and we looked through it and there was no mention of any band called Sex Pistols. Someone suggested that we phone the *NME*, so we phoned them and they had no idea where the Sex Pistols were playing, but they did know that their manager was a guy called Malcolm McLaren who had a clothes shop in the King's Road.

So we started walking down King's Road. By the time we arrived there it was almost closing time for the shop. There was this guy with red hair, and we walked in and he said, 'Oh, we're closing.' And we said, 'We're looking for Malcolm McLaren.' And he said, 'I'm Malcolm McLaren, what do you want?' – he was eyeing us a bit suspiciously. We said we'd read the review and wanted to know if the band were playing. Anyway, they were playing two shows that weekend, so on that night, the Friday night, and Saturday night we saw two Sex Pistols shows.

During the conversation, Malcolm was saying how he wanted to get outside of London and do some gigs, and Howard used to compile the pub-rock column for the *New Manchester Review*, which was like a Manchester version of *Time Out*, and so he was in contact with all the people who put on pub-rock gigs. He suggested to Malcolm, 'Well, maybe I could phone up and ask the people who put on the gigs whether they're interested in doing something.'

We went back to Manchester knowing that we had a new band who were doing music which was the kind of thing we were thinking of doing. So we tried to put on this gig. Anyway, we asked at the college, and they weren't interested in the Sex Pistols playing.

Howard's leads dwindled away to nothing, but because I'd been doing gigs myself and actually hiring halls and putting on things, I suggested, 'Well, why don't we try that?'

C. P. Lee: Then, more importantly, Music Force began to promote gigs. They opened venues that had been closed for nearly a decade. It's where Howard Devoto went for advice on how to put the Sex Pistols on in Manchester, and they said, 'The Lesser Free Trade Hall, this is where you go.'

Pete Shelley: So Howard found that the Lesser Free Trade Hall was available for £32, and although £32 was a lot of money, it wasn't too much. We reasoned that if we sold tickets at £1 each, it wouldn't be too long before we could get thirty-two people to come and see the band, and we also thought it would be a great opportunity for us to play. So Howard spoke to Malcolm about this, and he said, 'Yeah, it's a good idea, let's go for it.'

Tony Wilson: So we started our series as a comedy series, with Clive James doing a comedy routine, and with bands like Be-Bop Deluxe and Eddie and the Hot Rods and other nice crap, and then right in the middle of recording the series I sat there in the Lesser Free Trade Hall and saw the future. I always say that moment when I saw the Pistols in '76 at that first gig in Manchester, what it does is it reminds you why Robert Johnson sold his soul, and it reminds you that it was a good deal.

3

JUNE 1976 – JUNE 1977

Derelict 1930s estate, off Collyhurst Street, Manchester, October 1977 (Jon Savage)

Peter Hook: I went to work at the town hall. Because I didn't feel I was cut out for it, I had to have myriad distractions while I was working, and basically it was reading. I used to read all the music papers from cover to cover, and I became one of the kids waiting for them to come in on a Wednesday morning. What happened with the Sex Pistols was that somehow the whole thing leapt out, because it was unusual after reading about heavy-metal bands for so long.

It was unusual and it was a different culture. It was yobbish, which obviously appealed to me, being a yob. I cottoned on quickly to it. I remember going on holiday to Devon, three, four of us, in my Mark 10 Jag 420G, and we slept in the car for three weeks. We'd wake up in the morning and walk out somewhere looking for breakfast and trying to find somewhere where we could have a wash.

I spotted a *Melody Maker* and I bought it just to kill the time, and on the front page was the Sex Pistols, and it was the shot of Johnny Rotten fighting with the audience. I thought, 'That looks interesting,' so I showed it to the lads. When I came back to work, I was going through the little adverts and the classified in the *Evening News*, just scanning them for anything of interest: 'The Sex Pistols, 50p, Lesser Free Trade Hall'.

I phoned Bernard and Terry and said we should go, which we did, and I've still got the ticket – 50p. I thought it was shite, it was just like a car crash, it was like . . . oh my God, I'd never seen anything like it in me life. I'd been to see most groups – Deep Purple, Led Zeppelin, loads and loads of bands – and I'd never seen anything as chaotic or as exciting and as rebellious as that. It was how I felt: you just wanted to trash everything. It sounded awful, and for some insane reason you had the blinding realisation that you could do it.

Pete Shelley: I think there were about forty-two, forty-three people. I'm not quite sure whether that's counting me and Howard, or even the Sex Pistols. I was taking the tickets and the money in the box office, and so a succession of people would come up. Me and Howard really didn't know anybody in Manchester. It wasn't like we were part of a Manchester music scene, and we didn't have many friends who lived there – it was just a big city to us. All these people who were walking through the door, it was a completely new experience for us seeing them, and for them seeing us as well.

Because of the nature of the gig and because there weren't all that many people there, it was a thing where people afterwards were more likely to go over and have a chat with that person – 'How are you? Because I remember seeing you at this' – just to break the ice. So it got people actually networking in a way which was impossible with the way that the music scene was, because there really wasn't anywhere for people who were interested in music which wasn't of the Yes variety or the pop of the day.

Bernard Sumner: We eventually ended up at the famous Sex Pistols gig at the Free Trade Hall. It wasn't that the Sex Pistols were musically brilliant and I thought, 'Oooh, I really want to be like them.' It was the fact that they were not musically brilliant and could just about play together and it was a right racket. I thought they destroyed the myth of being a pop star, or of a musician being some kind of god that you had to worship. In fact, a friend who was with me said, 'Jesus, you could play guitar as good as that.'

Previous to that, in the seventies music was all based on virtuosity, Rick Wakeman playing a thousand-notes-a-second solo. A lot of that prog-rock and West Coast of America stuff was a bit soft and soppy: you were supposed to bow down. They were kind of gods, musicians: 'Oh, he can play it so well, it's amazing' – almost a jazz mentality. When they came on, the Sex Pistols trashed all that. It was like, you don't need all the crap, all you need is three chords, right? Learn three chords, write a song, form a group, that's it.

And that's what we did, me and Hooky. I bought *How to Play the Guitar*, he bought *How to Play the Bass*. We went to my grandmother's parlour, which was just across the Irwell. I remember we didn't have any amps. She had an old gramophone from the forties, and I took the needle out of it and wired two jack sockets on it. It sounded good, plugged into the gramophone – we didn't have any money, that's all we could do – and then we just started writing stuff together.

Peter Hook: So we formed a band that night. It's easy – 'Let's form a group' – it's all the rest that's difficult. Bernard had a guitar that his mother had bought him. I can't remember what position Terry took because he had the dubious honour of fulfilling every position with Joy Division, from singer right through to manager to lighting guy, roadie, guitarist, drummer. I went to Mazel's on Piccadilly and walked in. 'I want a bass guitar like that.' And they only had one: an SG copy for £35. Me mam lent me the money, had to pay her back. That was it then. Then we were a group.

Terry Mason: I dragged them there. At that point Hooky and Barney weren't reading the music press, they weren't listening to Peel. They'd settled down, they both had regular girlfriends and were quite happy with their world. All of a sudden the blinkers were off. Before that there was never any shortcut to being in a band; you really did have to put the hours in. Punk was more attitude than number of chords, and if you play it fast enough and loud enough, no one knows anyway.

Bernard Sumner: Terry was just one of the gang really. He's quite eccentric. I think, to give him his due, it was him that may have turned us on to the Sex Pistols, cos he'd read in the *NME* about them fighting onstage. He said, 'Let's go and see this group. They beat each other up onstage, could be a laugh.'

Iain Gray: Bowie and the Velvets spoke to me, as did Iggy Pop, but it didn't inspire you to do anything. That was the cathartic moment, going to see the Sex Pistols. I can remember it like yesterday. I thought, 'Christ, I could do this.' I do remember Ian being there. Hooky was there, and Barney. They reckon Mick Hucknall was there, but I didn't see anybody that looked like Charlie Drake. I was in a band from Wythenshawe at the time called Ram. We went away thinking, 'We could do this.' We didn't, and I left that group.

Alan Hempsall: It was an early-starting gig: it was billed as 7.30 start. It was the Free Trade Hall, so they had no option – it wasn't a club venue. We'd gone into Virgin Records that day, and Virgin had printed off these photocopies of the very early *NME* piece about the fight at the Nashville gig: they described Johnny Rotten as a dementoid and the group as beating up their audience. We had to go and see that for fifty pence, and then we just went along that evening, found out what time they were on, and although I was fifteen, I was home for about half past ten, eleven o'clock.

They were supported by a hippie band called Solstice, who did a cover of 'Nantucket Sleighride' by Mountain, so this was lulling us into a false sense of security. Then the Sex Pistols came on, and they immediately looked weirder than the bands of the day. I had a friend of mine sat next to me who, obviously with the name Sex Pistols, just blurted out, 'Oooh, you're not very sexy, are you?' And Johnny Rotten immediately fixed him with the glare and said, 'Why? Do you want some sex?' My friend responded, 'Oh, didn't expect that for fifty pence.'

They then launched into this set, and they were very proficient musicians. Don't be fooled: the Sex Pistols could play, and play very well. There were probably about forty-five people in the audience, fifty tops: a mixture of Bowie clones and hippies. I identified with it straight away. We were up at the front when the encore came on and we chatted to John Rotten for a couple of minutes when he was getting ready to gear the band up for one last hurrah.

Paul Morley: I just think of them as being weird music lovers that were crawling out of their bedroom where they spent all their time, because they would be social retards, and the only way they could ever get on with anybody else is to be in a pop group. So we found ourselves, and the funny thing about Manchester, of course, is there wasn't really any centre to Manchester, everybody came from somewhere else: Stockport, Chorley, Oldham, Macclesfield, Salford. Everybody came into what was almost like a little village.

I do remember going into the first one, when there really wasn't very many people there at all, and it was an incredible kick. Suddenly it was with us, it was in our surroundings, and everybody looked really odd. It's only now when you see the footage that of course they weren't: they looked quite ordinary, their haircuts weren't mad, they were just slightly shorter, certainly in that first one. We were just semi-hippies still and hadn't quite yet made the move into a new world.

When the Sex Pistols turned up, that's when it went a little bit bizarre. They were queasy in the way they looked: not so much the four members of the group but their entourage, hanging off the side of the stage, this weird combination of bondage get-up dwarves out of some weird thirties horror movie, *Freaks*. It just seemed so exotic.

The Pistols themselves didn't look that far removed from the Faces, to be honest. The way they played was different: it was more theatrical and it was more knowing about its theatrical nature, and that seemed somehow far removed from rock. It was something else. It did seem more surreal and more weird, even though the patterns they were playing and the chords they were playing and the songs they were playing were quite traditional. It was trad, but it had this weird avant-garde edge.

I went on my own. It was like going to see Faust or Beefheart, because you could hear rumours coming up from the south that made you think, 'It's like the Stooges, something really strange is going to happen here.' Strange unformed half-boys all gathering in this peculiar little theatre, but you wouldn't talk to anybody, you'd kind of look and get a sense. The support were Solstice, the hippie rock group from Bolton that played covers of Mountain, so you didn't quite get the sense it was a revolution. That happened six weeks later.

Tony Wilson: The first night, I didn't know what the fuck was going on, until they played 'Stepping Stone'. As soon as they did that, it was clear that they were deeply and remarkably and fabulously exciting. I went back to Granada and said, 'We must put them on the show,' and the researcher, Malcolm Clark, was asked to check them out with me, and we went to Walthamstow Assembly Hall, and that again was a completely non-attended gig: maybe eighty people, of whom forty were in a large, single-line semicircle, just out of gobbing range.

Peter Hook: After the Sex Pistols, there were so few people there that you just talked to them, because if something awful had happened, you'd talk to the person next to you, wouldn't you? If you watched a crash, you'd say, 'Oh Jesus, that was bad, wasn't it?' Normally you wouldn't ever talk to people, but because you'd witnessed something awful, which was the Sex Pistols, you'd talk to the people round you. You just got caught up in the excitement of it.

Richard Boon: Manchester seemed like a vacant set. Some kind of neutron bomb had been dropped, leaving derelict buildings. There was no centre of gravity; it was the cradle of capitalism and was rapidly becoming its grave. There was no scene, there were no bands. I did music listings for a fortnightly called *New Manchester Review*, a very slim volume. To fill the music listings you had to include places like Stalybridge, for heaven's sake. There was really nothing happening.

After the beat boom, when Manchester had a fantastic number of bands, as did Liverpool, a couple of things happened. The Beatles moved to London, shut down Liverpool effectively. The police shut down Manchester. There were hardly any places to go: there were the universities, the polytechnics, but they were not necessarily open to people who weren't students back then, and there was the debris left over from prog rock doing the Free Trade Hall.

It was like some disaster area, and there was hardly anywhere to go. There was no one to see. Something had happened. All the bands that would have filled medium-sized halls had gone, and then you just had really crap imitations and the few pubs that put anything on. It was a challenge because Manchester had a spirit which was in the place and in the people, but hadn't been energised.

Pete Shelley: By the time we did the second show on 20 July, we had managed to get a bass player and a drummer. In fact, I was introduced in the first Sex Pistols gig by Malcolm McLaren to this guy who'd just been standing outside waiting quite innocently to meet somebody else, and Malcolm said, 'Are you a bass player?' And this guy said, 'Yes.' And Malcolm said, 'Well, they're inside,' and he came up to the box-office window and said, 'Here's your new bass player,' and there was Steve Diggle looking quite bemused.

So I said, 'Well, Howard's upstairs, so you'd better see him,' and by the time we found out that he was there to meet somebody else, we said, 'Well, the Sex Pistols are just about to play, why not watch it?' This is the kind of ballpark of what we were trying to do, and the next day he came for a rehearsal. Then we had a sixteen-year-old drummer called John Maher, who'd only had a drum kit for about four or five weeks before he joined the band. Me and Howard had been writing songs since late 1975, so we had a few songs that we could play and so we managed to do a set.

Slaughter and the Dogs had bent Malcolm's ear and said how they were a huge band and that they thought they would pull more people than Buzzcocks ever would. And so there were more people, but they tended to be either people who were Slaughter and the Dogs fans or other people who'd been at the first gig or who'd heard about it through their mates and actually thought, 'Oh, let's go and see it.' And by then the news of the Sex Pistols was growing, so they started to attract more people.

We went on and did our half an hour, and then finished the set by leaping off into the audience, because we thought that was a different way of doing it, since it was all about trying new things and messing with the preconceived perceptions of what a gig should be. In rehearsal I was playing the sawn-in-half Starway guitar, but it wasn't actually sawn in half: one day in a rehearsal I was doing wild guitar, the chaotic random bit, and took the guitar off and threw it on the floor, and it split, and we thought, 'Well, we could easily do another one of those.' So I bought an Audition Guitar from Woolworths which was about £20. I thought, 'Well, I can destroy that, it's worth doing it,' and so me and Howard decided that at the end of the last number we would both attack the guitar, and he was there ripping off the strings, so it was a chaotic end. We smashed the guitar and it all looked good.

The Sex Pistols had actually got a lot better. I think it was that night the first time I heard them play 'Anarchy in the UK', and from the moment it started it was like a frisson of hearing something which is really a landmark. It was like opening the door and a herd of elephants rushing in.

Paul Morley: When I went a few weeks later, somehow I had turned into a hooligan and I almost got thrown out for throwing peanuts at Wayne Barrett, the lead singer with Slaughter and the Dogs – who already seemed fake. Six weeks after the Pistols arrived, we were making decisions about what was and wasn't fake and bandwagon-jumpers, and Slaughter and the Dogs seemed like bandwagon-jumpers. Whereas Buzzcocks, who were bottom of the bill, they already seemed to be the real thing, and they were local.

Pete Shelley: After the second one there were people who you'd seen from the first one, and of course they'd come up and start talking to you, and there were lots of people interested in starting bands or starting a fanzine. Because punk was very inclusive, it didn't say, 'We can do it, you can't, and that's the way it's going to stay,' which is what most forms of art were about. With punk, it was saying, 'Well, have a go, you know, why don't you do it?'

Because it was also something which had so much humour in it as well. People had more fun thinking about all the outrageous things that you could do than was perhaps ever attempted in the end. Most of the time you were just thinking about all the crazy things that you could get up to, if you allowed yourself this freedom.

Peter Hook: We went to see the second Sex Pistols gig, when the Buzzcocks supported them, and we were in it then, we were actually in the scene. I mean, we got pushed out a bit later because we were just too working class for Howard Devoto and all that lot. I think they thought we were yobs, which we were. I think it was just cos of our friends and the way we'd been brought up and the place we'd been brought up in. They'd all sort of escaped to art college, and so they had this freedom, if you like, whereas we hadn't found that freedom yet.

But it was a great scene. It was like going to the Ranch in the early days with the punks, there were so few of them. Me and Barney didn't know them, but they all seemed to know each other, yet we still used to go.

Pete Shelley: We heard that there was this bar called the Ranch Bar, which was a small bar in the basement of this building in Dale Street, and it was next door to Foo Foo's Palace. Foo Foo was a female impersonator, very much along the lines of Lily Savage, a very acerbic wit. It was basically an underage drinking den: if you looked over fifteen, you could get in and get a drink. The drink of choice was Carlsberg Special Brew, a bottle through a straw, so that's what everybody used to drink, and you used to have about two or three of those and it made for a good night.

In August of '76, after we played at the Lesser Free Trade Hall with the Sex Pistols, we went to see Foo Foo at his massage parlour and sauna. He came in for this meeting and he was wearing a towel around his shoulder, so it was very seventies gangster type, more like a scene out of *The Sweeney* than anything else me and Howard were used to. We said, 'We'd like to put on a gig at your club.' He listened to us and thought we were a bit weird, but said yes, it was a good idea.

So in August we had a gig which was a draw for all the people who normally go to the Ranch Bar and all the new people who'd started hearing about the Buzzcocks and wanted to hear more about the music. I think we got through a few songs before Foo Foo came in in full regalia and said, 'Better stop that infernal racket.'

The Ranch was full of Bowie and Roxy kids who probably couldn't get into Pips. I think it was just Fridays and Saturdays at the beginning, but then Sundays became a good night as well, and people used to meet up. I remember the first time I saw the people who then became the Fall. They were in there and I'd seen them in the bar. It was always a small place and it held about, I don't know

... if we had fifty people it would probably feel very crowded and so it was just about the right size. It was the kind of place which didn't mind the way you looked.

A lot of bars when you tried to get in, if you were anything remotely unconventional they'd have a fit and they wouldn't let you through the door. Because it was a drag act we were under – a club in a basement – there was a more liberal door policy, and therefore people could come in and listen to music which nobody else would entertain.

Tony Wilson: Then we put the Sex Pistols on *So It Goes*. We decided to make a virtue out of our last show, with three unsigned bands. They behaved pretty badly. They had a row with Clive James. They had drunk quite a bit. They were meant to do three and a half minutes – they agreed that and rehearsed it – and there was five minutes left, and they just kept playing for seven minutes and kicked their equipment apart. Two days later, the director edited it down to three and a half minutes. The next day, I was in trouble at Granada, there was bad feeling.

Pete Shelley: On the surface you wouldn't think that a jean-shirt-clad TV presenter would be the one who would take an interest in what was going on in punk. He was the man on the telly, he presented the local news programme on Granada. It seemed really strange him turning up at punk gigs, but in a way it was exciting because they had somebody who had at least a passing association with what goes on on the TV, and then when he started doing his programme *So It Goes* he invited the Sex Pistols up to play.

Paul Morley: There was a strange gap after the Sex Pistols gig in July. There was a pause as everybody got themselves together. I think Buzzcocks did a gig on Deansgate with Chelsea. I remember having a drink with Billy Idol and Tony James and Steve Diggle. It all seemed very exciting because suddenly I, the lonely weirdo, was speaking to Howard Devoto on the phone. I asked him his five favourite words, and he said, 'I like eating ice cream,' because it turned out he was eating ice cream at that moment.

At these places the guys looked exactly like me in a way – especially after I'd had my hair cut short – and they were wearing their granddad's clothes, as if this was our fashion statement because it was all we could muster. But there was this gap while people like Warsaw wandered off to work out how to respond, and suddenly they could, they could respond because they'd seen it, certainly with Buzzcocks as well: a bunch of local people, about their age, liked the same kind of weird music they did and had formed this band that were really good.

Richard Boon: I met Ian Curtis on 10 November 1976 at the Electric Circus, where Buzzcocks, in the tradition of doing it for yourself, had hired the Electric Circus and brought Chelsea up from London. I was doing the door. Ian came in talking about having a rubbish time at the Mont-de-Marsan Festival, which had been hyped in the summer as being some legendary French thing which he found ultimately disappointing, but he was obviously coming from the same kind of idiot enthusiasm that we were sharing.

Pete Shelley: The Electric Circus started off as a heavy-metal place. It was a fair-sized hall, it had a proper stage at one end. It was painted black, it was very dark, there was a bar at the top, on one side and towards the back. As punk started, they realised that they could get more people in by catering to the punk audience, and over time they got to be the primary venue for anything to do with punk or new wave in Manchester. It was in a place called Collyhurst, which was a run-down council estate. It took you about forty minutes to walk from Manchester city centre, but you needed a bit of an escort, at least a few of you to frighten away the dogs which were prowling.

Richard Boon: There were very few venues. There was the Electric Circus, which was like at the end of a bomb site up Oldham

Street. Then there was Pips, which was a disco, post-Bowie, post-confusion, post-glam, post-apocalypse. There was the Band on the Wall, which was trad jazz mainly but had its off nights; you could get it cheap if you could persuade the booker to let you have it on a Monday. You had to find these places that were left over, such as the Holdsworth Hall, which once upon a time had classical music and stuff; it was idle.

Peter Hook: The first Sex Pistols gig at the Electric Circus was really good. We had all the publicity for the 'Anarchy' tour. I had a poster of that for ages, and then my mum threw it out. Then there was Bill Grundy, and then they played it again because they had all the shows cancelled. That was just a riot, there was so many football fans and lunatics waiting in the queue outside, throwing bottles from the top of the flats. It was really heavy, a horrible night.

Richard Boon: The move towards recording *Spiral Scratch* came out of the fact that we'd had to put on our own gigs, but when the 'Anarchy' tour swept through, there was a real sense that the original punk impetus was dying out. It was becoming clichéd and tabloid, which we really didn't feel part of, but we wanted to document what we'd been doing. A record had to be made just for that moment, and with a little basic research and some fund-raising from friends and Peter's family we pressed a thousand copies, not really knowing what we were going to do with them.

John Webster, who was managing the Virgin Records store at 9 Lever Street, said he'd take a couple of hundred and phoned some of his regional colleagues: obviously Virgin had a central buying policy, they would have taken more persuasion. Geoff Travis at Rough Trade rang up, and suddenly we'd contributed to the unleashing of potential that we saw as the core of the early punk movement. We kept re-pressing until we reached about sixteen thousand.

Martin Hannett: I went to the second Free Trade Hall gig, in July. I thought the Pistols were very competent, tight rhythm section.

I enjoyed it. I thought the Buzzcocks were great too. I was involved with Slaughter and the Dogs, who I thought were barking up the wrong tree, cos they were doing glam stuff. I was really looking forward to the first Pistols record, and when I got it home I thought, 'Oh dear, 180 overdubbed rhythm guitars. It isn't the end of the universe as we know it, it's just another record.'

The first punk record I produced was the Buzzcocks' *Spiral Scratch*. Richard came in and said, 'We've done some gigs, we've been in the papers, what do we do next?' So I said, 'You make a record next.' Mr McNeish, Pete's dad, came up with the money, and we went into Indigo, sixteen-track. Again I was trying to do things, and the engineer was turning them off when I looked round. 'You don't put that kind of echo on a snare drum!' It sounds like it was done on a four-track.

It was never finished. I would have loved to have whipped it away and remixed it, but the engineer erased the master because he thought it was such rubbish. It sounds like a monitor mix these days. The guitars were really trebly. I just compressed them and added more treble. I loved guitars. That's what they sounded like, it's a document.

Paul Morley: At the end of '76, I guess the Electric Circus had the Pistols come twice, with the Clash, and Buzzcocks played with that, so our local boys were actually right in there, which was incredibly exciting. I don't think I really came across Warsaw until they were Warsaw, and then the strange clubs that started to open up in peculiar cellars and strip clubs and odd parts of the university, they would just be there and they'd be playing, and that's when I would start to notice them.

Iain Gray: I was trying to put another group together and I advertised in the old Virgin Records for a high-energy singer. Somebody had written on it: 'Must be able to withstand 10,000 volts' – Manchester wit. Ian Curtis was the only one who answered. We met up in a pub in Sale called the Vine Inn. Ian turns up with a

Ian Curtis and Iain Gray at the Electric Circus, Collyhurst, Manchester, late 1976
(Courtesy of Linder Sterling)

jacket with 'HATE' on the back, which was a pretty dangerous
thing to do in 1976 Manchester. He walks into the pub in a donkey
jacket. I'd already been getting daggers from the locals, like, 'What
the hell's this? What's he?'

Then Ian walked in, and he was a really sweet, nice person. You'd
look at him and you'd think, 'Christ, quite a frightening-looking
guy': leather pants, this combat jacket with 'HATE' on the back – a
bit like De Niro in *Taxi Driver*, because I know he was really into
that film. I remember talking that night, and he seemed a lot older
and more mature. I was eighteen at the time, and Ian would have
been about twenty, twenty-one. And I was going like, 'The punk
ideals, Ian. Being married – boring.' And he went, 'Oh, I'm married,' and he shows me his wedding ring.

I'd go round to where Ian and Debbie lived with his gran,
Stamford Street, in Hulme. Because it was around Christmas, his

gran had put all these balloons up, two round ones and a long one in the middle, so it was phallic shapes all round. His gran was totally naive to it, but Ian was laughing. He was a really nice, sweet guy – flowers for Debbie, chocolate. I've never met a couple before or since who were so happy. I envied it.

Ian was the picture-postcard happy guy. He didn't have kids then, but it was roses round the door. He'd be there smoking his Marlboros, he smoked a lot. He drank Colt 45, but he didn't really drink much. He'd sit with Debbie, and they'd watch telly together at his gran's and have their tea together on their knees. He was a young civil servant; he was upper working class, which existed then. It's pre-Thatcher, but he was a Tory: he had aspirations, he was motivated. He had more of a fire in his belly that he was going to do it.

Debbie would stay in. We'd always go to the Electric Circus or early Buzzcocks. We saw the Damned in 1976 at the Electric Circus, and both nights of the 'Anarchy' tour. We just swapped records at the time. He was well into Iggy Pop, like I was, but he also had a deep love of heavy dub, Jamaican reggae: Lee Perry stuff, U-Roy, I-Roy. He was just like me: he talked about going to that Sex Pistols gig and thinking, 'I've got to do this.' He'd gone to the French punk festival with Debbie. I'd never even realised that was on at the time.

We decided we'd go to London about two weeks after we'd met, just to see what was happening there. We did the King's Road: we went into Sex, Malcolm McLaren's shop, and we went into the Roebuck. Didn't see any of the Pistols, although we were hoping we'd bump into them. We bumped into Gene October, who played with Chelsea, and we were going to get a gig for them in Manchester and we'd play with them.

I remember we spoke to Don Letts. He stood out with his dread-locks, he looked pretty cool at the time. He says, 'I know a band' – which must have been the Clash – 'but they're not ready yet,' because we said we could get gigs for London bands in Manchester, i.e. we could support them. Ian just went up to Don Letts and went, 'Do you know any bands in London? Because you look dead cool.'

Ian would initiate conversation with people; I was a lot shyer. Ian was shy but could do the chat as well.

We hadn't actually rehearsed at this point. There would be sheds in people's gardens and pubs. I was the guitarist and Ian was the singer, with his little briefcase full of lots and lots and lots of lyrics. After about a month I started looking at them, and I remember 'Day of the Lords', 'Leaders of Men' and a rough draft of 'Candidate'. At the time – it was 1976 – he was really into these punk Nazi fiction books by Sven Hassel about German tank commanders, and his favourite one was *Wheels of Terror*. 'Leaders of Men' just made me laugh because it was straight out of the pages of Sven Hassel. You wouldn't admit to reading that by 1979/80, we were all very left wing by then.

We were rehearsing, me on the guitar, and Ian did the very first dead-fly dance. I'm playing this crap song, really going for it, and Ian's giving it this – like his head going back and eyes going up in his head. As far I knew then, he wasn't suffering from epilepsy; if he did, he kept it very well hidden. I never saw any indication, but he would have these kind of void moments, and when he did that there was something of the night about him. It was very strange because he was such a sweet, warm, generous person.

Around that time we met a bass player. We were just jamming at the time. We played in the Great Western pub in Moss Side, where we rehearsed. I'd phoned up and said, 'Could we play there?' We set up in this pub, and all these locals in a really rough working-class pub are really staring at us. Ian's there with his jacket and screaming away, and they chucked us out – 'Get out!' Ian hadn't really developed his singing voice. You never heard him singing, he was more kind of grunting, hunched over his lyrics.

We got through Christmas time. We could never get a drummer. We toyed with a few names, and he picked Warsaw, because that Bowie album was a big influential record with Ian at the time. We had great ideals but it never really took off, so around about February it just fizzled out.

Bernard Sumner: We got so far down the line, and we thought, 'Right, we need a drummer now and a singer, obviously.' We didn't know where we were going to rehearse, couldn't put a drummer in my gran's. And we advertised for a drummer and singer in Virgin Records, which was then in Piccadilly, so that was the punk thing. We were going out to loads of punk gigs by then: there was the Ranch and there was a bit of a scene forming, you'd get to know people on that scene.

Unfortunately, I was the only one with a telephone, so I put my number down, and we ended up with a load of cranks. Me and Terry went in his Vauxhall Viva over to Didsbury, met this guy who was a total hippie, and we were punks, right? We went for a pint with this guy before, and we went to his flat. I remember him sitting down, and he didn't have chairs, he had a cushion, sat cross-legged, and we had to sit on cushions opposite him. We were glancing at each other, going, 'What's going on here? What's going on?'

Terry Mason: Barney already had a guitar and an amp, so he was pretty much set up. Hooky went off and bought a bass guitar, which was a shame because I'd thought about that one myself because I'm taller – bass guitars go for the taller man. Then I was going to get a guitar, and it was just a matter of getting the money together to do that. In the end, it was once we'd met up with Ian and he decided that he was going to be in the band that I actually got a guitar.

We tried within our circles for a singer, one of them being a guy called Danny Lee, who was a friend of Hooky's. Danny was fantastic, he looked more like Billy Idol than Billy Idol ever has done – he had the lip going, the sneer – and he thought he was ready to sing, but never did. So then we decided that we'd have to talk to other people, which was new to us – we were quite quiet and shy people – so we put up the advert in Virgin and we had a few responses.

One in particular was this complete madman. He looked like Mick Hucknall is now. He had long red hair in a ponytail, he had a bit of a Catweazle growing on his chin and he appeared to be wearing a cushion cover as a jumper, as if he'd just cut holes in it to put his arms and his head through. We're there in this madman's flat, and he then pulls out a three-string balalaika and starts strumming it and singing to us, and we basically ran out of there. After that we thought, 'God, this is going to be difficult,' but fortunately Ian responded to the ad.

Bernard Sumner: I first met Ian at a gig at the Electric Circus. It might have been the 'Anarchy' tour, it might have been the Clash. Ian was with another lad called Iain, and they both had donkey jackets, and Ian had 'HATE' written on the back of his. I remember liking him. He seemed pretty nice, but we didn't talk to him that much. I just remembered him. About a month later, when we decided to try and find a singer, we put an advertisement in Virgin Records in Manchester, which was the way that all groups formed during the punk era.

We put an advertisement in there, and I got loads of headcases ringing me up. Complete maniacs. Then Ian rang up, and I said, 'Weren't you the one I met at that gig, that Clash gig? With the other Iain?' – 'That's me,' he said. So I said, 'Right, okay, you can be the singer then.' We didn't even audition him. We asked what sort of music he liked, and it was the same kind of music as us, so we gave him the job. Ian and Debbie were staying at Ian's mother's at that stage, near Ayres Road in Moss Side, and me and Hooky went over to see him in person and gave him the job then.

Peter Hook: The first time I met Ian was on the stairs in the Electric Circus, cos there was a kid in front, he had 'HATE' on his back in white letters in masking tape, and he used to peel the masking tape off when he went to work in the morning. Let's hope he remembered. He turned round, and it was Ian, and we went, 'Oh, bloody hell, you've got "HATE" on your back.' It was a bit extreme, we thought, but I suppose we were all at it. We'd seen him at all the gigs and it was that childish enthusiasm.

He formed his band with his mate, but there was some unwritten law about how punk bands didn't have two guitarists, you just had to have one. He had a singer and a guitarist, we had a guitarist and a bass player, so he couldn't join. We had to wait until it changed, and that meant that Bernard and I were trying to get a singer. I can't remember how wholeheartedly we were doing it, but everything seems to click into place once Ian joined us and we became the three of us. We met him at a gig, and Ian had lost his guitarist, and then we joined up and he became our singer.

Terry Mason: I think we were just glad at that point that he wasn't wearing a cushion cover. We vaguely knew him, more on the grunting terms that young men do. The punk situation in Manchester was you basically knew most of the people who went to every gig by sight, you didn't know what their name was, but you'd [*mumbles*]. He seemed okay. We got talking to him, he came out with his books of lyrics, and he had a lot of index cards with songs or bits of songs on, and he actually owned equipment: a couple of column speakers and a tiny amp.

It was obvious that this guy was serious. He was prepared for it and he didn't scare us, so we decided to see if we'd like him. So Ian's audition as such was we invited him to come out with us one Sunday afternoon, and we went to Ashworth Valley, in Rochdale. Basically, we spent a couple of hours just acting like kids, throwing bits of wood into streams and jumping over them. On reflection, it wasn't a bad audition technique. It worked. I'm not sure what Ian thought of it when he went home and told Debbie what he'd been up to.

Ian went and saw Iain Gray and told him that he wasn't with his band any more, and just to rub salt in it, would he mind selling his amp and speakers to me? So I bought Iain Gray's equipment, but I just can't play guitar. Every time I try I just can't do it. The problem was, there was already a stagger in the competence. Barney'd had his guitar for a couple of years, he could pick out a few chords. Hooky had got his bass guitar and was learning. By the time I got round to that, I was, what, two months behind Hooky, but maybe two years behind Barney.

We then had the problem of finding a drummer, and real drummers are very hard to find. We went through a number of people. Later on, I traded in the guitar and amp and got a drum kit, but yet again I was then so far behind everyone that it was obvious it was impossible.

Peter Hook: Ian was much better educated for things like Can, Kraftwerk, Velvet Underground. I was a big fan of John Cale, because a kid I used to work with in the canteen at the Manchester Ship Canal Company was a mad John Cale fan and he gave me all his LPs. It was Ian that introduced us to Iggy and things like that, because Bernard and I were listening to pop reggae, Led Zeppelin, Deep Purple. Ian didn't push it on you, he wasn't pushy with us at all, and he was just great to be with, he completed your education.

Bernard Sumner: He brought a direction. Ian was into the extremities of life. He wanted to make extreme music, and he wanted to be totally extreme onstage, no half measures. If we were writing a song, he would say, 'Let's make it more manic! It's too straight, let's make it more manic!'

Tony Wilson: It was Debbie who introduced Ian to Iggy. I think it was the lads told me this. Debbie is the Iggy Pop fan. Ian met and fell in love with Debbie, and she started playing him her Iggy albums. The whole point of music is the coming together of influences, so in that moment you've got something as important as Ibiza. Because Ian took Iggy to the band.

Kevin Cummins: When we went to see Iggy in March 1977 at the Apollo, with Bowie on keyboards, I think that's equally important as the Sex Pistols at the Lesser Free Trade Hall. It really galvanised a lot of people. Iggy was mesmerising on that tour, he was astonishing. I'd never seen anything like it.

Bernard Sumner: We rehearsed at a pub in Weaste called The Swan. You know like you had the Freemasons, you also had the Buffaloes. I think they've got a secret sign. We rehearsed in their meeting room above the pub, and it used to be all like weird chests under the seats. When we pulled them out and opened them up there's like buffalo skins. They're a little-known secret sect. It's all based on Leonardo da Vinci's paintings. When the Buffaloes weren't having meetings, we rehearsed there, which was great, until the landlord threw us out.

What was going on then, I guess it was like when you first have sex, if you're a complete virgin, and the first time you do it you're completely hopeless at it, you get it all wrong. That's what happened then, in that period. The first songs that we started playing, maybe you've heard some stuff, but there was a previous set of songs before that that were absolutely bloody awful. Music's like anything else: you have to educate yourself, or be educated by it, until you're good at it. Those were the days of our education.

The first set of material we wrote was just us aping punk, completely aping it and doing it really badly. We were the musical equivalent of nine-year-old kids, so we wrote about seven songs. We got pally with the Buzzcocks, and they were really helpful to us. They helped us get gigs. Pete Shelley sent Richard Boon down to see us, and he came and we were playing, 'Yeah, yeah, yeah, yeah, fuck off, fuck off, yeah, yeah, yeah, bollocks, bollocks' – these really dreadful, dreadful songs.

He said, 'Well, I'll give you the gig, but you need to write a new set of songs.' We thought, 'Yeah, yeah, they're crap really,' so we wrote a fresh set of songs for the gig. I think it was at the Electric Circus, supporting the Buzzcocks. We wrote six songs which were much better, but we still weren't there yet. They were better than the first lot, and we wrote them in about six weeks. Some of them, I think, ended up on *Unknown Pleasures*, maybe two.

Pete Shelley: We had a meeting with them one Friday evening because they said, 'We'd like to start a band up, we need some help.'

Punk was an inclusive thing, and we needed all the similar-minded people that we could have to make it a growing concern. And so this Friday evening we'd arranged to meet at this pub in Frederick Road, in Salford. It was just basically having a drink and talking about the things which they wanted to do, and we were trying to think of ways that those things could be accomplished.

I remember going to Bernard's house, and he had these effects, but they weren't effects pedals because they actually plugged directly into the guitar, so it was quirky even for those days. And it was just basically encouragement, the way that things probably started in many schools and things. I mean, there was a sixth-form feel in a way, people just exchanging ideas about what could be done, and how.

Richard Boon: They were in a constant process of forming. We used to visit them in the rehearsal room near the bus depot in Weaste and drink with them afterwards, and they were just trying to get a handle on what they wanted to do. They just wanted to be in a band, which is no mean ambition.

Ian was possessed by burning youth. I wouldn't go as far as to say he was anything like Arthur Rimbaud, but he was enthused primarily by the Stooges and the Velvets and his own sense of alienation. He was obviously trying to work something out and he could be as laddish and as loutish as the rest of them, but you always sensed he's making an effort to be a lad, he's really a little more withdrawn, a little more thoughtful, which just made him charismatic, but he was no saint.

Bernard Sumner: Ian used to have this really thick hair, and he used to go to this dodgy barber's and ask the barber to cut his hair like a Roman emperor. We used to be quite into the Romans. He used to read a lot of Nietzsche. I don't know, I never read it, I just thought they were beautiful uniforms, and beautiful architecture. So aesthetically I was always attracted to classicism. Ian liked it through Nietzsche.

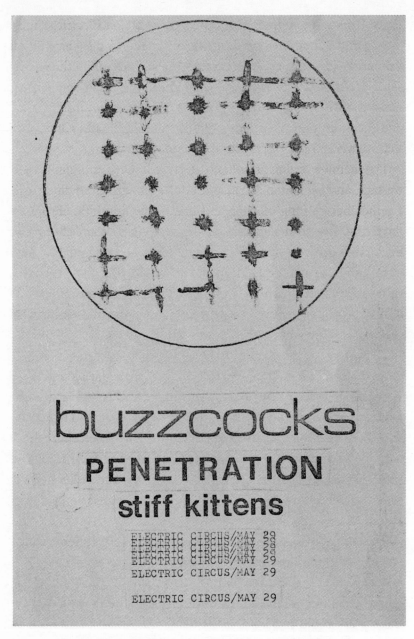

Electric Circus, Manchester, 29 May 1977, supporting Buzzcocks
and Penetration (Courtesy of Richard Boon)

Peter Hook: We supported the Buzzcocks at the Electric Circus. That was the first one. We didn't have a name, and Richard Boon wanted to advertise us. And we couldn't decide, and in the end he said, 'Well, what about Stiff Kittens?' Pete Shelley came up with it, and we said, 'Oh no, we don't like that.' He said, 'Oh, all right then,' and then put it on the posters. On the night, we had to announce that we were called Warsaw, and not Stiff Kittens.

I remember being absolutely terrified. One minute I went onstage, and I remember that and I don't remember anything else. I remember coming offstage and it was like, uhhhhh, absolutely terrifying. I've seen a picture of the first gig. Me and Terry had decided to dress up as tank commanders, and we'd bought a load of military German tank commanders' outfits. But that's the great thing about being in a group: you have a history of every ridiculous outfit you've ever worn, and every ridiculous haircut, and every ridiculous thing you've ever said.

Terry Mason: We thought we were doing the standard Manchester punk progression. You would do gigs with Buzzcocks in Manchester, and then go off and do gigs with them elsewhere, as had happened with both the Fall and the Worst, but we seemed to stumble on that. We did the first gig with them, and then we heard nothing more. We then got a string of gigs basically through Music Force: they tracked us down, and we ended up doing some support slots at Rafters.

The decision was that the band didn't like Stiff Kittens, which was the working title that Pete Shelley had given us. I thought it was a pretty cute name. Stiff Kittens as a punk band, it's a fantastic name: a box full of little kitties with their paws up in the air – how more punk could you be? But the band didn't like it, so it became Warsaw, mainly after the Bowie track 'Warszawa', because we used to go on to that at early gigs.

Iain Gray: When they supported Penetration, Ian did a very mild version of the full Ian moment. They were good, not great, then.

Ian always had great fashion sense. He had these really smart Tonik pants and he used to wear this RAF greatcoat all the time – it was utilitarian, Berlin 1935, that type of style. You had Barney with the moustache and Hooky dressed like a gay dancer, one of the Village People: it was quite odd at the time, his peaked cap, because he used to wear it at Pips. He had a leather collar with studs on, so it was a bit of a mish-mash.

Kevin Cummins: They weren't very good, but it didn't really matter because it was just so zeitgeisty. I think that was what we felt with nearly every band. We weren't that critical, we were just pleased that people were getting up and doing something. I shot about six or seven frames, but the negs have long since disappeared. I remember it had energy, but everything had energy then. You'd see Chelsea or the Cortinas or Eater, and they all had energy. The songs were quite interchangeable. I think that was the case with Warsaw for a while.

I always used to shoot the support band, even just three or four frames. I felt I was in the middle of documenting something that could be important. Not necessarily that band, but everything. I had a feeling that I was going to do something with it, so I wanted to be as complete as possible. I was really into glam, Bowie and Roxy Music. I didn't dress like a punk, I felt I was observing something. I did feel a part of it; it was very easy to feel a part of that group, no one was excluded. London was very cliquey, but Manchester was much more open at the time.

- 31 May 1977: Rafters, Manchester

Paul Morley review, *NME*, 18 June 1977
Warsaw have been searching for a drummer for many weeks, their stickman for the night uncovered only the night before. There's a quirky cockiness about the lads that made me think for some reason of the Faces. Twinkling evil charm. Perhaps they play a little obviously but there's an elusive spark of

dissimilarity from the newer bands that suggests that they've plenty to play around with, time no doubt dictating tightness and eliminating odd bouts of monotony. The bass player had a moustache. I liked them and will like them even more in six months' time.

Paul Morley: Rafters would be when Bernard had a kind of moustache, and so he looked a little bit more Pips: the shirt and the Roxy Music military thing, that was still hanging over slightly. There was a sort of odd muteness and smartness about it, it was fascinating, but they clearly dressed up too, there was a slight separation between off duty and on. And I remember them concentrating, I remember them taking it very seriously.

They were still unformed. There was no sense that there was going to be Factory Records, for instance, there was no sense that this would have any history. It was of the moment, and the moment was exciting. And here was another one, because you got excited about Manchester groups – Buzzcocks, the Fall – and in the middle of all this there was another one. I didn't like their name, and they sounded more ordinary than not, they sounded like a rock group trying, but there was something about the trying that was interesting.

- 3 June 1977: The Squat, Manchester
- 6 June 1977: Guildhall, Newcastle
- 16 June 1977: The Squat, Manchester
- 25 June 1977: The Squat, Manchester
- 30 June 1977: Rafters, Manchester

Richard Boon: They were very raw and unfocused, but there was an energy and a drive, which is essential. A lot of bands that formed in the wake of that early punk enthusiasm were basically talentless, but Warsaw had something: they had a spirit. Ian always struck me as being a very driven young man, and if Hooky and Barney just wanted to play a bit, he had something that he wanted to exorcise.

Bernard Sumner: I remember it being a terrifying experience because I never expected to end up on the stage when I was younger, so it was a complete surprise that it had actually happened. But it was both terrifying and very exciting at the same time, and the social aspects of it were very attractive: what it could do with your life, travelling around, going to different places, meeting people . . . It opened up a whole new life to me.

Peter Hook: From our first gig to the end of our first week as a group we did five gigs, and then we had a six-month lull. We did the Electric Circus with the Buzzcocks, then we had a day's gap, and we did The Squat with the Worst and some other band – I think the Drones. Then the next day we went to Newcastle and played with the Adverts and Penetration, and we came back and on the Tuesday we played Rafters with Johnny Thunders. It was a dream come true, absolutely wonderful. People would come up and say, 'Listen, there's a punk night tomorrow, do you want to come down and play? We'll try and give you some petrol money.' And we'd just go. It was dead free and easy.

4

JULY 1977 – APRIL 1978

Flyer for the last nights at the Electric Circus,
Saturday 1 October and Sunday 2 October 1977
(Courtesy of Jon Savage)

Bernard Sumner: You know lead singers are pains in the arse, right? They are, but drummers are just fucking weird.

Peter Hook: They were all arseholes. They probably might say the same about me. We just couldn't get a decent drummer who fitted in either personality-wise or playing style-wise. Firing people at the tender old age of twenty-one was awful. Invariably Bernard and I would go and meet them and tell them they were too good for us, just to get rid of them. Then we got Steve Brotherdale, who was the best drummer we'd had, but he dumped us for Rob Gretton's band, the Panik.

Bernard Sumner: We went through several drummers. All we wanted to do was find a nice guy that we got on with and we'd give him the job. We met several superstar drummers. One, I remember, auditioned us: it was basically, 'If you fulfil certain criteria, I'll join your group. Like, how much are you going to get paid for a gig? How many times a week are you going to gig? Who's your manager? What do you think your prospects are?' He interviewed us like that, and we were like, 'Yeah, yeah,' and then when he left: 'Kiss my arse.'

And then we got one who was a student studying to be a PE instructor, and he was a pretty good drummer, but we went round to his student digs and he had like a punk wig and a dog collar on and was practising to be a punk. We just thought, 'Knobhead, knobhead.' But we were too nice to sack him, so Hooky had this stupid idea of buying him a box of chocolates and going and telling him he's too good to be in the group: 'You're miles better than we are, you shouldn't be playing with a group like us.' That's how we'd sack people.

Terry Mason: I was still having lessons, because these early gigs, getting and keeping a drummer was very difficult. I thought in time I could pick up drumming, but it wasn't a situation where there was time, to be honest: with bands like that you don't know whether the lifespan's going to be three weeks or three years. We had a guy called Tony Tabac, who did the first couple of gigs. He didn't really like turning up for rehearsals and seemed to have other things on his mind, so I was basically learning in the background, and still was even when Steve came in.

Stephen Morris: I was in the bar at the Apollo and reading this magazine, and it said, 'Drummer wanted.' After the Sunshine Valley Dance Band falling apart, I'd gone to the odd adult audition and hadn't really been cabaret enough for the job required. I think the best that they said was, 'Have a few more lessons.' So, there you go – 'Drummer wanted.' There's two adverts: one was this band called the Fall, and the other one was this band called Warsaw. I didn't even know who they were.

As a sideline I started to make money reviewing the concerts I was going to for the *Record Mirror*. You got a cheque for about three quid, but it was Coutts bank and I felt great going into the bank: 'Look at this, the Queen's bank.' My first punk gig was Ed Banger and the Nosebleeds at Rafters. Vini Reilly was playing guitar, and I actually got an interview with Vini and said – this is bog standard – 'What's your influences?' And he said, 'We're influenced by revolutionary music of all kinds.' Right.

Anyway, I got talking to someone at this concert and I asked, 'Have you heard of Warsaw?' – 'Oh, I've seen them a couple of times, they're not much cop.' I said, 'What about the Fall?' – 'Oh no, no, no, not the Fall.' So I thought, 'Well, if I was going to join one of these two bands on the basis of a pissed-up conversation, I'd probably go for Warsaw.' I'm still sort of umming and ahhing, and then I was walking down the hill to the station and Jones's music shop had this notice in the window. Again it was the immortal words: 'Drummer wanted for local punk band, Warsaw.'

And I thought, 'I see the hand of coincidence in this.' And it was a Macclesfield phone number, so I thought, 'Well, you know, don't have to travel.' So I get on the phone, expecting some sort of oafish punk type, and it was a very mild-mannered, very chatty

Ian, and I said, 'You know, are you after a drummer?' – 'Oh yes. Can you do . . . play drums?' – 'Yes, I can play drums, yes, yes.' – 'Oh, do you want to come round to me house?'

He said, 'The rest of the band are on holiday, but come round and you can listen to a tape.' And I went round to Ian's house in Macclesfield, which was only just down the road from where I lived. I'd just given up smoking for the first time – I'd done three weeks smoke-free – and the first thing I got off Ian was being re-addicted to cigarettes: 'One won't hurt you, come on, come on, one won't hurt you, come on.' So that was it then, I was hooked on cigs for another thirty years, and managed to talk myself into a job.

He gave us this tape which they'd recorded at the studio in Oldham, and, 'Yeah, go and have a listen to it and see what you think.' And so I went away. It sounded like someone were play-ing a flute, but of course it wasn't a flute, it was the way Hooky played bass. It was just a bit strange. So fine, it wasn't too difficult, there was no 6/4, 7/14 Van der Graaf Generator complicated time signatures in there. I thought I could probably nail this one quite quickly. So, 'Yeah, okay, I'm in, if you'll have me.'

I'd been down this way before. I was half expecting to turn up and they'd say, 'Have a few more lessons, you'll be all right.' And he rang us up and said, 'Oh, they're back now from the holiday and we're going to have a rehearsal. Do you want to come?' So I bor-row me mam's car – I think they'd gone on holiday. I put me drums in the boot, and, 'Where are we meeting them?' – 'Strangeways.' – 'Strangeways . . . prison?' – 'Yeah, Strangeways prison.' – 'They've been on holiday?' – 'Yes, they've been on holiday.' – 'Okay. Where have they been?' – 'Oh, France, they've been on holiday in France.'

So I parked up outside Strangeways expecting them to come and open the doors, and then this Mark 2 Jag pulls up, and I'm think-ing, 'Oh, it's meeting somebody.' Bearded chap got out, and that's Hooky. 'Oh, he's got a beard, that's a bit weird.' Then Bernard turned up, then we went to Abraham Moss Leisure Centre at Crumpsall and started bashing about and did the songs that were on the tape, and that was it really. I don't think anyone said, 'You've got the job.'

But they said, 'Oh, we've got a gig next week, can you make it?' So that was how I got from Macclesfield to Warsaw.

Bernard Sumner: Terry's a bit of an oddball, so I guess he was drawn to groups that were oddball and outcast like him. He's gone through many things; he was a guitarist with us at one stage, second guitarist when we rehearsed at The Swan. I noticed after we'd been rehearsing for about a couple of months that you couldn't hear a single thing he was playing. So I went over to his amp, turned it up so you could actually hear it. Oh God, it was awful, he just couldn't play, and he said, 'All right, I can't play the guitar, I'll be the drummer.'

It was when we were looking for a drummer. So then he bought this drum kit that was so cheap that the legs were like wire coat hangers, so when you played the drums the legs of the drum kit would walk away from him. In fact, when Steve's mum wouldn't let him out of the house because he had a cold and wouldn't let him take his drum kit, he had to use Terry's drum kit, which was walking away from him. That caused a bit of political differences within the group, I must say.

Then he became the manager, and the first recording that we made, the one that Ian paid for with his twenty-first-birthday money, it was like, 'Right, Terry, sounds fucking great, send it out to record companies.' He sends loads out, and we have a group meeting. 'Had any response yet?' We did get a reply off a record company saying thanks but no thanks, give us a call in ten years. So we were like, 'Shit, fucking hell,' really dejected, so we put it in the cassette player and played it.

Terry lived with his mum. We heard [*makes drum sound*] drum beats starting, then we hear [*hums* Coronation Street *theme*], then we hear, 'Terry, your tea's ready' [*drum sound*] going over the music. And we were like, 'What, you've sent it out like that? You've got fucking *Coronation Street* on it and your mum telling you your tea's ready. How's that happened? How have you been recording them?'

He said, 'Well, I sit there, I'm watching telly and I've got one tape recorder here with the speaker on it and another one with a microphone, and I just hold the microphone near it.' So that's how he's making tape copies, just off the speaker of the other with a microphone. So it picked *Coronation Street* up and all sorts of shite, and he sent it out to the record companies. Fucking embarrassing. Then we promoted him to keyboard technician when we got a keyboard, because we never sacked him, we always promoted him.

Peter Hook: I mean, it was this very strange thing, when you think about it, because you couldn't hear anything, your equipment was dire. I never heard Bernard's guitar until we got in the studio with Martin Hannett, or Ian's lyrics, but the feeling was right: '[*makes guitar noises*] That feels right. Don't know what we're playing, don't know what he's singing, but it feels right.' It was the same with Steve's drumming: couldn't hear it, but it felt right, and the whole thing felt right, which is the interesting thing.

Stephen Morris: I'd spent so long sort of bashing about in me dad's bedroom. When you played with the cabaret bands, they were just doing their own thing, and you kind of had to fall in with them, and when you tried to do something different, 'Whoah, whoah, whoah.' But playing with Hooky and Bernard and Ian, we were all learning off each other. We coalesced really quite quickly and got quite tight. Then the first gig that I had with them was the last night of the Electric Circus.

Peter Hook: At the last night of the Electric Circus, we had a fight with the promoter, and then we nearly had a fight with the Drones cos they wouldn't let us on. It was that tosser, the singer of the Drones, and Ian kicked off like mad, absolutely mad at the door with the promoter and with the Drones and Slaughter and the Dogs, because they didn't want us on. They fucking stood there and said, 'We don't want you to play.' We were going, 'Fuck you, we've got as much right to play as you.' Me and Ian literally had them by the throat.

I think Bernard and Steve were in the car. We had to physically fight to get on. They didn't want us to play, and that's why they put us first on. Virgin recorded us while we were just checking the mikes. That's why it goes off halfway through 'Novelty'. We only recorded two songs, and I think that once they listened to it afterwards they thought, 'Oh fuck, these lot are better than most of the other bands that were on.'

The Drones and Slaughter and the Dogs stood there and tried to stop us playing. No one stuck up for us. Bleeding Buzzcocks didn't stick up for us. It was only us, sheer tenacity and Ian freaking that got us on that day. Ian could go like Krakatoa if something crossed him, and the only time I ever saw him go was when he was sticking up for the band, so it was great.

Stephen Morris: Up to that point I'd thought that they weren't really punks at all. There's nothing wrong with not being what I thought punks would be. They were just normal guys. For a singer I thought Ian was quite mild mannered and polite: you'd see Johnny Rotten and people spitting and all that lot, and then Ian's nothing like that. I didn't really pay much attention to what would happen when you actually did a gig. We just played and Ian mumbled into the microphone.

I should have suspected something really when we went to sort out playing at the last night of the Electric Circus. The last night actually was two nights, and Ian said, 'We'll go down on the Saturday and we'll sort out about getting on on Sunday.' We went in. Ian got very loud and aggressive with people on the door. I'd never seen him like that before, he was really aggressive and very passionate, and he got really wound up – 'Get us on!' – and eventually I think just to get rid of him they said, 'Okay, just turn up. You can play first.'

I thought that was a bit strange. And then we turned up with the gear, and they said, 'Right, you're on now.' And all of sudden it's, 'Whoah, he's turned into a whirling Dervish,' which spurred you on. Bernard and Hooky were playing the Ian sort of manic routine, and it wasn't a routine, it was passion. That was how he got whatever it was. I got it out of me by hitting drums, and Bernard and Hooky got it out by playing guitars. He got it out of him by doing that, which was just being Ian onstage, and until I saw it, it wasn't at all what I expected. It was a bit of a revelation.

- 2 October 1977: Last Night of the Electric Circus, Collyhurst, Manchester

> **Jon Savage review, *Sounds*, 15 October 1977**
> Hip disco segues into Warsaw. They look young and nervous. Desperate, thrashing, afraid of stopping/falling: 'What are you gonna do when the novelty's gone / You'll be back in the gutter where you came from' ('Novelty').

Terry Mason: We'd got so far and we were really stuck. At that point, Warsaw had become possibly the most unpopular band in Manchester. No one seemed to have any gigs for us to do. We weren't even getting last-minute cancellations. 'The support band at Rafters hasn't turned up, who have we got on the speed dial?' We certainly weren't on the speed dial. We just weren't getting out of Manchester, and we weren't getting much traction in Manchester.

The punk explosion was based around Buzzcocks, who were based in Lower Broughton, but the rest of the Manchester scene, the venues were still run by the Didsbury mafia, by C. P. Lee and by people like Bruce Mitchell. We were outside that. People didn't like us because we weren't musos. So we were on the wrong side of Manchester and on the wrong side of a number of people, just because a lot of it was down to location.

Richard Boon: What was the Manchester punk thing? Spearheaded by Buzzcocks, and then there was very little until the Fall. There was always rumour and gossip. Bands were forming just for thirty minutes, and never doing anything because they hated each other. It could have been regional, I don't know. South Manchester was

something else. That was kind of ruled by what was left of Alberto
y Lost Trios Paranoias. Warsaw didn't hang out in quite the same
way as other people hung out. They were very insular, they had
their thing going.

C. P. Lee: The Albertos were a kind of Dada cabaret band, and we
formed in 1974 in order to fight back against the leviathans of rock.
Then, when punk rock came along, it happened to coincide with a
stage show that I'd been writing called *Snuff Rock*, and the idea was
that kids were unemployed, nobody wanted to go and see groups
any more, they needed a gimmick, and so *Snuff Rock* was born.
The idea was to get an unemployed kid every night, then get them
to commit suicide onstage as part of the band, so live or die they'd
make a million.

- 7 October 1977: Salford College of Technology

Martin Hannett would come round and say we're going off to see
somebody at such-and-such a place – the Bierkeller, Band on the
Wall or whatever – so yeah, I did go out with him quite often to see
groups. In a way it was like A&R spotting, because Rabid Records
was just beginning, and the reason we went to see Warsaw at Salford
was because Slaughter and the Dogs were playing – they were on
Rabid Records. There was a fight at the gig, and the evening got
kind of curtailed by the brouhaha that was going on.

   Within the next few days, Martin was enthusing a lot at Cotton
Lane, where Rabid was, but Tosh Ryan was very, very worried
about the association with Nazi imagery. I remember Martin saying, 'This is the dance music of the future,' and that was Martin's
split-off from Rabid, I think, his pursuit of what he saw as the
dance music of the future, and it amazes me, because that was a
very un-hippie thing to do. It was some indication of his genius
that he saw it even then. They certainly were embryonic, but he
recognised something within it.

Martin Hannett: I was a partner in Rabid. It was put together as a vehicle for the Slaughter and the Dogs single, and it got used till we got up to 105, which was Jilted John. 103 was John Cooper Clarke, 102 was the Nosebleeds, 104 was 'Kinnel Tommy'. Ed Banger was a complete lunatic, but a gentle lunatic. Came from Wythenshawe. He came with the Faal brothers. Mike Faal stuck posters up for Factory. They were part of the Slaughter and the Dogs crew: Vini Reilly, Rob Gretton, me.

Terry Mason used to come into the office looking for a PA, and I went to see them one night supporting Slaughter at Salford Tech. They were really good. The PA broke down, and Steve and Hooky busked for about fifteen minutes. One of the things that drove me to drum machines was the appalling quality of drummers, and Steve was good, so immediately they had a red-hot start. They were different from punk. There was lots of space in their sound initially.

- December 1977: Pennine Sound Studios, recording the *Ideal for Living* EP

Bernard Sumner: When we made our first record, *An Ideal for Living*, we didn't have a manager. We were just making this music and we wanted people to hear it, and it was very much the punk ethos of doing it yourself, independence, forget big labels, forget the superstars, just a cottage-industry kind of thing. It was Ian's twenty-first-birthday money, and he very bravely and very kindly decided to book studio time with it, and booked us into a studio called Pennine Sound in Oldham.

The guys that were running it offered us a full package. 'You pay so much, and we do the full package. You record the track here, we'll mix it for you, and then you'll get it back on vinyl. We'll cut it for you and do the artwork and everything.' So we thought, 'That's great, that's really kind of them, we'll do that, yeah.' So we did it and we recorded it, and first time in the studio, '[*makes noises*] Come on, lads, time's money. You're running out of time, you've only got half an hour left.'

Joy Division, sleeve of *An Ideal for Living* 7″ EP, spring 1978 (Gareth Davy)

Peter Hook: I think that was because everybody did it, all the groups did it, and you helped each other to do it. If you needed to know something, you could phone up the Buzzcocks and they'd tell you. They might not crave your company, but they would tell you. You looked after each other, and also with the studios, you'd go along and you'd pay your money, and they'd give you the finished record – which is what they did.

Stephen Morris: That's after we'd done a few rehearsals. We did the songs on that original cassette, then we wrote some more songs. 'Novelty', I think, was an old song on that tape. Then we did 'Leaders of Men', 'Failures', 'Warsaw', 'No Love Lost'.

We started writing because we could. Ian had the lyrics. The way that the songs happened, they just appeared like out of thin air. We'd just start a song and then finish it, and then, 'Right, we've written another song, we'll go through the set.' And so you start: you'd have three songs, four songs, five songs. If you played for longer than twenty minutes, you were overstaying your welcome. Well, that's what we thought anyway.

'No Love Lost' was the start of moving away from thrash. It was an example of, 'Oh, hang on, we've got a good bit here, but it doesn't really go anywhere. Hang on, that's another good bit, so why don't we put that bit there and then that bit there' – which is what Ian was very good at, he could spot things and do bits of arranging. Also, he didn't mind the fact that he wasn't singing for a lot of it, because he did like the idea that our intros are our trademarks. The other thing was that the guitar riff in 'No Love Lost' is off 'LA Woman', which me and Ian thought was really good.

Peter Hook: There was another group in London called Warsaw Pakt that were famous because they'd done a direct-to-disc record. They'd played it in the studio, mixed it into stereo and cut it straight onto a disc, and they got loads of press for doing it. So when we were phoning up for support gigs, everyone started saying, 'Oh, are you the Warsaw Pakt?' We should have said, 'Yeah,' then we'd have got the gigs, but we didn't. We just said, 'No, no, no, we're Warsaw from Manchester' – or from Salford.

It just got too much really, so we had to change our name. We were racking our brains looking for other names, and the favourite was the Slaves of Venus and Joy Division. Ian brought it from a book, *House of Dolls*. It was round about the same time that we decided we were all going to dye our hair blond as a gimmick to get us noticed, and I came into rehearsal the next day with me hair dyed blond, and them three bastards hadn't done it. I got stuck with it for years and years and years.

Bernard Sumner: We had about a week to come up with a name, and some guy at the animation place where I was working gave me a couple of books. One was called *House of Dolls*. I knew it was about the Nazis but I didn't read it. I just flicked through the pages, saw this name Joy Division, and it was the brothel that the soldiers went to, and I thought, 'Well, it's pretty bad taste, but it's quite punk.'

Everyone I told the name to went, 'That's a great name,' so we just went for it. We knew it had connotations, but we just thought, 'Well, we're not Nazis, so fuck it, it's still a great name.' We were very determined, and it was a bit of 'Fuck you, we'll do what we want' as well in our heads, but I guess it is pretty bad taste.

Stephen Morris: It came out of 'No Love Lost'. Bits of that were taken from one of Ian's books that he was reading at the time, which was *House of Dolls*, which is about how the Joy Division was the regiment of prostitutes looking after the new Aryan super-race or Nazi thugs or whatever. That was what they were called, and it sort of stuck. That was the start of people thinking, 'Oh bloody hell, they're a bunch of Nazis.' I mean, really we should have seen that coming.

Bernard Sumner: I was born in 1956. I lived in my grandparents' house, and they used to talk about the war all the time. One grandparent's sister had been bombed, house had gone. We had a room full of gas masks and tin helmets, British flags and old radio sets – paraphernalia from the war. My granddad used to watch war programmes all the time. I was interested in what it was and what had made it happen, because for a young mind like mine it was quite a bizarre thing for the whole world to be up at each other's throats, and violence on such a mass scale.

Obviously, I thought it was dreadfully wrong what the Nazis had done, but it was like the whole world had gone mad. I think the only way you can deal with that is to study human nature and find out how to take the aggression out of people, because it's aggression at the end of the day, and it's also people being macho and not being prepared to stand down.

Living in Salford I saw quite a lot of violence, and so I thought that was part of the norm. I'd seen people getting beaten up with iron bars and people getting the shit kicked out of them. My uncle got stabbed forty times. My cousin got kicked in the face so much his eyeball fell out and he had to walk to hospital holding his eyeball, which must have been a nauseating experience. So I had all this violence surrounding me. I was not violent myself, so I just wanted to understand the causes of why people acted like that.

- 25 January 1978: Pips, Manchester, first concert
billed as Joy Division

Jeremy Kerr: I used to go to Pips regularly. The Roxy room right at the back used to play David Bowie and Roxy Music, and then there was a commercial room which played all sorts of soul, and then later on there was a room downstairs called the Future or whatever – they played Kraftwerk, *Trans-Europe Express* – but it was good, all in one place. You could walk from one room with David Bowie and Roxy Music down into heavy soul music, and in between there was a stairway going up to the girls' toilet – that was a good place to stand.

Kevin Cummins: I went to see them at Pips, when Ian got locked out. He went out for a cigarette, and they wouldn't let him back in, they didn't believe he was in the band.

Paul Morley: The change of name seemed to be good actually to rinse away Bernard's moustache and Hooky's leather cap and the slightly camp element that there was at the time. You probably would have thought there was a gayness about them because it did seem more Pips than anything else. A lot survived the Pips dressing-up business into punk, but they held onto it for quite a while. But I do remember Joy Division being something very early on, and not being Warsaw any more.

- 15 April 1978: Rafters, Manchester

Terry Mason: We got to a phase, and we were stuck with what we were doing. The whole thing about that night was, although it was supposed to be the Stiff/Chiswick Challenge and it was about new bands, it was still primarily being run by the music mafia over in Didsbury. Getting onstage that night was paramount. If we wouldn't have got onstage, we would have called it a day, because it looked as if so many things were against us. We knew that we were owed a shot.

We were there early, and we just got given so much crap served up to us by people, and funnily enough the same people not long after that all became our friends. We were there, we wanted to go on, the night was going on and on and on, and we just thought we would never actually get onstage. We were getting wound up and we were getting drunk at the same time. Thinking about it nowadays, the stuff that we used to drink was awful. We were on Special Brew and blackcurrant. I'd rather drink diesel.

Kevin Cummins: At the Stiff/Chiswick Challenge, I had an argument with them. At the time it didn't seem like they were part of what we would consider a Manchester scene. There wasn't a scene as such, but they didn't live in Hulme, they didn't go to all the gigs like everybody else, and they also had an arrogance that was kind of misplaced at the time. Like a lot of bands, and a lot of young kids, they thought they were miles better than they were, and I thought, 'I've got a few shots of them. I don't need anything until something else happens.'

It was justified in a way, but they wanted to be outsiders as well. They didn't want to be like the Drones, who would turn up every week, or Slaughter and the Dogs. They felt they had more to offer than that. Even though they didn't necessarily at the time.

Paul Morley: That Rafters Stiff/Chiswick Challenge was really bonkers, because no group in their right mind would have wanted to have been on Stiff because it was kind of a novelty label. But everybody including Joy Division turned up to win, like some weird prototype *X Factor*, with some awful judging panel deciding who would be on this rather strange London label. There was a violence about that night, because for whatever reason, it looked like Joy Division might not get a chance to appear.

Terry Mason: The most annoying people on there were the Negatives, which is Paul Morley, Kevin Cummins, Richard Boon – it's funny how the same names come up on the good side and the bad side on this – and it was those guys that had basically spoiled our Saturday night at the Electric Circus. The whole point of the Stiff/Chiswick Challenge was that at the end of the gig there was a possibility to travel the country. At the end of it the winner would get a single out.

They were basically just taking the piss. We were struggling to get gigs, we were struggling to get any sort of press, and these people were there basically laughing at us. We got mad at them, and I know Ian got mad at Paul Morley over it. People took the hint that we were less than pleased, and eventually we went on. I'm not sure if it was after two, but it was ridiculously late. By that point, because people had seen nine, ten bands already, none of them being particularly inspiring, the room was getting a lot thinner, the crowd wasn't there.

Peter Hook: If you look at the other bands, they were softer than we were. We were heavier, musically and in personality, compared to Howard Devoto or Pete Shelley, who were very effete. That was what estranged us from them. We had so much aggro. Just because people didn't like us. We were a working band, practising, and the Negatives come along, get pissed and think, 'Oh, let's play.' And because they were so well in with everybody, on it went. You had to threaten your way to get anywhere.

Bernard Sumner: This was when I first saw the other side of Ian. He was a really lovely, really nice, polite, intelligent guy, but if he didn't get what he wanted, he would explode into this kind of frenzied thing, because that's the only way he could get what he wanted. I remember him kicking the door down of the Negatives' dressing room and going to Paul Morley and Kevin Cummins, 'You're not fucking going on, you're not fucking going on, we'll kill you if you go on, and we'll bottle you. We're going on.'

We just threatened them so much that we ended up going on. Because Ian was so wound up by that stage, his performance was amazing. He ended up ripping the stage up. It was like sections of wood, and he just ended up ripping it up, throwing them out at the audience. It was an explosive performance. So Tony was there and Rob was there, and we just did the gig and thought, 'It was a good gig that,' and then went home and thought, 'At least we got a chance to play.'

Bob Dickinson: I was working for the *New Manchester Review*, which was a really good place to meet musicians and bands and artists and all sorts of people. It was like a kind of railway station in a way, in that you saw everybody and got introduced to lots of people as well. I saw Joy Division for the first time in 1978, in April at the Stiff/Chiswick Challenge. The *New Manchester Review* used to promote Band on the Wall and Rafters, and I used to get paid something like £20 to DJ down there once a week.

There were lots of local ambitious new bands wanting to get signed, but it was '78, so they were all pop bands or pub-rock bands, and I didn't really like any of them. I can't remember who any of the other bands were. I think about half past one in the morning Joy Division came on, and they played a pretty short set, about twenty minutes. You didn't expect something like Joy Division to be on the bill and they were a bit of a shock to the system, and I enjoyed it because they were violent and hypnotic at the same time.

I didn't know what to make of them when they came onstage because they were wearing biker gear. I think two of them were wearing leather trousers and I thought we were in for some kind of heavy metal because of the leather, but they had short hair, so it was confusing at first. And then they launched into this very uncompromising, crude music that was completely unlike anything else that had been on that night.

After the audience had left, I remember standing on the dance floor. I knew Rob Gretton because he was one of the other DJs at Rafters, and I just have this picture in my mind of him ranting at me, right in my face, really ecstatically – the floor was covered with broken glass and fag ends and the detritus of a gig – about how wonderful he thought they were and weren't they the best band you'd ever seen in your life, and he was going to manage them, and he was going to take them to all sorts of places you wouldn't believe. It was something I'll never forget.

Terry Mason: Afterwards, Ian came over and collared Tony Wilson. I'm there chasing after Ian and thinking, 'Oh God, don't do anything too stupid,' and he goes over and has a go at Wilson, and Wilson, being an educated man, decides he certainly doesn't want to get on the wrong side of Ian, me and all the people who were sort of closing in on him. He becomes all nice and says, 'Oh no, yeah, we'll get you on *So It Goes*, next series, don't worry.' And after that things changed.

Peter Hook: It was like seeing an alien with tentacles and eighty eyes when I first met Tony Wilson. He was from another planet. It was quite odd because my mother used to take me into Tony's dad's tobacconist's on Regent Road, next to Smith's, the toyshop. She used to go and buy her cigarettes there every Saturday morning, and I used to go in with her and she'd go, 'Hello, Mr Wilson,' and he'd go, 'Oh, hello, Mrs Hook, how are you?' and they'd have a right proper chat, and I'd be sort of, you know, four or five years old or summat.

So I knew Tony's dad before I knew Tony, and then years later I found out that his dad had the tobacconist's on Regent Road, so that was a weird one, cos he might have been in there. That was weird, innit, both of us there, just five-year-olds. I just didn't get Tony. He was showbiz. And he was a star, so you rebelled against it straight away, your thuggery – grrrrr – came out straight away. It's funny that when he was pissed Ian called him a cunt for not putting us on, and we were like, 'Oh, bloody hell, Ian, we're never going to get on now.'

Mark Reeder: Rob came into the shop one time and said, 'I saw the best band in the world last night – Joy Division,' and I didn't know who he was talking about, cos I thought they were called Warsaw. 'Best band I've ever seen,' he said. 'I want to manage them.' At that time he was managing a band called the Panik, and I think they'd just released their first single at the time, 'It Won't Sell'. It was right, too: we could hardly shift any of them. They stood there like lead.

Then, the same weekend, Tony Wilson came into the shop and said exactly the same thing. And it was then I realised they were talking about Warsaw. They'd changed the name because of Warsaw Pakt releasing that horrible record they recorded in twenty-four hours. I remember saying, 'Everyone's going to be identifying you with this group, are you not going to change your name?'

Anyway, I told Rob that Tony had said he wanted to manage them, and he was like, 'No fucking chance! I'm gonna go give him a piece of my mind.' And he went off to the telephone boxes in Piccadilly and phoned him up and swore at him, and came back and said, 'Well, that's done and dusted.' He was really happy with himself. Apparently he'd told Tony Wilson to fuck off, to get his fingers off 'his band', and he was going to manage them. He was quite determined. After that, it was dead obvious what was going to happen.

Tony Wilson: I can remember seeing Warsaw at the Electric Circus one night and thinking, 'What a bloody din.' Then again, most of it was a bloody din. I remember obviously being taken by the lead singer, by the fact that he had something special about him, so it just goes to the back of your filing cabinet: 'No, this isn't the band I'll put on television right now.' Obviously, at the back of my mind

I thought, 'The lead singer's really interesting, I'll be aware of this,' but that was it because it was caterwauling – I think is the correct phrase for how it sounded.

Whether I got a copy in the post of Little Drummer Boy or not, I don't know, but I was aware they'd changed their name to Joy Division, and sure enough, there was this Stiff/Chiswick test at Rafters. That night various things happened. Number one was walking down the stairs some girl said, 'When's *So It Goes* coming back, Mr Wilson?' And this voice says, 'He doesn't fucking want it to come back, he wants it to go away so he can become a legend.' And that was Gretton, it was my first meeting with Robert Leo Gretton.

Then I sat at the back of the place at the pool table, and a young boy in a long raincoat sat next to me and went, 'You cunt, you've not put us on television, blah blah blah.' It's the only time that Ian ever did this to me. The fact that he spent the rest of his two or three years working with me behaving like a thoughtful sixth-form schoolboy and being lovely was just my fortune. That night I got the other Ian, which was the 'you fucking bastard'.

At the time I didn't answer him, but I know I remember thinking, 'You're next on the list, you fucking idiot. You don't even know that I've already listened to this seven-inch single. It sounds wonderful. You're the next.' I could put one band a month on. At this point, there was no *So It Goes* and there was no *What's On*. I would just have to put a band on occasionally on the local news programme, and they were next on my list.

I remember thinking the difference is that every other band that night at Rafters was onstage because they wanted to be onstage, they wanted to be rock stars, they wanted to be in the music business, but this lot were onstage because they had no fucking choice. They were driven by something inside them, and you could see it in their eyes. That night it was clear to me and my dear partner, the late Mr Robert Leo Gretton, that this was the most important band in Britain.

It's my luck and fortune that I ended up working with them, and Rob as well. I mean, Rob's story's a different story, about going to them and wanting to manage them, but it was chalk and cheese. Chalk and cheese doesn't describe this: chalk and cheese are the same colour, this was night and day. There was this searing light, the sun, and everything else was just dimness throughout the entire evening.

5

MAY – JUNE 1978

Cassette, Joy Division RCA album, summer 1978 (Courtesy of Jon Savage)

Bernard Sumner: The next day I remember being in a phone booth in Spring Gardens in Manchester, just outside the post office. There was a knock on the booth. I opened the door and went, 'Yeah?' It was Rob Gretton. 'Are you out of that band Joy Division?' I went, 'Yeah.' He said, 'Well, I'm the DJ at that club, I'm Rob Gretton, and I've actually been sacked from my job. I work in the day for an insurance company, but I've been sacked for being too bolshie. I'm on my way now to get a temporary job cleaning toilets in the Arndale Centre, but I'd rather be your manager.'

So I was like, 'All right, yeah, what do you want to do?' He said, 'Can I come to one of your rehearsals and we'll have a meeting about it?' I said, 'We're rehearsing like next Sunday or next Wednesday, come along.' It was in this old factory that we used to rehearse in. I forgot all about it, so I didn't tell anyone. We're rehearsing and Rob walks in the rehearsal room, so we just carry on, and he sits down and everyone's like, 'Who's that? Who's that?' And then we stop. 'Who are you?'

He was really embarrassed, and I went, 'Oh, I forgot to tell you, this guy wants to be our manager.' Rob was a bit paranoid because everyone seemed to be unfriendly to him, so he said, 'All right, let's go to the pub and have a meeting about it.' We went to the pub, but in those days you didn't buy a round of drinks, you just bought yourself one. We all used to go to the bar: 'I'll have a sweet martini please, Hooky'll have a brown ale.' Steve would have a Coke and Ian would have a Special Brew, but we'd all buy our own drinks. Rob was just sat there without a drink.

By this time he's completely paranoid that he'd been set up by the band, that we were taking the piss out of him, but we weren't. That was just the way we did things. But the meeting went really well and we desperately needed a manager, so Rob got the job. He seemed to have some good ideas, and he was the missing link that we needed to move forward. He was pretty punk in the way he thought. When he was DJing he was playing soul music, but his ideology was really punk.

- 3 and 4 May 1978: RCA sessions, Arrow Studios, Manchester

Stephen Morris: The RCA record was before us bumping into Rob. Ian was hanging about Piccadilly Gardens, where RCA at that time had an office in Manchester, and cos Iggy and Bowie were on RCA and I think he just thought maybe Bowie would turn up one day to see how many records he'd sold. He got talking to Richard Searling and Derek Bramwood: this was another side of Ian that I'd never seen before, this schmoozing side where he was kind of, 'Oh yes, I'm friends with Derek at RCA.'

Richard Searling had this friend of his in King's Lynn who was starting a punk-rock label. He'd done a northern soul label called Grapevine, which had some sort of connection with RCA. We got roped in as being the token punk-rock band and ended up making an album at Arrow Studios, just off Deansgate. It was an interesting experience. It was all a bit of a cock-up, we shouldn't have done it, but someone comes up to you and says, 'Hey, guys, here's a contract, you can make an LP,' again, it's like you're climbing up that ladder, and so we went and did it.

Bernard Sumner: We'd met a guy called Richard Searling from RCA Records. RCA weren't interested in us, but there was a record that came out in the seventies by the Floaters called 'Float On'. It's that one: 'Hi, my name's Larry, I'm Capricorn,' and then the whole band introduced themselves and their star signs. Classic record. It was corny as shit but it was massive. And this guy was the guy that put that record together, and he thought punk was the next big thing and wanted to record an album with us. He was going to put the money up. I think he worked for TK Records, and he wanted us to do a cover version of this northern soul record called 'Keep on Keeping on', which when he played it I was quite impressed by, it had a really stonking guitar riff. We thought, 'That's a pretty good record. We know Richard Searling from RCA, he's a decent guy, so we'll do it.'

Richard Searling: Ian was a regular visitor to the RCA offices. The main reason for that was that he adored Iggy Pop. Derek looked upon him almost as a son. Ian was a shy guy, unassuming, but somebody that would keep coming back, as a lot of people did, because the office was a central point. It was very close to Piccadilly Radio, Derek had got it positioned perfectly. I think CBS was the only other label at the time that was in Manchester, so Derek pushed very hard to get that office against a lot of political resistance in London.

At the time we were running Grapevine Records, run by John Anderson in King's Lynn, whom I'd helped get a deal through RCA, and we had a splendid launch in London. Northern soul really was that big, you were going to sell some copies. I remember on the same week that we did the Joy Division sessions – the sales used to come through on a Tuesday – we'd sold thirty-eight thousand of a record by Judy Street called 'What', which is a classic. For some reason it didn't chart, because in those days if it was regionalised, they'd just pull it.

John Anderson's partner in America was a guy called Bernie Binnick, who was a bit of a legend. He'd owned Swan Records in Philadelphia and signed the Beatles there. Bernie had a connection with Henry Stone, who ran TK, who were really hot, with people like George McCrae and Jimmy 'Bo' Horne, and they wanted a punk band. I didn't know anybody other than . . . 'Oh, Ian's got a band.' They'd just been up at Pennine, they'd done a thousand copies of an EP. I seem to remember him showing me a shrink-wrapped copy and saying, 'We've got 999 left.' They'd just changed their name to Joy Division.

Manchester was awash with bands at the time, and nobody could have predicted that they would be where they ended up being. But Bernie wanted to get a band, and it seemed worth having a go. I can't remember exactly how we did it. I do remember that it took a little bit of convincing, because none of us knew what the hell we were doing. Somehow we managed to cobble together about £1,400, and off we went at £35 an hour into Greendale Studios.

We did the sessions, with a little bit of John Anderson saying,

'You need to use a synthesizer,' which they didn't want to do. We laid the tracks down remarkably quickly. I think the engineer must have been pretty good. I was there, but it was John and the engineer that were doing the work. I seem to remember playing pool upstairs most of the time. The tracks sounded fantastic. By the Wednesday we hadn't got the vocals down in any way, shape or form. I think we tried to loosen Ian up with cider, which I seem to remember he liked drinking, but only to get his vocals right.

On the Wednesday night I can distinctly remember John saying to me, 'We're not going to complete these sessions, these vocals aren't really right. Can you get Paul Young in from Sad Café?' Which is absolutely abhorrent, isn't it? But if you think about it, we'd got till Thursday night to get it finished. But it all came together, it came together so well that when we played people the cassettes, they were absolutely astonished. Even RCA sat up and took notice, and that's when the rot started to set in, because the band didn't want to be within RCA. That was the last thing they wanted.

Bernard Sumner: So we went in the studio with this guy. He wanted to cut an album with us in two days – a day to record it and a day to mix it – and the guy was a pain in the arse, he was not on our wavelength at all. We went into central Manchester, we recorded this album in a day. My guitar amp was playing up. It was a fifty-quid amp and it was buzzing and farting and the speaker cone was damaged, and he was pulling his hair out: 'Look, you've only got a day. Time's money, we're running out of time. You fix your amp, get some Sellotape or something.' The whole thing was a shambles.

Just as we were leaving, he said, 'Right, we should have done the vocals today, but we're going to have to do them all tomorrow morning before we start mixing.' He said, 'What you want to do is get a load of James Brown records, play them tonight, learn how James sings, and sing like James tomorrow morning.' Ian just went, 'Let's just fuck it off now.' And we were like, 'What? Fucking first opportunity of being in a studio?' We had a bit of an argument, and

Ian was going, 'This guy's a knobhead, we should just fuck off.' But we turned up, and Ian didn't bother singing like James Brown.

I remember us sat there in the morning in a really bad mood, and they'd double-booked the session in the morning with a guy that was singing an advertising jingle, and he kept singing this jingle for Littlewoods Lotteries: 'Littlewoods, Lotteries, more and more win Littlewoods, Littlewoods, Lotteries, more and more win Littlewoods,' in a phoney American accent. We were in the worst mood, and the guy would go, 'Right, you've lost another hour, get in and do your vocals.' Like, an hour to do all the vocals. And then we started mixing, and it just turned out dreadful.

Stephen Morris: I can always remember him trying to get Ian to sound like James Brown, and the best way to get Ian to sing like James Brown was to get him absolutely paralytic. Apparently, James Brown did the same thing, so we just got a bottle of whisky and were plying him with whisky and telling him to belt it out like James Brown. It's not the way really; he just got kind of very fractious and started yelping like a dog. Anyway, it was a learning experience, the RCA record – it's not the way to do it – so that when we did do *Unknown Pleasures*, we knew what to do.

What we did get out of it on the plus side was – this might have been hedging their bets a bit: 'If it doesn't work as a punk record, we can probably salvage it as some sort of northern soul/punk crossover.' – 'Why don't you do a cover of N. F. Porter's "Keep on Keeping on"?' Which was the first of our many ill-fated cover versions, because every time we try and cover something, it ends up being something else, and in this case it ended up being 'Interzone'. It was their idea to cover it, so we did, but we did it a bit differently. I mean, N. F. Porter's 'Keep on Keeping on', it's a great song anyway.

Richard Searling: N. F. Porter's is a really powerful record. As the insistent, urgent lyrics would tell you, it's a black man's plea to his fellow man not to give up: 'Keep on, don't let the system get you down.' It wasn't a typical northern soul record actually, it was probably more or less a new release – it only came out in 1971. The suggestion of 'Keep on Keeping on' came from my wife, Judith. I think we must all have had very fertile minds in those days about how we saw this session going at Greendale. The band didn't have any resistance to that. I think they probably raised their eyebrows a little bit. As I said, there were varying degrees of cooperation. Ian was very positive. Steve was quite a nervous guy, didn't really say too much. Bernard was quite suspicious, which, as he was a businessman, an old head on young shoulders at the time, I think he would have thought, 'What the hell are we doing with these guys?' They worked at that, and to give the band their due, having heard the track they got on with it and did a fantastic track. I don't know what they ended up calling it, but it was great.

So 'Keep on Keeping on' was done. There was a track called 'They Walked in Line' as well on there, and that was funny because there's a pub opposite Greendale and we took them for a drink, and my wife was there, and they wanted lager, and I went and got the drinks and got back, and they wanted lime as well, and Judith said, 'They wanted lime, they wanted lime,' and we sort of sang the thing. We gave them the opportunity when nobody else would, and I hope they look back on it as a positive week.

- June 1978: release of *Ideal for Living* EP on Enigma Records
- 12 June 1978: release of *Short Circuit: Live at the Electric Circus*, featuring Joy Division, 'At a Later Date'

Peter Hook: That last night at the Circus album was a complete farce. It was a real stitch-up. The contract was the funniest thing I've ever seen: 'All groups shall receive 5 per cent off Virgin.' We thought that meant we got 5 per cent each, and what it meant was, we got half a per cent. Ten groups between them got 5 per cent, and Virgin got 95. Then, six months later, it was out with the big sticker: 'Including Joy Division!'

Paul Morley, *NME*, 3 June 1978
Joy Division were once Warsaw, a punk group with literary
pretensions. They're a dry, doomy group who depend
promisingly on the possibilities of repetition, sudden
stripping away, with deceptive dynamics, whilst they use
sound in a more orthodox hard rock manner than, say,
either The Fall or Magazine. They have an ambiguous appeal,
and with patience they could develop strongly and make
some testing, worthwhile metallic music.

**Alan Lewis, review of *Ideal for Living* in *Sounds*,
24 July 1978**
Another Fascism for Fun and Profit mob, judging by the
Hitler Youth imagery and Germanic typography on the
sleeve. But interesting, and definitely worth investigating
if you're gripped by the grinding riff gloom and industrial
bleakness of the Wire/Subway Sect Order.

**Jon Savage, review of *Short Circuit: Live at the Electric
Circus* in *Sounds*, 24 July 1978**
Joy Division (then Warsaw) run through 'At a Later Date'
which, like their EP 'Ideal for Living' hints at a promise yet
to be fulfilled.

Bernard Sumner: We got the vinyl, *Ideal for Living*. I'd drawn the
sleeve. 'I know what we'll do, take it to Pips, the local club that
we go to, we'll play it.' By that time they had a punk room, so we
went to the DJ and it was like, 'Play our record, it's us, just play that
record.' So he said, 'No, fuck off.' – 'No, no, we've been coming here
for years. Play it.' He said, 'All right, give it here.'
   There were loads of people on the dance floor. He put it on,
and the pressing was so bad it was completely muffled, so quiet
that you wouldn't believe it, and it just cleared the dance floor.
Everyone just walked off, and he took it off halfway through. It
was like, 'Oh shit, what have we done?' I blamed it on the pressing,

but it could have been the music actually. It didn't go down very well at all.

Peter Hook: It was a simple matter of physics really. If you put that much time on a seven-inch record, it's going to sound shite. I know now that the monitors in the studio were distorting and that made it sound better, but when you put it on a record it didn't sound anything like the studio. It was probably one of the most disappointing moments of my life: getting that record, taking it home and playing it, because it sounded so bad I wanted to die. All that effort and work, and all the hopes and everything you'd put on it, and it was just terrible.

Stephen Morris: Then we're stuck with all these records. 'What are we going to do? Oh God.' I tried selling them. I actually did sell quite a lot – more than ten anyway – in the public houses around Macclesfield, so some people in Macclesfield must have a copy of *Ideal for Living* somewhere.

Mark Reeder: When they released the EP, no one wanted to stock it. I thought it was brilliant, I loved it. I knew Ian was interested in history, especially the Second World War and Germany. And since I'd been to Germany, he wanted to know all about it. I tried to explain to him, 'It's not like you imagine it to be, people goose-stepping around everywhere.' That's how people imagined Germany to be, just full of Nazis. But to have that on the front cover, I thought it was quite brave really. And when you opened it out, you had the Warsaw ghetto child inside.

Trying to sell the record, it was just at that pivotal moment, wasn't it? You had Siouxsie on TV wearing a swastika armband – that definitely sent out the wrong signals to everybody. They worried about people thinking they were fascists and all the right-wingers suddenly coming out of the woodwork. It was sending out all the wrong signals. And the pseudo-Germanic lettering and doing songs like 'They Walked in Line' – I knew it fascinated Ian, the mythology and the occultism, because we'd talked about all that when we were teenagers.

Deborah Curtis: Ian was intrigued. I think he liked all the pomp and the uniforms and the strutting around. He thought Margaret Thatcher was fantastic. He liked to have his own way, to be in control, and it worked. He flattened me, to some extent, not that he was trying to flatten me, but he knew he could easily get his own way with me. I don't think he could have married someone who was bossy.

You couldn't have an argument with him about anything, because he'd just back down. He'd stick to his beliefs, but he wouldn't upset anybody. Like this Nazi thing. He wouldn't discuss it with me. I think that was because he knew we didn't think along the same lines, so rather than have an argument – he didn't like confrontation – he'd just keep quiet.

Paul Morley: Warsaw shouting 'Remember Rudolf Hess' at the Electric Circus and all that kind of nonsense: at the time, whenever any of that happened those of us within it had not a moment's doubt that it was anything dicey; you just trusted somehow the instincts of locals that it was not. It could have been dangerous, but you just felt that it was them looking for some kind of dangerous energy rather than being actually fascinated in a sleazy, disastrous way. It just seemed clumsy rather than terrible.

Bernard Sumner: The Second World War left a big impression on me, via my grandparents. So the sleeve was that impression. It wasn't pro-Nazi, quite the contrary. I just thought that people shouldn't forget. As I was growing up, I felt that I was being taught by other people, my teachers, how to act and how to relate to the world. The generation before had gone through a period when the whole civilised Western world had gone through a world war. People had behaved in a completely insane way, killing each other.

One of the first things that Rob Gretton did when he came along was to say, 'That fucking record you've done, get rid of that fucking cover. Everyone thinks you're Nazis because of it. Whose idea was that, you tossers?' So he said, 'We're going to do a new cover and we're going to press it as a twelve-inch so it sounds loud.' Rob was a DJ at that stage. So he did it and we played it, and he was right, it sounds fantastic, it sounds really good.

Another of the things Rob did, which was really good, was to raise two grand to buy the RCA tapes and the contract off this guy – we'd signed a bloody contract. Two grand was an enormous amount of money then, don't know where he got it from. And we got the tapes, but of course it ended up coming out anyway as a bootleg after Joy Division became well known. It suddenly appeared, this crap album. So Rob gave us a togetherness.

Richard Searling: I remember them saying, 'We're bringing a manager in, any objection?' I said, 'No, you need one, you should always have had one.' It was Rob Gretton. He needs all the tracks remixing, which was a bit of a shock to us, because we hadn't really got any more money to do that. We felt it was good enough. I can't remember who made the offer or whether we said, 'Well, we need to get our money back.' John thinks we got £700 back. I'm sure we didn't, I'm sure we got all our money back.

All RCA were bloody bothered about was pushing a guy called Gerard Kenny. He was going to be the new Elton John. They weren't really interested about some band in Manchester that could have made bloody millions if they'd treated it right at the time. God, Iggy Pop could have produced them, thinking about it. But I think at the time if you'd said, 'Do you think the band are going to make it or not, Richard?' I would have said, with everything else that was going on, 'No, I don't actually.'

Rob Gretton (as 'Rob', from *Manchester Rains* fanzine): This is a Slaughter and Dogs fanzine – it's called 'Manchester Rains' because we've heard that London's Burning (hooray!). We've decided to devote it to the Dogs because we feel that too many poxy bands, particularly from 'The Big Smoke' – it's called that because it's burning, see? – are getting a lot of exposure that they don't really deserve.

Lesley Gilbert: We'd been to Israel on kibbutz for about six months, and we came back just after the Pistols played the Free Trade Hall, so we missed that, and obviously neither of us had a job when we came back. I got one pretty quickly, but Rob didn't, so he had a lot of time on his hands. When Slaughter and the Dogs were starting up in Wythenshawe, which was where he was from, he knew somebody who knew them, and we went to see them one night and that's what started it really. I'm not too sure why, but it really excited him, much more than it did me.

I was interested, but there was something that grabbed Rob. I think he just felt it was very exciting, and it came at a time in his life when he was really open to something completely new and completely different. I don't think he was consciously wanting to change his life, but this really got him excited. He worked with them for a while, and then their manager, who was the brother of Mike Rossi, Slaughter's guitarist, had to step down for a while, so then Rob took over managing them with Vinnie Faal.

We saw Joy Division together for the first time at the Stiff/ Chiswick band thing, and they were on really late. We stayed to watch them, and they were just amazing. Their presence and the atmosphere they brought. I mean, after standing for a few hours and watching band after band after band, you would have thought, 'Oh God, it's the last one, thank God for that.' But their presence was . . . I can't describe it any other way, it was just, 'Wow, these are amazing.' Maybe not so much at that time the music, but it was purely a feeling.

Bernard Sumner: We needed a manager badly, and Rob was great. He wasn't a businessman, and he could be belligerent and he'd treat us all like his children sometimes. I think he might have been a bit older than us. I think he felt me and Hooky were a bunch of thick tossers from Salford, cos he's from Wythenshawe, and apparently people in Wythenshawe look down on people from Salford. Rob was a City fan. Everyone in Salford are Manchester United fans, everyone in Wythenshawe are Manchester City fans, so there was a bit of that, even though we weren't that bothered about football.

He just thought we were a pair of Salford tossers. I remember the first time we stayed in a hotel together: 'Excuse me, sir, would you like an alarm call?' – 'No.' – 'Would you like a newspaper?' I said, 'Yeah.' And he said, 'Which one?' I said, 'I'll have *News of the World* please.' I remember Rob going, '[*snorts*] *News of the World*? You thick Salford bastard.' Of course, he had the *Guardian*. And I was like, 'What's wrong with it? What's wrong with the *News of the World*?' I know now, but he thought that was just so typical, and that summed up what he thought of us.

But he was a good laugh and he was very into the punk ethos and doing things that way and not being mainstream, which suited us down to a T. I think if we'd been left to our own devices, we would have signed to anyone just to get our records out, but the fact that we ended up on Factory was really Rob stirring. Ian thought it was a good idea as well. Me and Hooky weren't that bothered, but it gave us a great deal of creative living space.

Terry Mason: Barney had put in the least amount of effort of anyone. Me and Ian had gone down to London to try and get into record companies, we'd mail stuff off. We were the people who believed in the dream as such, that there's something big there, and Barney was going along just as he felt. Rob turned up, and I think Ian was really upset by the way it was done, because he was a very honourable man. That didn't seem right by Ian.

As a manager, I didn't have a phone, which makes life a little difficult. Rob didn't actually own a phone at that point, but the flat where he lived had a payphone outside his front door, so that was that. It was a weird situation: I'd gone from one of the founders of the band, put so much effort in, and then Rob comes in just as the first major hurdle had been cleared and I'm out on my ear. I was pissed off at that happening and I put out an injunction, not that I knew what an injunction was, but I knew it's what people did.

There was never anything in writing, and things in writing with bands don't mean anything anyway. But then I was left with the decision: do I give up everything – give up my mates basically – do I spit the dummy out, or do I stay with them? It was a fun hobby. Anyone who's thinking about being in a band, no matter how awful, try it. It's good, it's fun, it doesn't have to be for life, but try it for a while. I stayed with the band.

I had a meeting with Rob. He still wanted me around. I was still useful: I didn't mind humping equipment up and down stairs, I was a driver, I was quite sensible about doing things. Then Rob said, 'Well, what you can do is, the band can't afford to bring in a sound engineer, you can learn.' And from that point basically it was me doing that. You're still very much part of it; these people were my friends, you don't write off a bunch of friends over something like that.

Stephen Morris: Rob did make a difference. I think the fact that we'd got a manager was a step up on the road, because we'd done the record, we'd done the gigs, and now we'd got a manager, and it was like these are essential building blocks to the big time, and we'd just got another one. Rob made us . . . I was going to say take it more seriously, but I don't think we ever took what we were doing that seriously. We were passionate about it, but not to the extent where we were very, very serious about it. We were doing it because we enjoyed doing it. It was from the heart.

Terry Mason: There was this phase where, although we were the most unpopular band in town, it didn't stop the band rehearsing and getting better. More of Ian's songs were coming through. Some of the early songs were Hooky songs, and then all of a sudden Ian's writing comes through, and it's a different league. Everyone else in the country's doing simple rhymes, and Ian's putting these poems together, not that we could usually hear or understand what they were.

Bernard Sumner: I can't remember exactly how it happened. We'd just pick our instruments up and play. We'd have some kind of crappy cassette recorder. Ian would usually go, 'Oh, that bit's good,' because obviously we were concentrating, he was listening to it all the time. So I'd go, 'Oh, you like that bit, right?' So I'd probably arrange it. 'How about going to here?' And then we'd jam on that, and 'Okay, we'll use that for the verse and we'll use that for the chorus.' It was quite simple really, but I guess because we didn't know what we were doing, we ended up doing things in an unusual way.

You'd search for something that was easier to play on the guitar, and so you'd just go, 'Right, try these two strings. Oh, that sounds good, I'll just use that.' My amp was so incredibly loud: to get any distortion out of it I had to have it incredibly loud or else it sounded awful. I used a strange amp that I found: I think it's called a Vox U30. It's not the Beatles Vox and it's not an AC30; it's a weird hybrid of a transistor amp and a valve amp, and it's got a really biting, loud, angry tone to it, and I just love that amp.

I like to feel that I've got a good inherent sense of rhythm, so I'm quite a strong rhythm player. Because of punk and the thousand-notes-a-minute thing, I always thought it would be great if you're doing a guitar solo, it was a better solo if you could play it with just one finger. It's easier for people to understand what you're getting at, so I always try to keep it simple. Hooky couldn't hear himself play low down, so he started playing high up, so it was just a happy accident like that that gave us our sound.

I'm a pretty laid-back person, I'm not hyper by any means, and to play punk you have to be hyper or aggressive or mad, so it didn't really work out. Then I developed my own style, which was slow and considered. I liked sound, and I used to play on the neck of the guitar where it sounded really nice. I'm more rhythm and chords, and Hooky was melody. He's got a really good talent for melody.

He's got this powerful, barbaric part of his personality that people like, a strident quality that comes out in the music.

The strange thing is that we never used to talk about it, you just did it. A very unconscious way of writing music. There was no method that we used. We just used to wait for the inspiration. Ian was pretty good at riff spotting. He'd go, 'Oh, that bit's good, that bit's good.' And I'd go, 'Right, okay, let's play that bit round and round, right?' And I'd suggest, 'What if we went here to this?' Everyone would try that, going to this place, and then someone else would come up with another idea, so then we'd end up with a track, and he'd play it on the cassette.

Ian would take it home, where he had a big box of lyrics. I can't remember if he used to mumble any melodies on the tracks or not. I've got a feeling he did it all at home and he'd come back next rehearsal and we'd have finished lyrics. He used to sit at home writing anyway, that was his thing. He was a writer. He would always have a file box with him, full of lyrics. He'd sit at home and just write all the time, instead of watching telly, he'd stay up – I don't know this, I'm surmising, because he'd come in with reams and reams of lyrics.

We talked about other people's music: 'Have you heard Iggy's new record, "China Girl"? Let's do something like that.' But we couldn't because we weren't good enough. 'Have you heard this track by Love, "7 and 7 Is"? Put that on.' We'd go, 'Yeah, do something like that,' then we wouldn't talk, we'd just do our thing. We wouldn't go, 'Yeah, it needs a middle eight,' or anything like that. We just wouldn't talk about it, you just didn't. Sometimes for days nothing would happen, but some days we'd get some great ideas.

It would just happen, cos we didn't know how to do it, we didn't have any craft or skill, so it was a very naive form of writing. We just did what we thought sounded good, with the simplest of methods and the simplest of chords and the simplest of music. We thought the rhythm was very important, so we would always make sure that we had a good rhythm out of Steve before we'd start on the guitars. We'd sit around like, 'Come on, Steve, give us some drum riffs.' And we'd all sit around listening to drum riffs and go, 'Right, that one. Okay, we'll jam to that riff.'

Tony Wilson: It was all four of them, without any question. People talk about drummers being important to groups, and there's no Joy Division without Stephen driving it that way and Bernard's slash guitar, and clearly the core melodic element is Hooky's high-fret playing of that bass, which no one had done before then. All of them had something to say, and they'd all been freed by the Pistols. And I don't understand why that should glue together, that amalgam of those four people – it wasn't just Ian, it was all four of them.

Stephen Morris: I started off doing kind of punk drumming. I didn't really know what punk drumming was. I thought it'd be something like Maureen Tucker out of the Velvet Underground. The drummers that I was listening to were John French out of the Magic Band and Jaki Liebezeit out of Can. I tried to be what would happen if John French lived in Germany for a long time and listened to a lot of Krautrock. I wanted to do something different.

Maureen Tucker's style of drumming was one of the things that you noticed about the Velvet Underground. It's very, very minimalistic and quite dark. I liked that aspect of it, I liked drums being kind of hypnotic in a way – in the way that some of the Velvet Underground is – and that you could set some sort of a background and then put other stuff on top of it. I just wanted to play tom-tom things: I don't know why, I was making it up as I was going along.

There were arguments. I mean, everybody argues, but we were almost a democracy. You were influenced by your limitations. We all depended on each other, and if you took one of us away, then it would stop sounding like Joy Division. It was just all of us together. Hooky couldn't tune his bass, Bernard had to tune the bass and the guitar, and things like that, we did depend on each other quite a lot. I locked in with Hooky because he was trying to play melodic rhythms, and Bernard was filling in, he didn't really do big guitar riffs, what he did was not intricate but textural.

Peter Hook: It's funny, as a musician I always felt quite inadequate because I used to watch people slap and play reggae bass and think, 'Oh, I can't do that.' I can't play along to people's tunes, I find it impossible. Like my mum used to say, I couldn't carry a tune in a bucket. I think I'm partially tone deaf, so I can't play other people's music, so it used to really frustrate me, and it always seems to be the things you want are more important than the things you've got. I suppose in my mind or subconsciously I wanted to be like Jean-Jacques Burnel or Paul Simonon.

We used to rehearse twice a week, for three hours on Wednesday night and for two hours on Sunday, and in that time you'd invariably get a song. You had no way of recording it because we couldn't afford a tape recorder, so the songs only existed in your head. It's an amazing thought these days to think that *Unknown Pleasures* for the most part only existed in your head, and it only existed when the four of you played it together. It was mind-blowing to me that if one of us had died, it would have just gone. It's absolutely bizarre.

I bought a bass capo off an old teacher in my school who played bass with the Salford Jets, Diccon Hubbard, and I couldn't hear it when I played low, cos of the row, cos Barney's amp was really loud. When I played high I could pick it out. Ian just latched onto you playing high, and he'd say, 'That sounds good when you play high, we should work on that, that sounds really distinctive.' And I'd go, 'All right, which bit?' And he'd go, 'That bit you just played there.' And all those songs – 'She's Lost Control', 'Insight', 'Twenty Four Hours', 'Love Will Tear Us Apart' – 99 per cent of the time started with the music.

Terry Mason: Very early on the band realised that they needed a tape recorder. They'd basically jam along, and from that they would pull out snippets, and as they were going along Ian would pull out one index card, have a go at those lyrics, see if they fit. It's like an eye test – 'Is it better with these lyrics? Is it better with these?' – and they'd work it out that way. Because they had a tape, they could always go back and pick out what they'd done. At one point the band were churning out songs. They'd be working on bits and they had a lot of work in progress, and Ian would go back, rework it, throw something out, try something new; if they weren't happy, leave it for a while.

Stephen Morris: You couldn't tell what the hell Ian was going on about, because it was Ian's PA. I had no idea what on earth he was singing.

Bernard Sumner: It was great because Ian could come up with the words just like that on top of what we'd jammed, so you'd end up with a song in a day. Once we got the initial riffs, then it was more up to me, Hooky and Steve to work on the arrangements, and he'd step out a little bit while we made it into a fully arranged song. Then he'd come in with the vocals. We were not bouncing off each other; we just completely ignored each other, we were all on our own island, and we just made sure that what we were doing sounded great, and we didn't pay any attention to what the others were doing, not consciously anyway.

Obviously, subconsciously there were moments, but we didn't talk to each other about it and just did our own thing. We didn't know what we were doing, but something happened. We just knew we liked music. If you really love listening to music and it moves you passionately, like you hear a song and you play it over and over again and you absolutely love that song, to write music you just reverse that process: you feel a passion inside you, and then you get the passion to come out through your hands and through your minds.

I've also got to try and imagine what I'm going to play before I play it. I try to hear it in my head first and then try and translate it to my hands, and then it's just a reversal of that really. We were all really into music: Hooky was, Steve had an enormous record collection, probably bigger than anyone, and Ian obviously did. But

Ian was the writer of words as well. He was very into books, very bookish. I think if he'd have lived, eventually he would have become a writer. I think that would have happened quite soon actually.

Peter Hook: I suppose I'm more aggressive than Bernard, and a damn sight more aggressive than Steve, God bless him. Steve's not aggressive at all, apart from when he does go, and when he goes he goes like a volcano, fucking hell. What I liked about Joy Division was that it was very equal: it was the four of us and you were all going in the right direction. Joy Division was balanced perfectly, which made it perfect.

6

JUNE – DECEMBER 1978

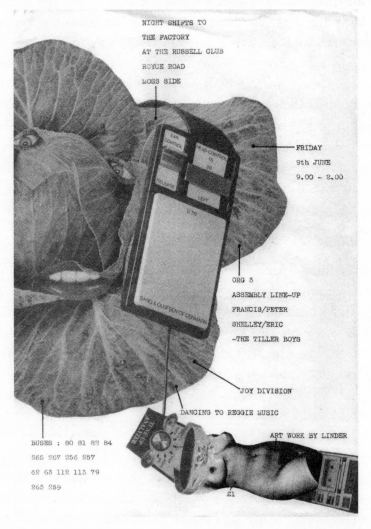

NIGHT SHIFTS TO
THE FACTORY
AT THE RUSSELL CLUB
ROYCE ROAD
MOSS SIDE

EAR CONTROL
HEAD CONTROL
10
20
RELEASE
LEFT
U70
BANG & OLUFSEN OF DENMARK

FRIDAY
9th JUNE
9.00 – 2.00

ORG 3
ASSEMBLY LINE–UP
FRANCIS/PETER
SHELLEY/ERIC
–THE TILLER BOYS

JOY DIVISION

DANCING TO REGGIE MUSIC

ART WORK BY LINDER

BUSES : 80 81 82 84
265 267 256 257
62 63 112 113 79
265 259

£1

Factory handbill, June 1978 (Courtesy of Linder Sterling)

Richard Boon: Despite all these little places that you could hire and set up your own event, there was no focus. But all these hit-and-miss, drive-by-night punk-rock events in odd places stimulated something. Tony Wilson was very quick to pick up on that when Factory launched their night at the PSV Club, another club which had its off night. PSV was the Passenger Service Vehicle Club. It was for the bus drivers and clippies, set in by the crescents in the heart of Moss Side, which actually gave the venue an edge as well, so the environment really made it the focus.

Moss Side was edgy because it was on the borders of various competing cultures. Down the road was a heavily Asian culture – the famous Curry Mile; there was a large Afro-Caribbean element; and there was a lot of white people who had been forced into what possibly was a huge design mistake: the crescents in Hulme. It meant some people were going into an area they were unfamiliar with, felt cautious about. There was a lot of crime and drugs, so it was exactly the right place. But that's what was needed: someone had to take that initiative and say, 'Here's a place that we can go, reliably, regularly, rather than be frustrated and waiting – "What's going to happen?"'

Tony Wilson: Although I was putting bands on *Granada Reports*, my main music show was *So It Goes*. Basically, I'd annoyed my bosses. Iggy had done his version of 'The Passenger' at the Apollo, which we televised in October 1977, and there was a whole bit right in the middle when he's sitting there with my cameraman, Mike Blakely, and he goes, 'So I said to Camille, "Camille, I'm going to buy you a Rolls-Royce." And she said, "Iggy, I hate fucking cars," blah blah blah.'

So we cut the film, it's wonderful, but 'You got to get rid of the "fucking".' And I go berserk. 'No, no, this is like telling Mozart.' So basically my bosses at Granada had to have two weeks of this moron Wilson screaming that getting rid of the word 'fucking' from the middle of this Iggy Pop classic version of 'The Passenger' was like interfering with the Holy Bible or cutting a line out of

Shakespeare – 'You can't do this.' So they got all this bollocks from me, and I don't blame them for saying, 'That's it, we don't have to deal with this shit any more from Wilson.'

I got pulled upstairs and told, 'Right, no more music shows, and by the way, if we see that guy with the horse's tail coming out of his arse one more time, you're fired' – that was a reference to Iggy. So I accepted that as far as putting music on television, that was it, *So It Goes* was over. But for me the passion of my life, which in the sixties had been the obsession of every British child, come the seventies I'd become connected to it. Suddenly I was touching this wonderful world, and suddenly it was like, 'Take your hands away now!'

I wanted to stay connected in some way or another, and around this very month when I was told this – January 1978 – one of my best friends, Alan Erasmus, got sacked as manager of a band, as did the drummer and the rhythm guitarist. This happened one particular day, 24 January 1978, after which we named all our companies. I rang Alan up and I said, 'Alan, I'll join you in managing this band, the Durutti Column.' So I became a band manager in partnership with Erasmus, a partnership that lasted for thirteen, fourteen years.

You're managing a band and you're on the band's first gig: 'Well, we could play Rafters, but everyone plays Rafters. Why don't we set up a new club?' And Erasmus knew a club in Hulme. One of the secrets of life which I now tell people is: go and find a local bar or club that's doing bad business on a Thursday or Friday night, and say, 'Can we just borrow your club?' The club owner doesn't mind one little bit because he makes the real money off the bar. If you can make enough money by putting on bands and taking the door, so be it.

We thought we'd start a new club just for four weeks, four consecutive Friday nights at the Russell Club in Hulme. The story is entirely true: that Erasmus and I were walking round Manchester one day and Alan saw a sign saying 'Factory Closing' and said, 'Let's call the club the Factory, because we can have a factory opening instead of closing.' So that is actually quite true, and the fact that me as a typical sort of sixties Oxbridge type didn't for one second think about Warhol; it just seemed a very Mancunian northern industrial thing.

So it was Erasmus's idea: start a club. Then this tiny young graphic design student who looked a bit like Bryan Ferry approached me at a bad Patti Smith concert – this was when Patti Smith had gone from being a New York poetess being a rock star to being a rock star claiming to be a New York poetess – and said, 'If ever you want any graphics doing, Mr Wilson . . .' He didn't say, 'My friend Malcolm Garrett does the stuff for Buzzcocks, and I'm jealous as fuck of him, and I need to get into this to rival Malcolm.' He didn't tell me that.

So I rang him up, and three days later he arrived in the Granada canteen, and typically Peter didn't bring any of his own work at all, he brought this book of Jan Tschichold, and we spent half an hour poring over this book – wonderful – and Peter became the graphic designer. So that was how the Factory came about, and posters and the relationship, and that was the original three partners, which is Erasmus, Wilson and Saville.

Peter Saville: You couldn't avoid him in Manchester. Tony had *So It Goes*, so he had one of the only television platforms. Tony loved what was going on and he was an amazing champion of it, and strangely a champion within the Establishment. There's nothing more Establishment, particularly to young people, than television. There was this anchorperson for the current-affairs news programme, political television journalist, who had a late-night music programme that championed punk and the new wave.

That was wonderful, because television was giving exposure to something that you believed in and validating it. And also you knew it was being quite provocative and challenging as well. *The Old Grey Whistle Test* hadn't quite got its head around this – it failed to get its head around even Roxy Music. We would see Tony at a gig at least once a week, with a cameraman from Granada in tow filming something, and it was a fabulous feeling of endorsement.

Everybody knew Tony, and we often feel that we know people

on television; actually, we don't know them at all, but we think we
do because they're familiar, and Tony was somebody that we felt we
knew. I think everybody had mixed feelings, but they were grate-
ful that he was there and interested and cared. I met him because
Richard Boon said, 'Go see him.' My kind, closest friend at college,
Malcolm Garrett, had managed to actually start working with the
Buzzcocks, which I was incredibly envious of.

Malcolm deserved it, and I actually didn't, but I was still terribly
envious and wanted to be involved in what was going on as well. So
I would harass Richard Boon every week when I saw him, hoping
that perhaps he'd take on another band and that it would be too
much for Malcolm to cope with, or whatever. I did my weekly har-
assing of Richard: 'Have you got anything you would like doing?'
And Richard said, 'Go and see Tony Wilson, I've heard he's trying
to get a club night organised. Perhaps he'll need something.'

A club night was necessary because all of the amazing venues in
Manchester – there'd been so many of them through '76, '77 and
'78 – had been systematically closed down by the authorities for
one reason or another, because punk was destabilising and a concern to the greater Establishment, a little bit the way rave culture
was in the early nineties. People were worried. And so venues were
closed, licences denied and neighbours upset about noise or whatever, and suddenly by early '78 there was almost nowhere for bands
to play in Manchester.

In his champion-of-the-young-people role, Tony took it upon
himself to organise a venue. I went to see him, and I was confident
enough to just go and say, 'Can I do something?' We had a meeting
in the canteen of Granada Television, and I hadn't done anything
worth showing. I'd been very happy in my first couple of years at art
college, air-brushing glamour and doing pretend Roxy Music covers, and then I'd hit this non-period in '76, where suddenly all of
that didn't seem to matter any more. I began to find where I wanted
to go, courtesy of Malcolm Garrett's influence.

I went to see Tony with a couple of books under my arm, and
I showed Tony the manifesto by Jan Tschichold called *Die Neue*

Typographie. I said, 'I want to do something like this. Do you need anything?' Tony looked at it. It's not really Tony's sphere, but it kind of looked right, so he said, 'Yes, why don't you do a poster?'

So it came to pass that I did a poster. He'd already done one, which he showed me: he'd done the two cowboys from the situationist canon, which I hated. I think it was on Alan's wall, and Tony proudly showed it to me and said, 'Well, I've done this just for fun,' and it was the two cowboys and their conversation in French about reification. I didn't understand it at all. It was twenty years until I understood it, and then I understood it so well that I quoted it in the front of my book, but I didn't get it then.

Tony Wilson: I remember going to Peter's flat in Hale, and he had these pieces of black and pieces of yellow squares and lines and was playing with them, actually constructing them on the floor. It wasn't very punk, but my obsession is working with people who are cleverer than I am. If you're working with people who are cleverer than you, why tell them what to do? 'You're a graphic designer, you're a clever kid, do what you want to do.' Musicians, the same; everyone, do what you want to do because either you can do it or you can't.

Peter Saville: I don't even know if Tony needs a poster, but he says, 'Do something.' He embraces the desire for someone to be involved, he sees that. It's just a fledgling thing, nothing's even happened yet, and it's only going to be a Friday night every couple of weeks at the Russell Club, but someone comes along and says, 'I want to help.' So he says, 'Fine.' So it comes to pass that I do a poster. At some point I say, 'What should we say?' And he says, 'These are the dates, this is who's playing.'

So I go away and do something that I want to do. I was both delighted and disappointed by the fact that it was going to be called the Factory. It immediately gave me a Warhol feeling, but this was not a good kind of sixties-quoting moment. Actually, we're sort of in the process of getting away from all of that: this is a point at which you're trying to put some distance between yourself and the immediate past. I was more interested in the twenties than in the sixties.

The coolly industrial understanding of Factory, that's the real understanding of Factory. There's two clear aesthetic channels running through postmodernism. One is the default remnant of sixties modernism, and that's high tech. The exuberant, modern, futuristic aesthetic of the sixties does drop out as the plastic furniture breaks and the waterbed leaks, but an undeniable truth of contemporary design was there in the commercial and the industrial, so high tech is the contemporary aesthetic that survives the sixties.

In postmodernism you see that radically juxtaposed against a contemporary pseudo-classicism. Classicism is part of that grand tour rediscovery. Actually, people quite like some columns and some pediments, and postmodern architecture sees a rather free form playing with those elements, moved away from their status as icons of privilege. They're plastic or they're pink, or in the case of the AT&T building, they're on top of a six-hundred-foot sky-scraper. It's a bit like the common people playing with the debris post-revolution.

Postmodernism is aesthetically defined by these two things, the interplay between high tech and neoclassicism. And Factory played perfectly into the high-tech aesthetic for me. There was a sign on a workshop door at the art college which I coveted for months. It was in the 3D department, on one of the workshop doors, and it was the 'Use Hearing Protection' head, and as soon as Tony said, 'I'm going to call this night the Factory,' I thought, 'I'm going to borrow that sign.'

The very evening I saw Tony I had to remove that sign from the workshop door, and that became the industrial symbol of sound that I wanted to quote in the context of Factory: a factory of sound. My notions of high-tech information were answered by quoting *Die Neue Typographie* from 1919, which is Jan Tschichold's manifesto of the new typography of the machine age, and so the first Factory poster is this funny hybrid of an industrial warning sign

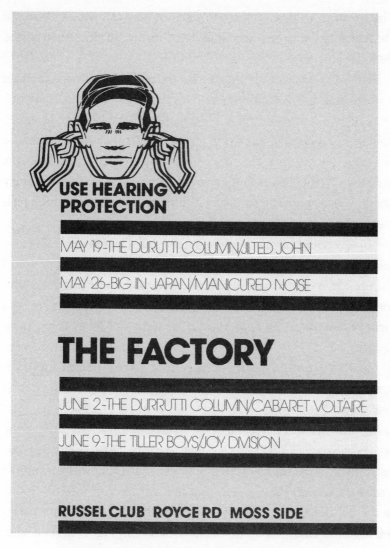

The Factory, 30 x 40″ poster, 1978 (Design by Peter Saville)

from the seventies composed together with a piece of rather strict, idealistic, modernist typography.

By virtue of being a calendar of things coming, that first Factory poster covers four nights across a couple of months. There was no specific thing for it to be about, other than a notion of a place that was called the Factory. I knew fully that when these posters were put up around Manchester, 99.9 per cent of the people who saw them would fail to register them, but they weren't intended for the 99.9 per cent, they were intended for the 0.1 per cent who would be interested in going, and I hoped that that 0.1 per cent would notice a visual statement of difference.

- 9 June 1978: the Factory I, PSV Club, Hulme, Manchester

Richard Kirk: Cabaret Voltaire were working in Sheffield. We sent some of our recordings to New Hormones. People in Manchester heard what we'd done, and Tony Wilson got to hear, and then we were invited to play at the Factory. I can't remember whether we played the opening night or the second night, but whenever we played, I think we played alongside Joy Division. They vaguely reminded me of the Doors, but if the Doors had been in Manchester in the seventies rather than in Los Angeles in the sixties.

Ian Curtis was a fan of writers like William Burroughs and J. G. Ballard, and that's where we bonded. We were interested in the Velvet Underground and the Stooges and Kraftwerk, so that's another thing where we had a lot in common. We were all working class, from similar sorts of backgrounds. Their music was very northern, a little bit like Cabaret Voltaire, a similar sort of take on life or the world – dystopian, grim, industrial.

Malcolm Whitehead: I'd met Rob Gretton in 1976, that great summer, and we really clicked. Rob had been to a kibbutz and come back, and I suppose he was trying to get himself together, so you had these two grammar-school boys trying to find out what to do with their lives. Anyway, we got on really well, and then he left early because he was going to Crete with Lesley, so post-'76 we lost a bit of touch, and I think we met up at the Moss Side Carnival the next year. He told me then he was managing a band.

I thought, 'Oh right.' He said, 'You're into wanting to do films,' because we used to talk a lot about what we wanted to do in the future. He suggested I film this band he was managing, the Panik, at the Electric Circus. They were absolutely awful. I was shooting, but it was so dark I gave up after a reel. I was working on that for about a month, and he rang me up and said, 'No, I'm not managing them any more, forget about it now.' He was managing this other group. I think they'd just changed their name to Joy Division, so he said, 'Come down and see them, see what you think.'

So I went into the Russell, and Joy Division were playing. They came on – there was nobody there because they were on very early – and they were just absolutely stunning. I can remember it, but not in my head, in my stomach, and it was that power, it was like, 'This is what I've always wanted from a band.' I was drained after seeing them.

I can remember to this day what I said to Rob. I said, 'I thought I was going to have to be like with the Panik. I thought I was going to have to come tonight and say to you, "Oh, they're very nice, Rob, we will do something with them."' But I was passionate about them: 'We've *got* to do something with these.' I didn't think they'd sell any records, didn't even think in those terms, but I thought they were going to be massive culturally. They'd just got it, just overwhelming.

Iain Gray: The shock of Ian was just immense. It was the first gig they ever did at the Factory, the Russell Club. It was beyond what the Sex Pistols did. Ian comes out, I can't remember what they opened with, but it was just unbelievable. Ian's just there and he starts that dance which I'd seen the very seeds of in a shed in Withington. It was otherworldly, and I was thinking, 'This is Ian who buys flowers for his wife, chocolates, he's the guy from *The Waltons*, and he's up onstage and it's totally inspirational and hypnotic.'

He was like a messiah, almost. I'm sold to it, I bought it totally. The weird thing about it was that I knew Ian. Usually it devalues star quality if you know them, but I saw him and I was just absolutely astounded. I felt so in awe of someone I knew, and I find that odd to this day. It was totally British, it was totally him, it wasn't an act and it was frightening.

Tony Wilson: They'd already become quite powerful. By May, June '78 they no longer had the caterwauling sound and the interesting lead singer. It had already become something rock-like, something honed like a diamond, and it was just getting more and more that way. They were stunning. Although my memory is of Margi Clarke being in this tiny dressing room and amusing Joy Division with stories, and suddenly going, 'Oh, I need to take a piss, I need to go to the toilet,' and the guys going, 'Okay, fine,' and Margaret hitching her skirt up and sitting in the sink, while two young Salford boys and two Macclesfield boys looked completely ashen. It was like they'd never seen behaviour like this before, never met anyone like Margi before.

Stephen Morris: When Tony started doing the Factory nights, there was this kind of void: there was the band, then there was nothing, and then there were some people lurking there. It didn't bother Ian that there was nobody there, that was just what happened, he'd go for it, and he did go for it in an empty room. And by the second time this void was getting narrower and narrower, so that eventually there was even the odd person dancing. Yeah, they'd sort of come to the front and, wahey, we've got an audience now.

- 28 July 1978: the Factory I, Manchester
- 29 August 1978: Band on the Wall, Manchester

Paul Morley, *NME*, 9 September 1978
Their music is mercilessly attacking, it rotates, persists, repeats, always well balanced . . . This could be Joy Division's peak.

- 4 September 1978: Band on the Wall, Manchester

Mick Middles, *Sounds*, 16 September 1978
They started with 'Exercise One' which immediately showed

that the band have improved immensely over the past year. It was a deep and doomy song with a killer bass line. The band careered through the set, gradually lifting the crowd from being just mildly interested to being pretty boisterous.

- 9 September 1978: Eric's, Liverpool
- 10 September 1978: Royal Standard, Bradford
- 22 September 1978: Coach House, Huddersfield

Bernard Sumner: By this time we'd play everywhere and anywhere. I had some dodgy agent, a small guy in a back office in the middle of Manchester. He'd put us on in places like Huddersfield, and we'd get £5 for playing. I remember paying to play at one place, a working men's club in Huddersfield, and somewhere in Leeds, all over in West Yorkshire, where no one else would play. It was a fantastic escape for us really.

In fact, Steve and Hooky got pulled in for questioning as Yorkshire Ripper suspects because we spent so much time driving over the Pennines – we played gigs in those areas where the Ripper was killing people. Steve had his Cortina, and they got his number and they got Hooky's van. The police came round to the house and took him in for questioning. 'Well, he's got a beard, hasn't he? Why did he bleach his hair all of a sudden, change his appearance? He's got a hammer in the back of the car as well.' Of course, we found that incredibly humorous when they got pulled in.

Going back to our little agent and us playing in West Yorkshire, we'd play that place like three times, and you'd go there once and it'd be five people, by the third time it was packed out, so it must have been word of mouth. I think the thing was, we weren't like other bands. By the time we'd stopped aping punk and discovered our own sound, we sounded unique and we looked unique. It was a gradual, slow-build process.

Malcolm Whitehead: Every time they were playing locally I went to see them, and it wasn't very long before it was absolutely packed.

I bet it was weeks, because things seemed to be so compacted into a short space of time then.

They had this magical thing. I've never seen it in any other band – you might get three members working and one not – but everything came together. It was like one of those wonderful accidents, because when you learn about how they got together, it was slightly random, and yet they were born to play with each other. They happened to be artistically right for each other. They're all different personalities, and yet they worked superbly together.

It was Ian connecting in that way: the way he laid himself bare. The massive courage of the man, that's what got to me. To be honest, I didn't really know what they were singing about because it was so loud. But I knew what he was singing about without hearing the lyrics. I don't know whether it was just a natural thing or whether he had to force himself to do it. I know he had to knock down a few Pils before he went onstage. I don't think that was just a bit of nervousness about being before an audience, I think it was, 'Ooh, I've got to do this and I've got to tell the truth, so I'll have to get a little bit pissed if I'm going to do this.' All the times I ever saw him I never thought, 'He's just going through the motions.' I think each performance that he gave that I saw was the real deal, the raw truth.

Bernard Sumner: Part of the time when Joy Division was forming, Ian worked in a rehabilitation centre for people with physical and mental disabilities trying to find work again. He was very much affected by those people. 'She's Lost Control' was about a girl who used to come into the centre and try to find work. She had epilepsy and lost more and more time through it, and then one day she just didn't come in any more. He assumed that she'd found a job, but found out later that she'd had a fit and died.

My influence was from my grandparents and from the war. Ian's influence seemed to be madness and insanity. He was interested in the sick part of life. He said that his sister, or his aunt or somebody, had worked in a mental home, and she used to tell him things about the people in the home – people with twenty nipples or two heads – and that left a big impression on him. He had moments of intensity, but he was fun. Primarily he was a fun guy, a good laugh. He wasn't a straight person.

Let me start with his moments of intensity, when he got frustrated. I remember him coming down from a hotel once, and he'd phoned Debbie and the phone call cost £10, and he didn't realise that hotels charge so much for calls. So he asked Rob to contribute towards it because he didn't have any money, and Rob was like, 'Fuck off, pay for it yourself,' and Ian going apeshit with Rob over that, just completely exploding in frustration at Rob.

I remember another time in the rehearsal room him getting so frustrated at Rob he just picked up a wastepaper basket, put it on his head and starting marching up and down the thing in a frenzy, and of course we found that extremely funny. He went fucking bananas, completely crazy. He went from being this nice, polite, pleasant, funny person to being completely insane. Ian was strong-willed when he was riled; he had an explosive personality.

But most of the time he was cool. He really was. His performance, I guess, was a manifestation of this kind of frenzy that he went into. He was Ian, and then suddenly [*snaps fingers*] he'd hit this threshold and become this manic person whose head was in another world. He was like that onstage, but he was like that if you had an argument with him as well. He was a very charismatic frontman because people never knew what was going to happen with him next – we didn't – and it just worked. He seemed to get carried away by the music.

A lot of people thought he was off his head on drugs, and he wasn't, never, ever, ever. Because he looked like he was on drugs, but the music seemed to put him in a trance and he just started dancing away and he'd go to another world. He was lost in the music, completely. You never knew what was going to happen next, whether he was going to start pulling the stage apart or smashing the drum kit up. It was just a very exciting performance to watch.

- 20 September 1978: *Granada Reports*

Bob Greaves: . . . called Joy Division. They were called Warsaw once, but Joy Division, I think, has a nicer ring to it, and we hope that we're launching them on a real joyride, as we have before with many others, haven't we, Tony, yes?

Tony Wilson: Seeing as how this is the programme which previously brought you first television appearances from everything from the Beatles to the Buzzcocks, we do like to keep our hand in and keep you informed of the most interesting new sounds in the north-west. This, Joy Division, is the most interesting new sound we've come across in the last six months. They're a Manchester band, with the exception of the guitarist, who comes from Salford – very important difference. They're called Joy Division, and this number is 'Shadowplay'.

Peter Hook: I was terrified. Rob took us out and bought us a new shirt each: 'Got to keep them on the lead.' So we had a new shirt for 'Shadowplay'. I watched it back on Granada, and I thought, 'Fucking hell, we're good.' There were very few occasions when I've thought, 'Oh, that was good.'

Bernard Sumner: It was bizarre, because we weren't allowed to touch our own equipment because of the studio regulations, the unions and all that. It was like go and plug my amplifier in, and: 'Don't touch that, you'll have them all off the set if you touch that, we'll shut it down.' I said, 'It's just a plug, I just want to plug my amp in.' – 'Don't touch it, sunshine.'

I remember seeing it and being pretty pleased with it; they'd cut a bit of footage in of cars going through a city.

Tony Wilson: I asked one of the directors to direct the afternoon session if he would, and it was the wonderful, lovely David Liddiment, who went on to be head of ITV. I was in the box, and David said, 'I want to drop something behind them, can you go and get me some backing, Tony, please?' So I said, 'Yeah, yeah, yeah, fine.' So I ran upstairs to the first-floor *World in Action* editing suites, where one of my friends was the editor. 'Can I borrow some stuff?' And they have these bins with little wire things. They'd been neg-cutting some documentary about the CIA in Langley, just outside Washington, and they said, 'Those are being thrown away, you can have them, Tony.' So we just glued together this series of black-and-white negative travelling shots of Langley. I ran down to telecine, and then David rolled it in the background and overlaid it, so it's nice suburban shots and there's no real meaning whatsoever. I think far more meaning is in the fact that Bernard looks so young and beautiful in it.

You see some very large beltway bungalows. It was totally chance; it could have been anything in the bin of that *World in Action* cutting room. It was by chance a suburban travelogue, it's that 'To the centre of the city where all roads meet, waiting for you' lyric, with the fact that Ian and Steve come from Macclesfield. Manchester was the big city just down the road, and they would go backwards and forwards, so it's that understanding of the northern city.

C. P. Lee: Joy Division and their ilk are among the first vanguard of groups who could actually use proper motorways, and there is a feeling of motion within Joy Division, the idea that there's a Mancunian Way which goes east–west. It doesn't actually go anywhere, but it's there and it's in the sky. We're very used to American groups talking about the freeway. Joy Division don't actually sing about that, but I think there's an undercurrent, there's a feeling of motion and of movement and use of roads. In the seventies you could actually criss-cross Great Britain, so there is the kind of free spirit which is associated with driving.

- 12 October 1978: Kelly's, Manchester

Bob Dickinson: Kelly's was a little basement nightclub in a tiny little street just off Hanover Street. It's not there now. It was a Rock Against Racism promotion and Phil Jones promoted it, which is how I knew about it, because he used to come round to my flat. There was hardly anybody there; it was the closest I'd ever stood to Joy Division, so I could look at them really closely. I don't think it was a terribly good gig. Joy Division weren't great every time; probably they were underperforming because there weren't that many people there.

Something that was different from the first time I saw them was that they had changed the way they dressed. They stopped wearing leather jackets and boots and so on, and they started wearing suits and ties and dark shirts, dark suits, and they started looking like 'Here are the young men'. They looked German, but they looked well-dressed and sober. They always looked serious, but the suits were part of this important image change that they went through that created the character of Joy Division.

I don't think they were Nazis, I think they were deeply aware of Nazism and the things that Nazism had done, and they were interested in Auschwitz, Warsaw, the ghettos, the way that the Nazis oppressed and killed the Jews. I think their music was very much influenced by this sense that they were haunted, that we're all haunted by the ghosts of Nazism and by what it did to Europe. The fact that they didn't come from formerly occupied Europe is probably what makes it even more powerful.

They were talking about it in dark, depressing Manchester. They were throwing up these echoes and these spectres of late Second World War Europe and the deaths of millions, and it's something that people still don't want to think about, so I never thought they were Nazis. When I bought *Ideal for Living* and looked at the artwork, that drummer boy on the front and Barney's haircut, I thought, 'That's just Barney cutting his hair deliberately to look like that and carry the guilt.' That's what I thought: 'Carry the guilt and not be ashamed.'

Bernard Sumner: We knew that we weren't Nazis, and that was good enough for us. At the same time, we were doing gigs for Rock Against Racism. We didn't feel we should defend ourselves, because we knew we weren't Nazis – quite the opposite. We didn't feel that we had to go out to the press, saying, 'Wait a minute, that first sleeve is actually anti-Nazi.' We thought that was a bit crass. Our attitude was, if anyone wants to know if we're Nazis, ask us, and we'll tell you the truth. But nobody asked us. We were also being naive, to be fair.

- 20 October 1978: the Factory I, Manchester

Liz Naylor: In '77 I'd have been fourteen, fifteen, and I didn't know what to do and I felt really frustrated. I was really into music, and I also loved Captain Beefheart and things like that, so punk wasn't too much of a leap for me to make. I'd been to see Beefheart at the Free Trade Hall in maybe '74, I'd seen Lou Reed in some kind of particularly grim Free Trade Hall moment, so punk was absolutely natural for me to latch onto.

I think about late '77, maybe early '78, the thing I'd do was go and stand in the Virgin record shops, which was where other punks were standing, and I didn't really do anything but stand in the shop. I thought something would happen to me and it would be a way to access it – of course nothing ever did happen to me there, but that's how I sniffed the punk atmosphere. All very frustrating.

I was absolutely the only punk where I lived in Hyde. I used to get chased by a gang of boys. They used to call me Punky and chased me down the road and terrorised me. I wasn't very hard; I was quite frightened by them. Hyde had one record shop, and it didn't really sell punk records, but it was there I saw a piece of A4 paper with a handwritten thing saying the Fall were playing at Droylsden Town Hall. Droylsden was a really horrible suburb between Hyde and Ashton and Manchester, and for some reason I'd heard of the Fall by then.

That was June 1978, and that was the first punk-rock gig I ever went to. It was fantastic. For somebody who was into Beefheart, the Fall totally made sense to me, and being there was just this amazing moment. I didn't think I'd be let in, but because it was a town hall gig, it was fine. They were supported by a band called the Distractions, and their bass player came up and talked to me, so I sort of felt like I was in the music industry. I knew that everything that I'd been standing around Virgin Records waiting to happen – that access to the punk atmosphere – happened in a tiny little way that night.

That summer of '78 I saw my first punk gig, shagged my first girl and cut my hair off, and it was just a great moment of 'I can't go back.' I really understood that. And then I started to hang out in places in Manchester, pubs and clubs that would let me in, which was remarkable because I looked about thirteen. It just shows you the kind of class of joint I was hanging out in that would let me in.

And I never had any money. I did a bit of babysitting, rather alarmingly, but I didn't really have any money, so I didn't buy a lot of records. All my trips to record shops were just to look at them and imagine what it would be like to buy them or imagine what they sounded like. That took me into Salford, into Robinson's Records, and the real edges of Manchester that were quite decayed.

On the Eighth Day, in All Saints, was a bona fide hippie shop that had a little café in it, and I ate things that I'd never eaten before because I'd just come from a common family that ate meat pies. I ate brown rice and sesame seeds and Mu tea. I was really intoxicated by the smell, which I suspect would have been patchouli oil, but it really excited me. They had second-hand records upstairs, and I bought my copy of *Trout Mask Replica* there. There were all these fusty records that I could touch and smell.

I bought a hessian bag, and I used to read *Mole Express*, which was a very important underground paper at that point. I didn't understand any of it, but it didn't matter: you know that you're stuck in the wrong world, and it's like trying to find a portal to the world that you should be in, and that was my portal to this possible world. On the Eighth Day was next to a radical bookshop called Grass Roots, where I used to stand and read books and not buy anything. I loved being in those places.

Summer 1978 is this big moment of crisis for me – or liberation. I go back to school, and that September it all collapses, everything blows up, and I get expelled very early on that term. I'm asked to leave in no uncertain terms. And then I have this period when I was drifting around and I was seeing education welfare officers and social services were kicking in. That's when I saw Joy Division at the Factory.

I used to run away from home and go to the Factory and stay out all night, because there was a flat opposite the Factory on Bonsall Street, in Hulme, where anybody could just doss down. I used to go to soundchecks at the Factory and just stay in, and I also discovered that there's a side bar, where I used to steal beer and open it with my teeth. The Factory was the place I could get in: when I saw Joy Division it wasn't a problem to just smuggle myself in and stay there.

- 15 November 1978: Brunel University, Rezillos tour, Joy Division supporting the Undertones and the Rezillos

Martin, joydiv.org: The gig was held in what was known as the Kingdom Room. I had seen numerous bands play there, it was always very dark inside and had low ceilings which added to the atmosphere. The venue was full that night, about 400+ I'd say, I was at the very front crushed up against the stage. Joy Division took the stage to a few muffled cheers and a lot of 'who the fuck are they?' Without any introduction they went straight into the set.

Being unfamiliar with their music I can only be sure of remembering two numbers – Walked In Line and Digital, this was down to the repetition of the chorus. The sound was harsh and disjointed and without any apparent melody, but very loud and furious. I was unsure if I liked the sound but it didn't matter, as I was engrossed in Mr Curtis who was no more than eight feet away from me and going like a fucking train! Ian kept locking onto people in the audience with piercing stares, including me, for a good ten seconds he made me feel quite uncomfortable.

Unfortunately the set was cut very short; there can't have been any more than four or five numbers. The reason being that a part of the audience was still into the spitting thing and took a big dislike to Ian. They covered the poor man from head to foot and shouted 'Rubbish!!', 'Off Off Off!!' At the end of Digital, Ian had clearly had enough and said quite politely to the audience 'I see you are not educated down south' and promptly walked off. He was quickly followed by Sumner and Hook, Steve Morris realised it was over and scrambled from his drums, unfortunately he had to walk past the front of them to exit the stage and he tripped on a speaker cable, the crowed jeered and heckled him, he picked himself up, hurled some obscenities and walked off.

> **Mick Middles, *Sounds*, 18 November 1978**
> On the record label it says 'songs by Joy Division'. Do you write collectively? Who comes up with the ideas?
> Ian: 'It varies a lot, musically anyway.'
> Bernard: 'We usually start with a drum riff and then add bass and guitar on top of that. Ian supplies the lyrics.'
> Ian: 'Yeah, I've got a little book full of lyrics and I just fit something in. I have a lot of lyrics in reserve so I'll use them when the right tune comes along. The lines are usually made up of all sorts of odd bits. "Leaders Of Men" for example, some of the lines are two or three years old.'
> What are the lyrics about?
> Ian: 'I don't write about anything in particular, I write very subconsciously.'

- 20 November 1978: Check Inn Club, Altrincham

> **Mike Nicholls, *Record Mirror*, 25 November 1978**
> Fronting the band is the pallid, hyperactive Ian Curtis, whose weird, wired mechanic dance routines are reminiscent of Lou Reed circa '74.

- 27 December 1978: Hope and Anchor, London

Nick Tester, *Sounds*, 13 January 1979

Joy Division try to be a grim group, but I just grinned. They stutter onstage wearing sulky, long looks. The vocalist, Ian Curtis, seems intensely irritated but he doesn't say anything between the songs other than to remark the band are going to tune up.

Terry Mason: We'd become this reasonable-sized fish in the pool that's the north-west and a little bit of Yorkshire, but this was like Jesus going into Jerusalem on a donkey. This was our first London gig, and it was at a gig that we'd heard of. We'd read the papers, and you always used to see the gigs in London were at the Rainbow, at the Nashville Rooms or at the Hope and Anchor. We got there: it was just after Christmas, it was a Sunday night. Not that many people turned up, and it was such a disappointment for Ian, and I think that maybe triggered what happened.

Bernard Sumner: Ian had this explosive personality: Mr Polite, Mr Nice, and suddenly, before anyone realised, about the third song in, you'd notice he'd gone a bit weird, started pulling the stage apart, ripping up the floorboards and throwing them at the audience. Then, by the end of the set, he would be completely and utterly manic. Then you'd come offstage, and he'd be covered in blood, going, 'Fucking hell, what happened then?' But no one would talk about it, because that was our way. We didn't question it. We didn't think he knew why he got himself worked up that way.

One day we were doing a concert at the Hope and Anchor in London. I don't know if it was our first concert in London. I was incredibly ill. I had tonsillitis or flu, I didn't really want to go. Steve turned up in his Cortina, and Rob was like, 'Come on, get out of bed. Come on, you're going.' I got in the car, and I remember Ian being in a weird mood – it was unusual for him, a little bit childish and brattish, which wasn't him – on the way down, and a little bit negative, not quite himself. This was in the morning.

We drove down and did the concert, and only about three people turned up, and it was horribly hot and sweaty, in a tiny little room. The sound was crap, and every time Steve hit his drums the room started spinning for me. We actually had something to eat after the gig: we went for a Greek meal. Ian was really negative and bratty and not nice, and I remember thinking it was unusual. I took a sleeping bag down with me and we got in the car to go back.

We started driving up. By then it was about two in the morning, driving back up the M1, and we got near Luton. Ian was in the front, Steve was there, and I think me and Rob were in the car; I think Hooky was in the van. I had the sleeping bag over me, and Ian was moaning about the gig and moaning about the sound, and he said, 'Hey, give me that sleeping bag,' which wasn't like him, because he wasn't a selfish person at all. He turned round, grabbed the sleeping bag off me. I said, 'Stop pissing about, give it me back,' and I pulled it, so he pulled it back. I pulled it back and then held onto it, so he just wrenched it out of my hands but put it over his head this time and wrapped himself in a ball, and then just started making this weird growling sound, just growling like a dog, and I'm thinking, 'What's going on?' And next thing a hand comes out the sleeping bag, lashes out at Steve, comes out, punching the windscreen, and then he just starts punching, and that punching turned into a fully-fledged grand mal fit in the car while Steve was driving.

So I was like, 'Pull over, pull over, he's having a fit, he's freaking out, pull over.' So Steve pulled over to the hard shoulder, and me and Rob dragged him for his own protection out the car and held him down flat on the hard shoulder in the middle of the night, and we just pinned his limbs down while he basically had a fit. We knew he'd had a fit, and we took him to the hospital in Luton, and they basically said, 'Go and see your doctor when you get home.'

We just thought, 'One-off, never happened before, it's a one-off.' After that he got diagnosed with epilepsy, and they just started getting more and more frequent, and then it never stopped. It was difficult for us to comprehend because we never suspected it was going to happen. It was quite difficult to accept that after that point, Ian's different.

Stephen Morris: It affected Ian in a really bad way because they put him on heavy tranquillisers, and the doctor told him the only way he could minimise the risk was by leading a really normal, regular life, which by that time wasn't something he wanted to do. He liked to jump around onstage, and he liked to get pissed. The first time I saw that side of him was one night we were trying to get into the Electric Circus, and he just ran off, and the next time I saw him he had his tongue down this girl's throat. He used to go a bit wild. He didn't like being told he couldn't do that any more: it was one of the reasons he got into the band in the first place.

Peter Hook: I was in the van in front with the gear, and they were behind in the Cortina, and the Cortina just disappeared and we stopped, but we didn't have enough petrol to go and look for them. We had no money – we'd each put in to go to that gig and we were running out of money – and so I couldn't go back. I thought, if they broke down, Steve was in the AA, so I knew he'd be all right. I knew they'd make it home eventually. It was only when I drove home and dropped the roadies Twinny and Terry off and did the gear and everything that I heard that Ian was ill.

Terry Mason: We didn't know what to do. We'd certainly never come across people who'd had fits before. We didn't know what to say to him. What do you say to your mate who's just thrown a massive fit in the back of the car and who's just been diagnosed epileptic? Plus, we're men, men don't talk, and we certainly didn't talk to each other. We were blokes: 'Oh, go and see the doctor, I'm sure he'll give you some tablets for it,' and Ian duly went off to see the doctor and had the tests, and from then he had more tests and bigger and bigger prescriptions.

Deborah Curtis: I think the trouble started when my pregnancy began to show: he had that first fit. It sounds awful, but I think he liked to have the attention. I think one of the things he liked about me was that I did stand behind him, a hundred per cent, whatever he did. I supported him so much. When I got pregnant, everybody made a fuss of me, and I think he was a bit jealous.

I think he had a row at the gig at the Hope and Anchor, but nobody has said it was a row. My mum remembers me telling her that they were talking about Ian leaving the band, so it must have been a pretty big event. But he took it all so seriously. I don't think he believed that the other lads took it as seriously as he did. It was all he wanted. I think he felt that other people weren't giving as much. They were, but they weren't making so much noise about it.

7

OCTOBER 1978 – MAY 1979

'Use Hearing Protection' Factory Records sticker inserted in *FAC-2, A Factory Sample* (Design by Peter Saville)

Paul Morley: I think they liked that sense of being outsiders, didn't they? They liked that idea for quite a while. I think it was something that was very important to them. That's what football cultures use to galvanise. It gave them something to really fight against. Did they have outsiders coming from Macclesfield? I remember at the time coming from Macclesfield seemed very strange; only your aunts came from Macclesfield.

That was a strange association, Salford and Macclesfield, and definitely part of the strange tension that eventually exploded into what it became. Salford would somehow be a metaphor for everything grimy, grotty and broken about Manchester in a way at that time. If you looked at Salford, it just seemed to be decrepit and gone. To go into Salford seemed quite dangerous. Occasionally you'd go to Salford University to see a gig, and it did seem like Brooklyn or Harlem or something, that you were going into the dark side.

Macclesfield was pretty much really in the country, it was a nice, lovely place. It was kind of dead, but it was the country. So one was smoky, industrial, all those classic clichés, and the other was open spaces and potential, at the edge of which was a world where you could make your escape very quickly, it seemed, because just through there was hope, just over there was Alice's Wonderland. You could almost see it if you lived in Macclesfield, whereas in Salford you had no sighting of that at all, so that was an odd coupling.

That's why they took quite easily to the Gretton/Wilson dynamic and the Hannett dynamic, which was all good because it was then even more every man for himself, and there was a few more of them and they all had to fight each other, and it was fascinating to watch that. Hannett was the first person I ever saw smoke dope, way back in the mythical early seventies, when he was just a sort of strange rumour of a character that seemed to be on the edges of the music business somehow, but I could never quite work out how. I'd met him a couple of times.

Tony Wilson – this man who was John Stapleton, Richard Madeley, Bruce Forsyth almost, it was quite extraordinary that he would suddenly come to be involved, and all the suspicion that there has ever been comes from those of us that remember Tony Wilson and Kamikaze Corner on *Granada Reports* in 1973. It's preposterous, wonderful but preposterous. It should never have happened, and yet it was great that it did. I suppose he was just another music fan in his way.

Gretton had put on some gigs at the Oaks in Chorlton: Siouxsie and the Banshees and the Slits. He'd managed Slaughter and the Dogs, so I was aware of Rob, and it took me a long time to get over that: Rob's strange switches of allegiance, from the crap to the mighty. For a while it was difficult to cope with. So yeah, you were aware of all these figures, Erasmus too, because Erasmus had been an actor in an episode of *The Liver Birds*, so he was quite something.

So it was an odd troupe, you know, and to an extent with them around you didn't have to run away to the circus, they were the circus. They had the ringmaster and the weird people with their party tricks, so it was an odd little crew.

- 11 October 1978: Cargo Studios, Rochdale, recording of *A Factory Sample*

Bernard Sumner: Martin just sort of appeared like that. I don't remember having a meeting about it or anyone saying it would be a good idea; it just seemed to be suddenly we had a producer and his name was Martin Hannett. Didn't know who he was.

Tony Wilson: First of all there was the three of us, equal partners, and then Martin became an equal partner because he was the producer. In fact, our group that Alan and I managed, the Durutti Column, broke up over our insistence that very first summer to use Martin. The musicians in the group wanted to use a guy called Laurie Latham, who turned out to be a great producer, but we're going, 'No, we believe in Martin,' so the group left and we were left with just Vini. We actually did the whole Pink Floyd thing, as in we had Syd Barrett and the group had gone off.

Stephen Morris: The first thing we did with Martin was the *Factory Sample*, which was the first thing we did on Factory Records. Tony started a record label, and it was going to be fantastic: 'I'm doing a double EP and every band's going to have a side – Cabaret Voltaire, Joy Division, John Dowie.' We'd done 'Digital' and 'Glass' at the time, the latest songs that we'd written, so obviously we thought they'd be best. 'And Martin Hannett's going to produce' – that's great, a proper producer.

Rob forgot to tell us that Martin was coming, so Martin just turned up and said, 'Play something.' We must have done 'Digital', and: 'Yeah, yeah. Right, right. I've heard enough, I'm off.' And he was a bit of a hippie, didn't strike you as being anything out of the ordinary, it was only when you got Martin in his environment. The studio was Martin's, and when you were in the studio you were working for Martin and his whims, and it was just his way of expressing them.

Memorably, he had the AMS DB 16 whatever – it was a digital delay line. With this one, once you'd recorded it you could lock it in, so the sound was always in this box, and you pressed the button or hit the snare drum: 'Oh, there's me snare drums in the box now. How have you done that, Martin?' That's amazing, and he was doing things that are commonplace now, but at the time it was like magic. I mean, literally he was some sort of shaman.

Martin Hannett: They were a gift to a producer, because they didn't have a clue. They didn't argue. The *Factory Sample* was the first thing I did with them. I think I'd had a new AMS delay line for about two weeks. It was called Digital, it was heaven sent. The ideas were always there, but at the end of the sixties a digital delay line was implemented using these things called shift registers, which were enormous, unreliable and used too much electricity. When little bits of memory started to arrive, those clever guys at AMS stuck 'em in a box.

The gig at Salford was very important. It was a very big room, and they were very badly equipped, and they were still working into this space and making sure they got into the corners. When I did the arrangements for recording, they were just reinforcing the basic ideas.

Tony Wilson: Hannett created the modern drum sound with the digital delay. What he did with that digital delay machine, he put a speaker in the toilet, and over the years you learned this isn't insanity, this is to take away all the signifiers of the room that the sound is in to render the sound naked, and then apply reverb and echo and the other signifiers of where you're listening to this particular sound. So I knew he did that. What I didn't realise was that Martin had been part of the vision behind the digital delay machine itself.

I met Stuart Nevinson, who owned AMS Neve. He told me how he'd drive up the hill out of Burnley and park in the car park, and this lunatic would drive his battered Volvo up from Didsbury onto the same car park, then get out of his car, sit in the back of our car and spend fifteen minutes describing the sounds he was hearing in his head. He'd then drive back to Manchester, and they'd drive back down to Burnley to create the machine that would create these sounds.

Jon Wozencroft: The lyrics of 'Digital' are actually digital. There's on–off: 'Day in, day out, day in, day out.' They're switching. They're also somehow weirdly related to Curtis's persona itself, which as we know now is bipolar: on the one hand we have the lad going down the pub with his mates, fooling around; and on the other we have the aesthete who is reading poetry and imbibing himself with all kinds of highfalutin ideas that he's going to be a romantic pop-star hero.

Peter Saville: The record cover was the holy grail of visual artists and designers in their teens and early twenties. Particularly in the UK at that time, it's the true manifestation of pop art: it's a public window, a common platform of mass awareness. Within a week of committing imagery to a cover that anywhere between five and five hundred thousand people would see, it would become a shared iconography among an enormous number of people, and there isn't anything else like that.

It's not like doing a magazine cover, which is a much more disposable item. You have this direct medium to an enormous cross-section of people, nationally and internationally. It's quite amazing. So the idea of being able to work in that space is incredible, and also the perceived freedom that there might be in that space. It's something that if you've got this ambition or ego or vanity to either do something that's noticed or to be noticed, the record cover's it.

So when Tony sat with Alan and I, Christmas '78, and said we could do a record from the club for the bands that haven't got contracts yet, this was just terribly, terribly exciting. Because the three posters I'd done so far for Factory I saw very much as within the limitations of Manchester, and I knew that if we did a record, then it would be a national thing. I had no idea how Tony was going to fund this grand project, but I put my hand up and voted for it immediately as a great idea, but entirely selfishly: I just wanted to do something that went beyond Oxford Road.

Lindsay Reade: We met in 1976, and Tony's mother died in 1975. She'd left him £15,000, which was quite a lot then. Tony had a good job working for *Granada Reports*, so he didn't need to dip into any savings to live. I was politically against the idea of having money in the bank; Tony's always been a bit left-wing as well, so it seemed like a good idea to spend it on the *Factory Sample*. We were both perfectly happy to write it off: I was absolutely 100 per cent certain it would be a write-off, but it didn't matter because it was good fun.

Peter Saville: We did a record. Even though the second and third Factory posters had gone off on an avenue of classicism, we felt it was appropriate with the Factory sampler – which had four groups and was a kind of a generic release from Factory – to quote the first Factory poster: the Factory house identity. So the Factory sampler is a derivation of the first Factory poster, and each of the groups had a sticker insert for whatever they wanted to contribute, and the outer form was of Factory rather than of the individual groups.

Joy Division gave a picture like a collage – I think it was a ventriloquist's dummy, a black-and-white image found somewhere. Even when I did the *Factory Sample* I hadn't established any kind of personal contact with any of them yet; it was done through Tony. Tony said, 'Cabaret Voltaire want this, Joy Division want this . . .' – 'Fine,' and I did artwork for it and did the cover that I wanted to do. I didn't need to meet anyone to do it, so I didn't meet them at that point.

The *Factory Sample* was a home-made product and low-budget. Tony had a little bit of money left by his mother and he invested that in the *Factory Sample*. And we didn't really know what we were doing. I had no idea how you got a record cover made. I didn't know who record-cover printers were, so when Tony said, 'I think we could make it using this heat-sealed polythene that I've seen in Taiwan with rice paper,' I thought, 'Great, because I've no idea how to get this manufactured. Tony's got an idea that you can do it with plastic bags – great.'

I designed a large piece of paper that was folded up and sealed together in plastic bags, which Tony did with Alan, I think, and I was delighted that he did it, because I didn't know anything. So luckily Tony and Alan made them in Alan's flat, all five thousand of them. I think I avoided that, I avoided that stage. I don't remember sticking any of them together.

- 13 January 1979 *NME* cover: Nationwide Ethnic Credibility Special '79, featuring Bob Last of Fast Records and Ian Curtis

Paul Morley: Two things sent me to London: one was that my father had killed himself, and I needed to get the hell out of Heaton Moor, this house that seemed like *The Texas Chain Saw Massacre*. The golden grail was a job on the *NME* – it was beyond any local affection or affinity. Whatever Tony Wilson would say about getting me a job at Granada, I needed to go to London. I remember going down in the late summer. I think the first thing I did was interview

Debbie Harry. And this was the cover and I'd got the cover, and here we go, it all seemed to make sense.

I would say from very early on, 'Ian Curtis should be on the cover.' There's a great picture that Kevin Cummins took very early on of Ian, far too early really for it to go on the cover, because there was a weird kind of apprenticeship. Back then it was Bryan Ferry, it was Bob Dylan . . . there was no way that had started to happen, that local kids, local characters would be put on the cover of these incredibly important, influential, London-based magazines.

Kevin Cummins: The *NME* had used a picture from the first gig probably two months later, just to go along with some news piece. Beyond that, I'd get printed in possibly the *New Manchester Review*, and then quite regularly in the *NME*, because I'd just bombard them with pictures. Every time there was a gig in Manchester, we'd send pictures in, or Paul would write a news piece or some review. We weren't commissioned. Well, sometimes we were, sometimes we weren't, but we'd do it anyway.

Paul Morley: The first time Ian made the cover of the *NME* it was two months after my father committed suicide. I did a big piece on Manchester; clearly a psychologist or whoever would tell me it was a cathartic moment. It was very important I did it and that I blotted everything out simply to talk about, to report this scene that was happening in Manchester with Joy Division, Fall, Buzzcocks, Slaughter and the Dogs. I would keep badgering them that there was a local scene.

Then there was the *Factory Sample*, and then I got to interview Joy Division as part of a second Manchester piece. My own feeling is that I also pushed very hard for Ian first of all; it was when Neil Spencer said no that I then changed tack, because I was desperate to put Manchester on the cover in some form. There were fights, and I was very passionate and I would just go bonkers and really get angry, to the point of almost being sacked for being so reckless, but it seemed very, very important.

I look at these photographs now and I can't believe it, because at the time it was me ringing up Kevin, who I'd found somehow to help me do the photos for these pieces I was writing about Manchester: 'Oh, I'm going to do an interview. Do you want to take the pictures?' We would all nervously gather in a pub, and I would do the most abortive interview with Joy Division, who had absolutely nothing to say, and I would find it so hard because I just wanted them to say something.

We would drink ridiculous amounts of lager and say nothing to each other really, but in a way I guess that inarticulacy was fascinating because elsewhere we could be quite articulate, but when we were all together we couldn't really talk about anything much. It was almost embarrassing. Then Kevin would go off and take these photographs that seemed to be more articulate, in a way, than our nervy, pointless interview.

Kevin Cummins (looking through the contact sheet of the Joy Division shoot for *NME*, 13 January 1979): Ian just looks straight into the camera while he's smoking. It's the eyes, this slight translucency of his eyes looking into the camera that sends a chill through people. 16, 17, 18, 20 and 21 – we are getting there. One was in silhouette, and there was one where they came slightly out of the passageway and we got some side light. Already by then I've shot two-thirds of a roll of film, and I'm conscious of the fact that I didn't really think I had anything.

I'm walking up to the bridge, and they're waiting for me. And I just felt that it looked so bleak and they looked so un-rock'n'roll-like that I took two frames, and then took an upright shot of the same thing. And that's all I did of that picture. And that's, I guess, become probably the most recognised Joy Division image.

When we did the piece for the *NME* in January 1979, we were commissioned to do a piece about three Manchester bands: the Passage, Spherical Objects and Joy Division. Paul felt that Spherical Objects were going to be the more important band of the three, I think because he liked Steve Scrivener, he thought he had quite a lot to offer, and he was intelligent about music, he liked dub reggae. Like Rob Gretton, he was an interesting guy. He had the credentials, he had the flat in Hulme with nothing in it, all that kind of stuff.

So we did maybe four rolls of film and spent quite a bit of time with them, a couple of rolls of film with the Passage, cos obviously Dick Witts was always quite interesting as well, and we left Joy Division till last. And it was only then, when Paul did the interview at the Brunswick, near Piccadilly Station – it was the first time that Paul had really spoken to them, and just then discovered their absolute passion and intensity for everything. That's when the idea for the feature changed. And when we realised that Joy Division were going to make something of themselves.

The picture of Ian at the long table was taken in a shop called Art & Furniture. It was off Cross Street, on Chapel Walk. The guy who had it was Jonathan Silver, who had a couple of clothing shops in Manchester where Ian got his wedding suit. Jonathan was great: he'd been at art school with David Hockney, they were friends, and he had this vision for Manchester, that Manchester could cope with all this great art and furniture. All classic design stuff. He was selling Allen Jones and Hockney, and various other things. And not selling very much of it. Even in Didsbury, Didsbury wasn't even ready for it. So he let us shoot in there, and it was great cos obviously he had some really nice pieces that we could work around.

But the picture of them on the bridge became the picture that defined them. People told me that they knew what the band would sound like from looking at that picture. It's quite humbling that a picture has such resonance. Whenever it gets posted anywhere, someone will say it's the best rock'n'roll picture of all time. And it was a deliberate attempt not to take a rock'n'roll picture. It was an architectural shot, with the band in it giving it some context. Everything about Joy Division is so inextricably linked that Joy Division couldn't exist without that photo, and the photo couldn't exist without Tony and Rob and the band and the way the city was at the time.

- 26 January 1979: the Factory I, Russell Club, Manchester

Alan Hempsall: Early '79 at the Russell Club, that was the first time I actually saw them. That really blew me away. The power on the stage was fantastic. It's been well documented Ian had a great stage presence, but the music was just so functional, almost a triumph of function over form. I don't know how you'd describe it, but everything's pared down to the minimum – the guitars were very economical, which I thought was what was needed in the music – and it was just like a well-oiled machine.

They were very clean-cut for the time, and there were a lot of short-sleeved shirts and ties, which was quite unusual: I suppose you would think of somebody like Bowie on the front cover of *Low*. You looked at the shoes, and the shoes were very much like demob suit Oxfords, and the green serge trousers and that sort of thing, it was all a very pressed, clean-cut image, which was very unusual, and the haircuts were, 'We go to the barber's once every three weeks, and if there's a hair out of place, we see to it.'

And then there was Hooky with his beard, he almost looked like some kind of U-boat commander or something, all he was missing was the blue turtle-necked sweater. But yeah, the image was very, very striking, and then when you coupled that with the music, the whole package set them apart.

Peter Hook: The look came as a combination from Ian and Bernard. We discovered that scout shop by the post office in Back Piccadilly and we used to buy the little scout shirts for 50p, and then there was a shop in Tib Street where you'd buy military gear cos it was dead cheap. We just had no money, it was necessity really, and we just got into it. Bernard latched onto the look. Ian had the look anyway really. Steve was always dressed by his mother, so he had a very individual style, which was like a geography teacher.

We just arsed about really. The punk thing was about ripping everything up: ripping your wardrobe up, ripping your life up, starting again. It was like that. Couldn't afford the good stuff.

Finding out that a Destroy T-shirt costs . . . how much was it then? Seventy quid or summat? That was like two months' wages for me. Unbelievable. It sort of took the tarnish off the Clash when I found out how much their clothes cost. I thought, 'What the hell's that about?' – you know? I didn't understand it really.

Bernard Sumner: It was Oxfam shops and Army and Navy Stores. When I was working at the animation place in Chorlton, there was a little Oxfam shop there, and I remember buying a nice tie with spots on it that you couldn't get anywhere. You were buying stuff that was from previous generations that people had slung out, and army surplus stores, which were like stuff from the forties and sixties and stuff like that, so I guess they were vintage clothes really. And tight jeans. It was just what we wore really.

Promo for *A Factory Sample*, December 1978 (Design by Peter Saville)

Jon Savage, review of *A Factory Sample* **in** *Melody Maker*,
27 January 1979

Joy Division wind their claustrophobic, abrasive yet precise
anger even tighter, a quality only hinted at in the previous
Ideal For Living EP: both Digital and Glass are strong,
massive and, as throughout the EP, make you want to hear
more (the acid test of a sampler).

- 2 February 1979: release of *A Factory Sample*

Tony Wilson: There's all these great myths: that the independent
British record movement was some kind of punk thing, a political statement, it's like, 'Fuck the majors, we'll do it ourselves.'
That is complete and utter bollocks written by people after the
event. If you were there at the time, what had happened was
through a series of accidents. Rough Trade records, run by a
bunch of clever kids in Notting Hill Gate, had become very good
at sourcing rare reggae twelve-inches, and suddenly other shops
in Britain said, 'You can get hold of these things, we can't. Can
we buy them from you?'

By default, Rough Trade became a record distributor, just when
this new punk thing happened and there was a market. I used to
go into this little bookshop on Peter Street to buy these little seven-
inch singles by these obscure American punk bands. At the same
time as this happened, there were people like Pinnacle, who – and
this is an important piece of history – sold dust bugs, spares, acces-
sories for playing records, so they had these estate cars going from
record shop to record shop with half a dozen dust bugs and half a
dozen anti-static cleaning dusters.

Suddenly they realised there was spare space in the back of their
cars, and in the course of 1977, '78 there grew up an independent
distribution system. I don't want to get all Hegelian on your ass, but
this is mode of production determines mode of consciousness. It
was wonderful. Suddenly you could put records out yourself, and
we all began to do it. People were doing it before me in Manchester,

Tosh Ryan did it with Rabid Records, and the cleverest label was Fast Records from Edinburgh. But the whole idea was to sell your band to a major.

Rob Gretton (notebook, January 1979): Paul Morley's question was around a new underground forming outside of the system – How do you see the role of the band? Do you want to work within or outside the system? Do we want to do long major tours of our own? Personally I would rather adopt a different role with regards to everything – try to approach everything from a different viewpoint – not having everything dictated by money.

Kevin Cummins: Rob was very meticulous in everything he did. You can see by his notebooks he was quite OCD about it. He was very good at giving them focus, at pulling things together: what would work, what wouldn't, and what would actually make them make some money. You get to a point with all bands at that level. You have to ask, 'What is the next stage? Are you happy just pissing about, or do you want to do this seriously?' If you do, there has to be one person who can pull that together. That was Rob. He did have his laddish side, but he was very serious when you talked to him about music.

Paul Morley: I did keep in touch because I would go up north a lot. Wilson would always be on the phone because he would be cajoling, as he did to us all, telling us all the same stories as if we were the only one – 'If you don't review the *Factory Sample*, we won't have a label, it's up to you' – and you fell for it. It wasn't a single or an album; the *Factory Sample* was actually very hard for the *NME* to understand, so I did have to get on my bended knee to please let it in, and then Tony thanked me for saving Factory, and you felt very proud.

- 14 February 1979: broadcast of first John Peel Session

Jon Wozencroft: One of the main modes of distribution was the radio – John Peel's radio shows on BBC Radio 1, ten till twelve – and there used to be among my friends a network whereby if one of us couldn't tape it, we'd make sure the other one would, and so there'd be this circular exchange of 'What was on last night?' 'Oh, there was a session by such-and-such,' and you'd build up very quickly a brilliant archive, which was also some kind of litmus test as to what the actual eventual releases were going to be like.

C. P. Lee: I can remember listening to Joy Division when John Peel played them very, very early, and at the end of it Peel immediately put on a Doors track and then at the end of it said, 'There you go, now we know what they're trying to sound like.' And I have to say to my shame that I felt a lot of the early stuff was too Morrison-esque, in that there was a scrabbling around for meaning within lyrics that really shouldn't be meaningful.

- February 1979: Bob Dickinson interview

Bob Dickinson: I interviewed Joy Division for *New Manchester Review*. The band were still relatively obscure and it was difficult to sell the idea because the *Review* was run by a bunch of guys who were a couple of years older than me, so they were really not quite in tune with post-punk or even punk. They'd seen it all happen, and you really had to try hard to convince them that new Manchester bands were worth interviewing. I think Kevin Cummins had a lot to do with convincing the *Review* that this interview ought to happen.

Anyway, the interview was commissioned, and we went ahead and did it, and I was on my own. Kevin had already taken some photos of the band, and I think the one that the *Review* actually used was one of the shots that he took in the snow in Hulme on the bridge. I went down to meet the band at T. J. Davidson's Rehearsal Rooms on Little Peter Street, and I suppose it was about six o'clock at night, six thirty or something, and they were rehearsing, and the rehearsal broke up in this stark, strange room which I'd never been in before.

We decided to go down to the pub at the top end of Little Peter Street, at the junction with Albion Street. On the other side of the road there was an old Victorian pub, and Barney didn't go. They said that he didn't want to talk to a journalist, but the other three came down with Rob, and we went into a back room where there was a TV on and I recorded the interview, and I've still got the tape and you can hear the TV in the background, and you can hear also the tension in the air, especially because Peter Hook felt to me like he was being very hostile.

It wasn't anything to do with what he was saying to me, it was more to do with the fact he kept flicking his fingernail against the glass ashtray on the table, and you can hear this pinging noise all the way through the interview, and it's a nervous thing that he was doing that felt like he was hostile in some way. I wasn't unduly surprised because a lot of bands were hostile to you as a journalist in those days, because they thought you were going to stitch them up, and also I think it was just part of the aesthetic of being in a band then.

But the other two guys, Stephen and Ian, were really relaxed, and Ian was very forthcoming about his life, because I asked him about his background and where he'd come from and what sort of bands he used to like. He talked about working in Rare Records and Iggy and the Stooges, his favourite bands and so on, and Rob was there as well, going on about how convinced he was that the way the band ought to go should be in the direction of these twelve-inch singles that he brought over that were imported from America.

Rob was a northern soul DJ originally, and he introduced Joy Division to northern soul. He wasn't a conservative, he was a real enthusiast for music. That night I remember him bringing a pile of records with him into the pub, and they were all new, imported twelve-inch singles from America and they were all dance-floor, early electro, really early hip-hop stuff, and he was going on and on to the band about it, and saying, 'This is the way, the direction you should go in, synthesised drumming, electronic drumming, dance-floor.'

They were odd sort of dance-floor records with electronic rhythm and seemed to be completely in contrast to what at that time I thought Joy Division were about, which was a manually operated drum kit. But when you think about it, Joy Division used rhythm in a machine-like way: they could harness rhythm and turn it into something that was unearthly and not quite human, except that human beings were making the rhythm, so there was this interest in interacting with the machine that you got a sense of from listening to their music.

The direction that Rob was foreseeing for them, he was talking about it as a kind of interrupted thing. There were two parallel dialogues going on at the same time in this interview: there was me trying to get an interview, and there was Rob trying to suggest to them in the strongest terms that this was a direction that they ought to take seriously, and so it was an interesting experience just witnessing that, hearing the way that the band and their manager were thinking about the way that the band were going to develop.

- 4 March 1979: Genetic demos, Eden Studios, London

Tony Wilson: The *Factory Sample* produced enormous interest in this band, Joy Division, so I was doing what I was there to do. With my friend Rob, I would get on the train to London and go and see a man called Andrew Lauder, who was a very bright A&R man. He was the man who had signed the Buzzcocks to United Artists, but he then moved to Genetic/Radar, which was some Warner Brothers imprint, with a guy called Martin Rushent, who was a very wonderful producer at the time.

And I was assisting Rob in going to Warner Brothers. Arguably for me the night that is the greatest night in British music culture and history is sitting in the Band on the Wall in Manchester one Sunday night with Gretton, who suddenly turns to me and goes, 'Why don't we do our first album with you and then go to Warner Brothers?' And I remember far from being, 'Wow,' it was like, 'Are you sure? Are you sure? How much is that going to cost?' 'Martin says it'll cost ten grand.' It cost twenty-five, the bastard, but anyway.

I went, 'Well, all right, maybe, it's quite a nice idea. Are you sure, Rob?' – 'Yes, I am.' Then Rob wrote down the deal, which was fifty–fifty because that's a wonderful way of doing it, but then he added in – the fact is, Rob is a fucking genius but doesn't let you know he's a genius at all – 'Oh, by the way, it's fifty–fifty, but we leave the publishing out of it, then you pay the publishing out of your 50 per cent.' And me, being a good Catholic communist, went, 'Yeah, yeah, fine, fine.' And that's what bankrupted us in the end.

And that was the moment that the British independent record industry started, the moment when one manager of one band said, 'Let's stay here and do it this way, and not go to a major' – even though this major, Warner Brothers, was crying out for them. And at the time I just . . . you know, when history happens you often don't see it, and I didn't see it, and I didn't know what was going on in Rob's brain, and what was going on in Rob's brain was very simple, and it comes down to Mancunian arrogance and Mancunian chutzpah or whatever.

His theory was, 'We've just done the *Factory Sample*. It cost Tony £4,000. £4,000 went out, £4,400 came back, and they gave me a hundred quid. That's on a really bizarre double seven-inch single.' He knew the reality: the album makes a lot more money. If we could do the same thing and get paid, then basically he and his band could have a great career and not have to get on a train and go to London every fortnight and talk to cunts. And that was Rob's basic philosophy, and in fact Rob then managed to not have to go to London and talk to cunts, and it worked.

Lindsay Reade: Rob was very driven. If you'd grown up in Wythenshawe, then you really are going to be driven, aren't you? He was clever as well, he'd worked it out. Did Tony tell you he worked the best business deal that's ever been done? They got the contract agreed between them; it was a complete rip-off really, and Tony didn't care, because Tony's drive was a different kind of drive. It was more intellectual and conceptual, it wasn't material in any way. I think Rob's drive was very much material.

Peter Hook: Rob decided that it was better to be in control than not, because Martin Rushent was a big character and it was obvious as soon as you dealt with him that he wasn't like Tony. I think there was a big north–south divide then, and I think that really, for all the glamour of being signed to a major label in London, we were scared, and I think Rob was scared of losing control. I mean, the great thing about Rob was that he could turn a lot of money down.

Pete Shelley: I think it allowed them a lot more freedom than they would have had if they'd gone down to London. In London, the record companies were still trying to get their own versions of punk bands. Luckily, we were with United Artists and our A&R guy was Andrew Lauder, who basically allowed us to do what we wanted to do, so we had freedom and also the support of the record company. Factory was just run by hippies in a way, and like I say, there was no business plan as such, just a sort of a mischievous spirit.

- 14 March 1979: Bowdon Vale Youth Club, Altrincham

Malcolm Whitehead: One night Rob came to talk to me. He came over to my place at Charter Road in Altrincham, and we were talking about 'What shall we do?' sort of thing. We decided to put a gig on at the Check Inn club, that was the first one, in Altrincham, which is basically a disco type of thing. So I thought, 'Well, we'll start off, we'll take some stills.' Anyway, I had a disastrous night: they played and it went down a treat, but unfortunately the still camera jammed.

So I said, 'Well, we've got to put them on somewhere else in Altrincham.' So, cos I'd been to a lot of these Merseybeat concerts at Bowdon Vale, I suggested, 'Why don't you put it on there, you know?' So they did, and I filmed it. I knew a couple of the guys who were on the committee, I worked with a couple of them, so I was able to get permissions and things like that dead easy. So then I just hired in some scaffolding, got Rob to organise some lights.

We needed real powerful lights because Super 8 film wasn't very sensitive to light, and that kept fusing everything. Then we did the gig. I think we were originally only going to have two songs and then do a short film about what was happening with Anderton and the repressive regime he was trying to run in Manchester. It was a bit like the situation with Mayor Daley in Chicago in 1968. That's how we felt about it anyway.

Anderton was a very vociferous chief constable, one of the first to get into the political arena of being obviously right-wing and wanting to crack down on the young: anybody who had any ideas different to the semi-detached Dunroamin' crowd he seemed to see as a threat. And this background was going on in Manchester all the time, and then we had the looming Thatcher thing, which we didn't really know about, but there's a hint of that in the film, where we're going away from trying to create a good society to creating this consumerist/fascist society.

Once you've got this sort of proto-Hitler that I saw Anderton as then, it would be the obvious response – well, it would be Joy Division. So you've got the references where you've got shots of the crowd, the normal sort of person, and then we cut to the underground feel of the rehearsal rooms, where it's almost like a resistance group. That was the idea to get across: this was resistance through art and culture, and that will someday be bigger than all these right-wing politics, because it's more human than that is, so it will win.

The rehearsal room was at T. J. Davidson's. At first I thought, 'I'll get a little bit of an interview, I'll just do a wild track on the tape machine,' but they couldn't think of any answers and I couldn't think of any questions. Film was about £6 a cartridge then, so we abandoned it pretty early. Then I started thinking, 'Well, actually they don't do it through talking,' because through conversation they were just normal blokes in the pub, but when it came to their art, then they communicated, so I thought, 'Well, we'll just do the music, cos that's a big enough statement.'

Liz Naylor, 'No City Fun', *City Fun* magazine, issue 3, December 1978
I think I hate the city. I think it hates me. I think I'm
   paranoid.
I hate, I hate, I hate. I hate every product; everybody;
   everygroup everyshop everybus everyclothing; everyfad
   everyfashion every 'scene'.
I feel like 1976.
my head aches. thank you god.
I am sylvia plath in reincarnation.
I hate – and that's the saddest thing.
by James 'don't call me scarface' Anderton
(HONEST)
xxxxxx

Liz Naylor: I'd always written at home. I had endless, endless stacks of kind of stream-of-consciousness writing. I wrote all the time as a way of expressing myself, and I got this fanzine called *City Fun* and I thought I could write something for that. It was kind of Roneoed, it was incredibly crude, unstylish, not very punk rock almost. It was like a community paper, run by a collective who were hippies essentially.

There was Andy Zero, who had a wholefood shop in Mossley, and a guy called Neil and a guy called JD, who owns the flat in Hulme that everybody dossed at, and the mysterious Martin X, who just drifted around, who was old – he was a sixties generation kind of person. So it wasn't like a punk fanzine as people imagine; it came out of a certain community-type hippie thing, and they used to have meetings where anybody could go because it was a collective, so I started to go to those meetings and got involved with them.

The city was in the dog days of something, and the only people left were the scum of the earth. Anderton was the chief constable of Manchester, and he looked around his manor and thought, 'Do you know what? The only people here are the scum of the earth. I'm going to wipe them out.' And it felt really genuinely threatening. If you read his biography, he believed he spoke directly to God every night, he believed that God sent him messages.

C. P. Lee: In the same way as in the sixties, when one specific chief constable, a Scotsman called McKay, decided to crush the beat clubs, we have the rise in the seventies of a chief constable who was originally regarded as a liberal: a guy called James Anderton. He was going to clean up the corruption that was supposed to have existed within the Manchester police force in the late sixties. It was a little later on, when people began to notice he was referring to conversations he'd had with God, that Jesus told him to do this, that alarm bells began to ring.

The people who run Savoy Books tell a fascinating story of one morning, very, very early, seven o'clock, spotting Anderton stood in civilian clothes opposite their bookshop on Peter Street, near the Free Trade Hall, by the site of the Peterloo Massacre, looking at their shop and nodding. Then, a few months later, they were all arrested and thrown in jail for obscenity and publishing pornography. Debatable points. Anderton would personally, physically go to these places, look at them, weigh them up and then go and do his business.

There was an atmosphere in Manchester whereby the forces of repression were given carte blanche to do what they wanted. Newsagents were raided for selling the *Sun*'s page-three girls calendar. Video shops were raided and copies of *Apocalypse Now* were seized: that's because they had the same title as *Cannibal Apocalypse*, but the vice squad couldn't quite understand that.

Now the thing was, they could take a shop's entire stock, but when it went to court you had to pay for a lawyer to prove that that stock was not obscene. The police didn't have to prove anything, so people just said, 'Oh, there you go, I give up, you've got it all.' Anderton tried to hit the clubs in the same way that McKay had, but there were certain strictures against him closing them down. It was a very, very tight-run thing, and there was a certain amount of police pressure.

Liz Naylor: Now when you're queer and punk-rock and got no money, it feels very like they're out to get you. We were paranoid, but I think there was a certain truth in that paranoia, in that his presence in the city was really malevolent. I think he really did look around the city and thought, 'This place is just full of you scum, and I'm going to wipe it out,' and he was that fundamentalist, and he really believed he was going to remake the city as a more wholesome place. It was a contest really: we were contesting space with quite a powerful force.

There was a bookshop called Savoy Books that sold porn and bootlegs, and when the police closed them down, Anderton stood outside and watched it happen, looking like Moses – at that time he had a large beard – and he'd do the same for Clone Zone as well, in the centre of what is now the gay village. I know at police raids Anderton would be personally present with a look of absolute immense glee on his face, and so he was a physical presence in that city. So anyway, my taking his name was my own little moment of irony.

> **Rob Gretton notebook, March 1979**
> Germanic One –
> Exercise One – very good – like new feedback
> Lost Control – excellent – nice + simple and also builds
>   up well – drums very important – build up – beat
>   emphasised

Shadowplay – good lyrics – very good lead guitar

Melodic One (Insight) – don't think that all the breaks will
 come across well – but I like it

Wilderness – no – don't like the disjointedness

Ice Age – good fast one – memorable but lyrics a bit simple –
 don't like the guitar bit at the end

Transmission – very good – maybe screams too much?

New One – possibility?

Day of the Lords – good lyrics

- April 1979: Strawberry Studios, Stockport, *Unknown
 Pleasures* sessions

Bernard Sumner: With the material for *Unknown Pleasures*, that
was about mark III. *Unknown Pleasures* took about six months
to write and was the second or third set of material that we'd got.
The first set, we were just having fun really, learning where to
put your fingers on the guitar and what sort of guitar picks and
amplifiers to use. *Unknown Pleasures* was our first outing into
the real world. It was our first effort, really; the rest of it was just
practice.

The first memories of Martin are from *Unknown Pleasures*: of
him being on the one hand fantastic, a catalyst really for experimentation, in that he really made it fun in the studio in that way.
On *Unknown Pleasures* we'd laid all the tracks down, we'd played
them all live many, many times, so I think we had three weekends
to record and mix it. So the first thing we did with Martin was
to get them recorded in the studio, and then it would be experimentation time and we'd start putting wacky noises on it. Like
he recorded the lift shaft, and he brought this machine that you
could do this thing called sampling into. Now in 1979 that was
quite amazing, so I think we recorded a 'dink' off my guitar into
it, and then it gave me a keyboard and it was a delay unit and you
could play the sound on the keyboard, so I did overdubs with
that. It was fantastic experimentation, and very, very creative, and

I loved that aspect of working with Martin. Straight recording bit, he could be very strange.

Tony Wilson: I was there the very first day, I was there the day when Martin made Steve take his drum kit apart. We're now doing an album, and somewhere during the second day he says, 'Right, Steve, disassemble your drum kit.' Martin's great ability was to unsettle musicians.

Stephen Morris: The studio was Martin's, and when you were in the studio you were working for Martin and his whims. There was an awful lot of pot smoked: whether Martin was completely stoned or did have a different outlook on what he wanted, he would be obtuse. He wouldn't say to you, 'I want you to do it like this.' It was, 'Great, do it again, but a bit more cocktail party' or 'a bit more yellow'. Whether it was pot or whether it was the Zen school of production, it was definitely interesting, because he turned us on to the studio being a musical instrument.

Peter Hook: The songs were great anyway. Martin didn't write them, he only produced them. He started chipping in when we needed him, but that's the job of a producer. When we first started working with him, we were just really wet behind the ears, you know; he could tell us what to do and he could get away with it. He was just difficult to work with, and with Chris Nagle he had a bit of a team going and it was petty and small-minded.

It was like working with Professor Stanley Unwin: you didn't know what he wanted. Martin was a typical A&R guy, I've since found out: he didn't know what he wanted, but he'll tell you when he hears it. Part of his charm was he didn't communicate well, it was his bag: 'Go in and be magnificent but humble.' And fucking hell: 'Oh God, I come from Salford, mate, I can't handle this.' It was hell really.

Stephen Morris: Martin knew what he wanted, but I don't think he knew how to tell you. You had to guess what it was that he wanted.

I think we managed all right. It wasn't a completely pleasurable experience. I know Bernard and Hooky didn't enjoy working with him, because what Martin wanted to do was some sort of a sound-scape, whereas what Joy Division played onstage was very aggressive, it was very raw and very passionate.

Bernard had a very strange but raw guitar sound, and Martin took it and turned it into something else. He didn't mean it personally, he's trying to make the best record he possibly can, but we did have numerous run-ins with him. We used to take it in turns, it was like Punch and Judy: 'Go on, you tell him, you tell him.' – 'Martin, Martin, can you turn the guitar up a bit?' – 'You tell him, you tell him.' – 'Have you turned the guitar up?' He'd just go, 'Phhhh, yeah,' and then he'd be gone again, you know: 'These fucking musicians.'

We were expecting it to be raw and rocking. It was live, but he'd taken our sound and made it into something else, psychedelic. What I gathered from him on our numerous spaced-out conversations was, he saw what he was doing as Factory's producer was creating a Factory sound akin to Elektra. The Doors, the early West Coast stuff had this specific kind of sound which he said was all boom and zizz. As well as establishing an identity for himself as a producer, he was trying to make one for Factory.

I liked what Martin did on *Unknown Pleasures*. I think Bernard and Hooky were a bit taken aback with it. I liked it because I've always thought when you went to a concert you wanted this visceral thing, you wanted it to be raw and you wanted energy, but when you were listening to a record, it kind of happens inside your head. Sometimes it's nice to have subtleties. I always liked Martin's little noises that your ear would just focus on and you'd think, 'God, I've never heard that before.'

Martin Hannett: *Unknown Pleasures* was half of the classic Hannett patch. I didn't have enough to do it on both left and right. I use basically the same patch these days. It's a very controllable space. I can take it up from a cardboard tube to a cathedral. Syndrums were just coming out then, and Steve bought one and had a good look at it. When the Simmons stuff arrived, he must have had one of those kits.

Stephen Morris: Why I started using syndrums was a mistake. What happened is, I've got the British cover of *Tago Mago* – it only works on the British cover, the German one is different – there's Jaki's drum kit and there's this thing next to it, and I wonder what that is. My brother says, 'Oh yeah, that's a drum synthesizer, that'll be what they used to get that sound.' – 'Drum synthesizer, you say? Mm, right, okay.' So I lock that away. And then I've seen these adverts and they say drum synthesizer. 'Yes, this is what I want to sound like.'

At the time there was a spate of these records which had that bing-boo noise on them. There was 'Dancing in the City' by Marshall Hain, and Rose Royce's 'Love Don't Live Here Anymore'. It was a fad. 'Of course, these people don't know what you can do with a drum synthesizer, so I'll get one and I'll show them what you can do, cos obviously they'd never heard Can.' I've still got the receipt for it. Two nine-volt batteries, and you whack it and it goes bing-boo.

I got over the initial disappointment, as you would, and decided that even though it was probably the best noise you could get out of it, there was more to it than that, yeah? So we got 'She's Lost Control' out of it, we got the tide coming in and going out, bing-boo on 'Insight'. Probably the reason why I'm going deaf in one ear was when Martin turned it up and it turned into a flock of marauding pigeons.

The drum riff on 'She's Lost Control' was stolen off a Phil Spector song: it's the same beat, but played with different sounds. It's just a classic Phil Spector beat, and if you listen to it and imagine it played on a big drum kit, it's the same thing really. See, I'm not original at all. The only original thought I had was: 'I'll go and spend some money on a flying saucer-shaped drum that takes two nine-volt batteries, and I've got to get it in there somewhere.'

Bernard Sumner: There's an interesting thing that Martin did on 'She's Lost Control', which is probably one of my favourite rhythm tracks of Steve's. Steve did a lot of it with electronic drums, which hadn't been used much at all before, certainly not by anyone in Manchester at that stage. Martin had a great idea of getting Steve in a vocal booth doing the hi-hat pattern with an aerosol spray. Unfortunately, I think it was fly spray or something, it nearly killed Steve – you know, psssst, psssst, all the way through the track. Poor Steve, he had it in for Steve, definitely.

But yeah, great. It's doing something new and not trying to just repeat what other people had done, and because it was new I really enjoyed the learning process. One of the strengths of Joy Division's music is that we were in the learning process, and what you can actually hear is someone exploring music and how to play it and: 'Don't really know what I do with it, but that sounds good.' That was an extension of getting into electronic music and synthesizers, and in those days they weren't widely used: Kraftwerk and Cabaret Voltaire were a big influence.

Peter Hook: There must be only me and Bernard in the whole bleeding world that don't like *Unknown Pleasures*, because it doesn't sound like we did live, it's purely one-dimensional. We wrote the songs, we listened to it, we thought. 'That's fucking great, that's how we want other people to hear it.' Now I realise that recording songs and playing live are different, and that's what's great about it. Then I was so young I just wanted us to be how we sounded live. I didn't want it to sound melancholic, I didn't want it to last.

I wanted just to lop people's heads off, like Iggy Pop live. I wasn't interested in depth or anything, I just wanted to kick them in the teeth, and that was it. But that's not the way that things survive. Martin had obviously been through that and realised there was a lot to be said for subtlety, and also a lot of depth and melancholy and sucking people in. Instead of screaming in their faces, you were whispering in their ear, weren't you? Martin Hannett whispered in people's ears, and me and Bernard wanted to scream in people's faces.

Stephen Morris: I was happy with all of it, absolutely all of it, because it was completely different to the RCA LP, which was a bit of a drudge, a bit of working for the man. With Martin it was like you were going on some sort of strange science fiction-based journey, and you weren't quite sure how it was going to end up. When you got it, it was nothing like you'd heard, because when you were recording it was all pretty raw, and then there were all these things he put on afterwards. I thought *Unknown Pleasures* was a very futuristic-sounding record and I was very proud of it.

Peter Saville: So sometime in January or February of '79 Rob and Tony had their discussions about Joy Division doing an album and Factory's commitment, or Tony's commitment, to doing a Factory album with Joy Division. All I know is that Tony told me we're doing a Joy Division album, they have some things they'd like on the cover. I don't remember who gave them to me, whether he gave them to me. Stephen Morris might have given them to me, Stephen being usually the person most communicative about things.

I got an envelope of elements that Joy Division would like for their album cover. I mean, the wave pattern is just brilliant. I mean, it's unquestionable, it's great. Stephen gave me, I think, a photocopy of this page, and I read in the caption that it was the graph from a pulsar. It was the jazziest one in space at that time apparently, according to this book. The rest of the brief was really free. I mean, I think I probably asked the obvious questions: 'Does anybody want the title on the front? Do you want "Joy Division" on the front?' – 'Not really.'

I think that's the most revealing. It's not very cool putting your name on the front. And it's a funny combination of shyness and arrogance. It's not cool to put the name on the front – that's like trying a bit hard, isn't it? And I think they felt like that, I think that's the sort of psyche that is part of the discreet elitist-image era, something from that phase before punk, it's something from that phase of visual codes – the silent, discreet identifying of things.

They thought it might be white on the outside and black on the inside, which I sort of converted. But I was just given the elements and asked to put them together, so I did to the best of my ability. The look of *Unknown Pleasures* is pretty much shaped by a very limited technical knowledge. I did it over in the studios of the *New Manchester Review*. I was using their studio as a place to work: they had a PNT camera that was useful for paste-up, and I just did what I knew how to do.

I was really limited by lack of experience, so I put it together in a very neurotic way. I decided that if the waveform was to be on the label of the record, it would be a particular size, and I couldn't cope with it being more than one size, I didn't want to have the same thing in two different sizes, so the outside of the cover is determined by the dimensions of the inside. The waveform is sized to fit on the label on one side of that record, or possibly even on both sides – I can't remember – so it's that size on the front.

I hadn't heard the music. I was concerned with my own work, I was concerned with the precision and the feeling, the mood, the quality of my own work. I'm often really handicapped by that sense of perfectionism, and it was a terrible responsibility. I hadn't heard the record, but it was just the fact that it was an album cover that made it terribly scary. I was twenty-four, and this was a public national work that I was doing. I was scared to do anything wrong, so I did the most I could as perfectly as I could within the narrow restrictions of my ability.

The marvel of Factory was by virtue of not being a company, by not being a business, by not employing anybody, by not investing any money in anything other than just manufacturing; there was no agenda of commerciality, there was no profit agenda. I think people wouldn't have wanted Tony to lose his money. I mean, the wonder of the *Factory Sample* was that five thousand were pressed and five thousand were sold, but I think people bought the *Factory Sample* the way one bought independent records at that time: as a gesture of support.

I bought Fast records. I mean, I didn't even know what was on it, but it was a Fast record, and you bought it because it was your duty to find a pound or two for it, because you were supporting the gesture of independence. The *Factory Sample* sold as a result of people supporting the gesture of independence, and this was it: you were just doing the best you could and making something the way you wanted it to be, and I made *Unknown Pleasures* the way that I would have wanted had I found it in a record rack, and nobody obliged me to do otherwise, so that's what I did.

And it must have been early summer, I took the artwork for *Unknown Pleasures* to Rob's house, and the afternoon that I did that he had received a test pressing of the album, and he said, 'I have a test pressing, do you want to listen to it?' You obviously do want to listen to it, and I was terribly anxious: I didn't really want to listen to it.

All I knew of recorded Joy Division were the two tracks from the *Factory Sample*, which were kind of listenable, more listenable than the rest of the *Factory Sample*, but it was tough going, and I was a little bit anxious. I didn't know if I could sit through forty minutes of Joy Division, especially in front of their manager, but I couldn't really say no: I was delivering the artwork for the cover, couldn't really say I didn't want to listen to it.

So I sat down on Rob's sofa, and he put the test pressing on. And within moments I knew that I had a part in a life-changing experience. Minute after minute was beyond anything I could have expected, I think beyond anything that most people expected. Joy Division with Martin was just beyond . . . it was the most developed thing that I had heard in the brief canon of the new wave, and I was buying things and listening to things, I had a context in which to place it. It was astonishing.

It didn't have the kind of rough rawness that so much of the punk new wave had, but it had integrity. It wasn't trying to please you; it had the spirit of post-punk, but without the crudity of it. It was perfectly its own thing. I think perhaps they grew into Joy Division; I think Martin proposed a way to understand Joy Division. He heard something, he saw something, he felt something from them, and was able to project in his mind what it could be. Martin obviously saw a path and he saw down the path, and that's where he took the material he had.

It's again only in retrospect that I've got a notion of what Martin did. At the time I didn't understand. It was the Joy Division album and Martin produced it; I just thought, 'Wow, this is great.' There'd been a transformation, but I wasn't able to understand at that point that it was Martin. I didn't know Martin. I remember Warsaw, I'd heard Joy Division tracks on the sampler, and now here was something truly astonishing, something's happened, I didn't know where it had come from.

I never sat with Martin and talked to him. I shouldn't think Martin and I ever exchanged more than twenty words. He was interested in his universe and I was interested in mine: we didn't really have much time for other people, either of us. Factory was a collaboration of people who didn't have much time for other people, but the unique role of Tony is as a body around which other bodies orbit. I don't like having to call him the sun, but a solar system is an analogy for what Factory was.

I was in an orbit around Tony, Martin was in an orbit, Alan was in an orbit around Tony, then there's Joy Division in an orbit and Rob Gretton in an orbit. I would be off in my own orbit, except once or twice a year when I would cross with Joy Division, and you can see the whole Factory experience as a system around a central figure, which is Tony.

The brilliance of Tony was to draw those individual talents into that system and let them exist and coexist. There were no rules, no agenda, just the product of passing orbits, and it continued like that pretty much all the way through. No one ever said what anyone else had to do, at least among the artisans of the products. No one ever said what anyone else had to do.

Ian Wood, review of Eric's, Liverpool, 3 May 1979, in *NME*, 26 May 1979

When Joy Division left the stage I felt emotionally drained. They are, without any exaggeration, an Important Band.

8

JUNE – SEPTEMBER 1979

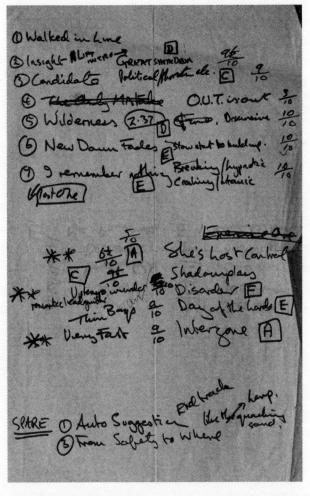

Handwritten notes for *Unknown Pleasures* assembly, spring
1979, Rob Gretton (Courtesy of Lesley Gilbert, Benedict
Gretton and Laura Gretton)

- 15 June 1979: release of *Unknown Pleasures*

Bernard Sumner: I remember me and Hooky being a bit frustrated at the sound of *Unknown Pleasures*, because we felt that the sound of the group playing live was a lot wilder and more rocky and aggressive than the sound that came out on the album. If you've got any live recordings, you can hear that. Martin didn't want it to be a straight-ahead sound: there's this straight recording band and that's it, finished. He wanted to warp it quite a lot, and sometimes we liked that and sometimes we didn't.

Unknown Pleasures was our first outing and we'd played it live a few times, and it was powerful, almost heavy-metal kind of stuff to us. Two things Ian said. One, he never wanted to get any bigger than the Kinks ever got. Two, that what he wanted to do was to get onto the heavy-metal circuit in America, which was really weird. He really loved the Stooges, and he wanted to get into what the Stooges were into.

So the music was quite loud and heavy, and we felt that Martin had toned it down, especially with the guitars, taken out the more raucous elements of it. So we didn't actually like *Unknown Pleasures*. It inflicted this dark, doomy mood over the album: we'd drawn a picture in black and white, and he'd coloured it in for us. We resented that, but Rob loved it, and Wilson loved it, and the press loved it, and the public loved it, so we were just the poor stupid musicians who wrote it. We swallowed our pride and went with it.

Peter Hook: Everything I've read about *Unknown Pleasures* says that the first pressing was five thousand, and it wasn't five thousand, it was ten thousand, because Rob and I carried them up the stairs into Palatine Road.

Stephen Morris: There was definitely an upward trajectory once we'd done *Unknown Pleasures*. We'd had all that time when we were just practising and practising, writing stuff, and then once we got to make a record of it, it took on a life of its own. After *Unknown Pleasures*, when people were trying to be nice to you, you were sort of, 'Yeah, yeah, yeah, you weren't like that the other week, were you?' We didn't exactly take the praise in the way that perhaps we should have done.

We did have a chip on our shoulders about the old Manchester mafia. We still had a bit of 'don't care' in front of the music press, because we couldn't understand a lot of the words that they used in the reviews anyway: 'What the bloody hell are they going on about?' It was just a record, so we took it all with a pinch of salt. When at gigs punters came up to you and said they really liked it, that actually meant something, but the reviews just baffled me.

Peter Hook: We just carried on doing what we did. In those days you were literally doing everything yourself. It was very difficult and it was really hard work. You had to set your own gear up, pull your own gear down, and it was very unglamorous. Even while you were Joy Division and *Unknown Pleasures*, travelling to and from the places was still really hard, and you didn't have any of the glamour, to be honest.

> **Charles Shaar Murray, 'Heads Down No Nonsense Mindless Poetry', John Cooper Clarke interview, in *NME*, 7 July 1979**
> Onstage, Joy Division ram dark slabs of organised noise at the audience while a scarecrow singer moves like James Brown in hell. Acidrock a decade or so on. It is whispered that acid enjoys considerable allegiance from a lot of the young postpunks in Manchester. As the bassist triggers a synthesiser and a skin breaks on the snare drum and the band's sound begins to resemble Awful Things carved out of smooth black marble, who could argue?

- 13 July 1979: Russell Club, Hulme

Kevin Cummins: They did two gigs quite close together at the Factory, in June and July that year, and Martin did the live sound at one of them. It was around the time that the album was coming out. Suddenly it all started to make sense. The band didn't like the sound: it was too arty. But for us, their sound was fuller, they'd hugely fulfilled their potential with that album, and we all thought that was going to be the album of the year. It was astonishing to think that about six or nine months earlier, we thought they were a bit of a joke band.

Alan Hempsall: Crispy Ambulance supported Joy Division at the Russell Club, July the thirteenth. It was one of the first gigs they did after the album came out. Joy Division started with 'Dead Souls', which I don't think I'd heard before. They were never ones to pander: if they had any new material, they would play it. 'Dead Souls' is still one of my favourite tracks. I like the way it builds and the way Ian holds back and doesn't launch in until the song's halfway over, which was something I always thought, 'That's a clever trick, there's not many singers with that self-discipline.'

> **Roger Mitchell, review of *Unknown Pleasures*, *City Fun*, issue 8, July 1979**
> It is a truly remarkable debut mainly due to their originality and their own policy of non-compromise. Probably the best debut album since 1977 and 'The Clash'.

> **Jon Savage, review of *Unknown Pleasures*, *Melody Maker*, 21 July 1979**
> 'To the centre of the city in the night waiting for you . . .' Joy Division's spatial, circular themes and Martin Hannett's shiny, waking-dream production gloss are one perfect reflection of Manchester's dark spaces and empty places, endless sodium lights and hidden semis seen from a speeding car, vacant industrial sites – the endless detritus of the 19th century – seen gaping like rotten teeth from an orange bus.

'Shimmy': Poster for Joy Division at the Factory, 13 July 1979
(Courtesy of Jon Savage)

City Fun **review of Joy Division at the 'Stuff the Superstars Special', Manchester, 28 July 1979**
Their manager reads a book during most of the evening.
No, it's not a pose, he's a genuinely serious bloke, well into
philosophy and such. He sees it as a job to do (and he's
rather good at it). He's not impressed by the hype, the 'next
big thing' bit. He knew they were a big thing years ago.
Joy Division, in one form or another, were in at the start.
THEY knew where they were going, even if we didn't.
THEY WERE BRILLIANT, I MEAN BRILLIANT!

Liz Naylor: I saw Joy Division a series of times at the Factory, leading up to the 'Stuff the Superstars' gig at the Mayflower, which was
promoted by *City Fun*. They were on a day-long bill with the Fall
and Ludus, and lots of also-ran bands and the appalling John the
Postman. It's interesting that Joy Division really crossed over. They
weren't like a snotty Factory band; they actually aligned themselves
with a certain other kind of group in Manchester, and I think that's
really evidenced by the line-up at that gig.

The Mayflower was fantastic. It was my all-time top favourite venue. It had been built as a cinema in the twenties, when
it was called the Coronet, and then in the fifties and sixties it
was a dance hall called the Southern Sporting Club. It's absolutely embedded in a very working-class area of Manchester
called Gorton, which is where Myra Hindley was from: terraced
houses, white working-class Manchester as it was in the post-
war years. In the seventies it used to hold gigs which nobody
else would put on: reggae gigs and things that were considered
a bit dodgy.

The venue was just crumbling, I mean it was absolutely dank. I
can remember going in, and it certainly had no house PA or anything, so it was just like a big, dank, old empty building with a
barely functioning bar – I think you could buy cans of beer – and
it smelled. It had an upper level that was shut because it was struc-
turally dangerous, so it was a big, black, empty hall. It was a really

melancholy building actually; it had plants growing out of bits of its walls because it was so damp.

When *Unknown Pleasures* came out, I went to Palatine Road and was given a free copy, but I didn't have a record player, so I took it to the Mayflower, and there must have been a *City Fun* gig there. I played it over the PA, so that was the very first moment I heard the album sort of booming through this bad PA in this huge damp room, and of course it was absolutely perfect. You fell in love with it, it just meant everything – 'This is the ambient music for my environment.'

I was just very swept up in them. I was young and I wasn't able to stand back and think, 'Mm, they were a good band.' They were like an extension of me, it just felt there was no boundary between me and what I was experiencing. They were really important to me. I think I saw them probably about seven or eight times. I didn't have any sense of a good or bad performance actually, they were just there for me. Other bands I'd go and see and I'd have an opinion on, but Joy Division were my ambient world.

That's the thing about Joy Division: they were a very interesting band about time because they're very informed by the past, but also you're always propelled into the present with them. So time stops a little. Ian's performance to me was like time just stopping. Joy Division were of a particular time and a place, and once you take them out of that their meaning changes. It's like collectively they relayed the aura of Manchester in that period. They are what Manchester was like. Subsequently, that kind of aura has been slightly pushed onto Ian as an individual, and I think that's errone-ous. As a band they're much more important than one individual or what his vision was, because I don't think it was his vision, I think it was the ambience of Manchester.

Bernard Sumner: Ian had a desire to explore the extremes. There's two types of people in this world: there's people who are extremists and they want to taste the extremes, get extremely drunk or not drink at all, and there's people who take the middle way. I'd say I'm pretty much the middle way, but Ian wanted everything to be

STUFF THE SUPERSTARS

FUNHOUSE AT THE MAYFLOWER CLUB

SAT 28TH JULY   DOORS OPEN 1.30 p.m. BANDS FROM 2.00 TILL LATE.

IN ORDER OF APPEARANCE.

HAMSTERS	**LUDUS**
ELTI FITS	**THE LIGGERS**
ARMED FORCE	**THE FALL**
FRANTIC ELEVATORS	**THE DISTRACTIONS**
JOY DIVISION	**JON THE POSTMAN**
	PSYCHEDELIC ROCK 5 SKINNERS

TICKETS AVAILABLE FROM:- DISCOUNT RECORDS (Underground Market)
PICCADILLY RECORDS (Piccadilly Plaza)

TICKETS £1.50   TICKETS £1.50   TICKETS £1.50

STUFF THE SUPERSTARS SPECIAL FESTIVAL.....SATURDAY 28th JULY
FUNHOUSE AT THE MAYFLOWER CLUB.............
BAR 1.30 - 3.00 & 5.30 till LATE. FOOD AVAILABLE ALL DAY......
RECORDS, BADGES, FANZINES, etc, ON SALE (CHEAP!!!)...........
ALL PROFITS AFTER EXPENSES WILL BE SPLIT EQUALLY BETWEEN THE BANDS

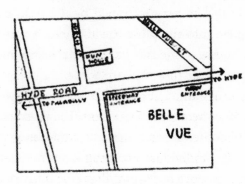

BUSES:-
From Piccadilly: 125,126,160,
204,205,206,207,208,209,210,
211,212,233,234,235.
From Cheetham/Clayton: 53.
From Old Trafford/Moss Side:53.
From Denton & Hyde.125,207-212
From Droylsden: 169, 170.
From Didsbury & Burnage:169,170

'Stuff the Superstars' gig at the Mayflower (from *City Fun*), 28 July 1979

extreme: extreme music, manic performances. So the music was extremely dark. Even after we recorded *Unknown Pleasures* I found it quite difficult to listen to because it was so dark.

I don't think the production helped because that made it darker, even darker still, but I felt, 'No one's going to listen to this, it's too bloody heavy, too impenetrable.' Also, I think in our lives we'd all had very dark experiences. We were only twenty-one, but for me, say, I'd had a very difficult upbringing and I had a lot of death and illness in my family: my mother had cerebral palsy; my grand-mother, who we grew up with, had had an operation on her eyes that went wrong, so she'd lost her sight; my stepfather got cancer from smoking.

My grandfather was ill as well – he had a brain tumour – and all this had been going on when I was very young. I had all this tragedy within my family. I'd had to witness a couple of them dying at quite a young age, and that definitely had an effect on me. To experience such things at a young age makes you quite a serious person. I was sixteen when it started, when my grandfather died. And being an only child makes it worse. I know Hooky had had a few troubles at home, and Ian, I guess, in his line of work was quite serious. For me, life was serious, so I guess that came out in my music, subconsciously.

I'd had quite a lot of loss in my life. The place where I used to live, and where I had my happiest memories – and let's face it, every-body's happiest memories are from when you're a kid and every day was sunny, there's no inhibitions and no hang-ups – well, all that had gone. All that was left was a chemical factory. It's all gone – the houses, the people. So there's this void that you can never, ever go back to. When I was twenty-two I realised that I could never go back to that happiness. So, for me, Joy Division was about the death of my community and my childhood.

Liz Naylor: I don't know how Joy Division managed to relate to Manchester. I don't think they were conscious of it. Bernard is somebody that was rehoused into a post-war development. They had the dislocated relationship with community and city just because of the age they were. I think it's purely an accident of history. Their experience of Manchester was of being in communities, then being rehoused.

Their experience of the city would have been not dissimilar from mine, going in there during the mid-seventies, pre-punk times, where it was really failing and emptying out, decaying and derelict. I think it was a really strange kind of hitch in time and place, the very last days of an industrial city. That created a really unique moment, an ambience, and that kind of ambience can be traced still through psychogeography in the city as it is now, because those moments are never, ever truly eradicated.

I suppose the environment totally mirrored my inner self. I felt really comfortable in it. It's interesting reading the Deborah Curtis book: the places, the clubs that Ian was going to and the places that I was going to – the New Union on Princess Street, which was the vilest pub, and the Mayflower Club, and I went to a club called Dickens, on Oldham Street. These were identified as gay places, but that doesn't really tell you anything, because the people in them were freaks, they were people who were left in the city after everybody who could had moved out.

C. P. Lee: The whole zeitgeist of the late seventies fed into Joy Division. You've got this group of young guys from these towns in the north-west of England who could not help but be informed by the atmosphere that was around them. When I hear them now I can see how it directly transmuted into the music that they were playing. There's a definite feeling of ritual in Joy Division performances and Joy Division releases – 'release' being the operative word, in that you can transcend and move beyond and get onto another plane of being.

Mark Reeder: I loved the Joy Division records. I was in awe. *Unknown Pleasures*, I couldn't imagine it being any better, it was just perfect for that moment. When Rob sent me the first box of

Unknown Pleasures, I couldn't believe my ears. The album just blew my mind. Everything about it: the cover, the mystique of the inner sleeve – the hand at the door. Fantastic. 'New Dawn Fades', I couldn't stop playing that. It just hit a chord with me, that song, but I loved every single song on that album.

Jon Wozencroft: *Unknown Pleasures* was such a devastating moment, because from the *Factory Sample* to the album within six months was an extraordinary development, and most importantly in the sense that there was a complete world in itself. It was like a really good long film that you didn't want to end. There was no question of a thirty-eight-minute album or a forty-five-minute album or anything like that; it was just exactly right for the experience that it sought to communicate.

It's very exciting because you have been taken on a journey. Ian comes on, track one, side one, and he says, 'I'm waiting for a guide to come and take me by the hand' – that's it, you're in it straight away.

Iain Gray: I found *Unknown Pleasures* a frightening album, and that was when Ian was alive. I can remember listening to it late at night and thinking, 'It's quite creepy.' It caught the essence of despair. You always think, even if you knew someone slightly, that you should have gone, 'Are you OK?'

Richard Boon: I thought it was a great Martin Hannett record. I thought some of it was very forced, some of the vocals were very mannered. I think the vocals were a bit too upfront, and you get the sense that the delivery is very sort of artificially intense, not really coming from his heart. Once Martin had reshaped them – he was their Svengali, much more than Wilson or Gretton – and they could achieve the sound that he'd brought out of them, it eased up a lot and wasn't as formal and forced as I perceived it to be.

Bob Dickinson: Joy Division sounded like ghosts and seemed spectral at the time, and their music still does have that quality about it, of something that's dead but it's alive, something that's there and it's not there. The other phrase that comes to mind is that technology has turned us all into ghosts; that the recording medium and the visual recording medium, as well as the audio recording medium, are turning you into a dateable object and they're killing you. I think that they were aware of it, and they were haunted by it themselves and they described that condition, which is what makes their music so relevant and still so powerful.

- 2 August 1979: live at the Prince of Wales Conference Centre, YMCA, London

Jill Furmanovsky: They were compelling. Ian looked like a schoolboy in his grey shirt and trousers. Then there was Hooky, with that low-slung bass. He had a particular way of playing that was quite unusual. Bernard, too – they just looked very un-rock-star-like. More like the Fall, from that point of view. I was very struck by Ian Curtis: he looked like he'd bunked off school and gone to join a rock band, which in a way he had done.

After the gig I went backstage and poked my head into their dressing room. They were in a good mood, the gig had gone well, friends were arriving, and I had a few minutes, and that was the extent of my shoot. I just whizzed in and whizzed out; I didn't get to know them at all. They must have known who I was, cos I'd worked with Buzzcocks and some of the other punk bands, and I probably just said, 'I'm Jill Furmanovsky from [whichever newspaper I was working for], is it all right if I take a few snaps in the dressing room?' And they didn't mind. I snapped, and I left.

They were all rather jolly, sharing out cigarettes, having a drink. They were in good spirits. The other bands – Monochrome Set was one of them – they were all popping in and out. I'm very quick at what I do; a lot of my best jobs are done very fast, in a hotel room or a dressing room, places like that. It was immediately after the gig, and the main shot, which we always use, it looks like they're exploding from one point. I always liked the composition of that, with Ian leaning over, but building up to that there was a lot of movement going on.

Seeing Ian Curtis with a towel around him and not minding somebody being in the room, there was a feeling of having cracked that gig. I think it was quite an important London gig for them at the time. There must have been a buzz about them.

Adrian Thrills, review of YMCA concert in *NME*,
11 August 1979
Joy Division were phenomenal . . . Each member is equally important. Drummer Steve Morris is undoubtedly the best 'thumper' since the sadly exiled Palmolive of Slits/Raincoats fame. His style is also remarkable for the combination of ordinary drums and electronic percussion and syndrums, particularly devastating on She's Lost Control and the Insight encore. Peter Hook swerves and dips on bass like a more menacing Paul Simonon, while guitarist Bernard Dickens [*sic*] remains sternly still beside Ian Curtis who sings and growls as he grimly jerks like a puppet on invisible strings.

Steve Taylor, review of YMCA concert in *Melody Maker*,
11 August 1979
Joy Division speak of apocalypse hopelessness and fragmentation, yet their music acts as an exorcism of passivity and neglect, as near a revitalisation of the spirit of primeval rock 'n' roll as I've experienced in a long while.

Dave McCullough, 'Truth, Justice and the Mancunian Way',
***Sounds* interview, 11 August 1979**
The irony was, of course, that even by, as they thought, remaining inscrutable and, ahem, Obscure, the band provided us with gargantuan evidence of their pseudness and, more to the point, their cerebral shortcomings. Ian remained contentedly silent as I became increasingly irritated by the absurd masquerade that was taking place.

Bernard Sumner: I think it was one of our first interviews. It was such a horrible experience we just thought, 'Fuck it, if that's what they're like, we won't do them.' So we just didn't do them. I think Ian might have done a couple, but it wasn't the fun bit. We were only doing it for fun, we had no idea of promoting ourselves. We weren't bothered about getting on *Top of the Pops* or selling vast quantities of records, we just liked it at that moment and that's all we were interested in. We didn't have any idea that if you do loads of interviews, you'll sell more records.

Dave McCullough was pretty off-putting, because he was just a knobhead basically. We weren't being unreasonable or anything, we were just okay with him, and when we didn't follow his little plan, he just went off on one, so we just thought, 'Fuck it. Stick to making records.' Of course, my opinion of journalists is totally changed now. I think they're wonderful.

Peter Hook: Rob was the thinker. He had the vision in the way we were portrayed. When the press came along, spouting this rubbish at you, in the same way that you annoyed the other bands when you began you annoyed the press, because basically they were a bunch of tossers. We wouldn't play the game. We'd answer questions with the word 'no'. They didn't seem to warrant taxing yourself. They'd ask you one question, and then expect you to fill their column inches for them with one answer. They got what they deserved.

Ian was very shy, especially early on. Steve didn't want to say anything, me and Bernard were a pair of pissed-up yobs, so Rob said, 'Listen, it's probably better if you two don't say anything, because you're both as thick as pigshit.' And we went, 'That's all right, yeah, we can agree with you on that one.' You didn't know what you were doing, you were just doing it. Ian may have known what we were doing, but he fell behind me and Bernard because we were mouthy, gobby.

Rob stopped us really. It changed later, because Ian used to hate it when people would only talk to him about the group, he hated people singling him out in Joy Division, so that again put you on a spot where you didn't want to talk to the press. Every interview that you see or read about a group starts roughly the same. They're all as boring as shite really. I'd rather not know where the music comes from, I'd rather it was magical and just existed like that, so I was quite happy to go along with not doing interviews. I think it breaks the mystery.

We were very insular. While it may annoy you, you still got strength from being together. Rob was really, really good at bullying us along. You know, 'Come on, come on, fuck that.' He'd keep us at it really. If something happened to bring us down, he'd boost the whole thing and push us along, and then we'd forget it because he'd stand up for you. If there was somebody there that he felt was doing something wrong, he'd say, 'Fuck off, you knobhead, you fucking twat, it's my band, this' – which was great. You really felt he was rooting for you.

James Brown, sabotagetimes.com
Stephen Morris: The first time I realised something had changed was when we played the Nashville. We went out and there was a queue of people like I'd never seen before, round the block to get into the Nashville Rooms. I said, 'Look at that, that's our first queue.'

Paul Rambali, 'Joy Division: Take No Prisoners, Leave No Clues', *NME*, 11 August 1979
Were you to shine a torch around this subterranean scene you would see the young, tidy faces of Joy Division and notice perhaps the ordinary neat cut of their clothes. An unremarkable image, with the barest hint of the regimental overtones of their name in the flap-pocket shirts two of them are wearing. You might also notice the growing excitement in the faces of the onlookers, by now all locking into the irresistible motion of the music. Easily the strongest new music to come out of this country this year.

- 13 August 1979: Nashville Rooms, London

Ian Curtis (interviewed by Paul Rambali, *NME*, 11 August 1979): You're always working to the next song. No matter how many songs you've done, you're always looking for the next one. Basically we play what we want. It'd be very easy for us to say: well, all these people seem to like such and such a song . . . it'd be easy to knock out another one. But we don't.

We don't want to get diluted, really, and by staying at Factory at the moment we're free to do what we want. There's no one restricting us or the music – or even the artwork and promotion. You get bands that are given huge advances – loans really – but what do they spend it on? What is all that money going to get? Is it going to make the music any better?

Terry Mason: It was like a snowball how they were growing at that stage. We were getting more and more press, and you start taking on what the press are saying. You've had this period where no one wanted to know you, and all of a sudden people are saying, 'You're fantastic,' and that brought more confidence into the band, and they started going onstage with more of a swagger about them. They were a lot more sure of themselves.

Tony Wilson: I don't think I saw them becoming world-beaters fast because I presumed from the very beginning they were world-beaters. I presumed they're the most important band of their generation, like the Pistols had been two years before. It would be nice to think I didn't know it at the time, but I did know it, and no, it was not a surprise. They just got better and better.

Bernard Sumner: We'd always relied on what we thought about ourselves. We didn't really care what other people thought. Because I think we were quite disliked at the start – I don't know, it could be my own paranoia – we learned to rely on ourselves. I mean, me personally, I was an only child, so I have that way of thinking anyway, self-reliance.

I always felt that was a wonderful strength of Joy Division – that

we only really cared if we liked it – and that gave us longevity. We
didn't know how it worked either, we were on an independent label.
We didn't think of it in careerist terms; we were just happy to be getting £50 a week, £100 a week or whatever and doing what we loved
doing: travelling around the country, travelling around Europe, playing gigs. It was fantastic. That was enough for us, because it was good:
we were having a great time on the road, partying and all the rest.

- 19 August 1979: photo session with Kevin Cummins at
T. J. Davidson's Rehearsal Rooms

Kevin Cummins: I'd been to see them rehearse a couple of times
and hadn't taken photographs; I'd just been along, because I was
interested in what they were doing by then. I'd already photo-
graphed Buzzcocks and the Fall in there. I thought I might need to
take some lights, to fill in a bit. Also, as you know, bands are notori-
ous for not turning up on time and starting work at midnight or
something. So I went in a couple of times to watch them rehearse
for an hour or so.

Then I went down that day and took the pictures. Most of it is
shot against the light. I liked the silhouette, shadow kind of feel
for them. Which kind of became the way other people shot them.
You can see lots of Coke cans and things in the shot, and the Coke
cans are all full of piss. The place stank, it was disgusting. The toilets were on the floor below, and they couldn't be bothered going
down there, they just used to piss in Coke cans, and they'd be dot-
ted around the place, so you didn't dare touch anything.

Bernard Sumner: T. J. Davidson was the guy that ran the rehearsal
space. He looked a bit like the drummer out of Frankie Goes to
Hollywood, with the Scouse perm, but he was a really nice guy. I
think his dad owned a jeweller's shop and bought these old factories in Manchester. We had an enormous factory floor to ourselves.
Half the windows were smashed in and there were rats in the toilets
and there was no soundproofing, so you could hear down below

you. Did we have Slaughter and the Dogs down below us?

In the winter we used to brush all the rubbish to one end of the room and set fire to it just to keep warm. There was a hole in the floorboards, and you could see Slaughter and the Dogs' drum kit. Hooky used to piss through the hole in the floor onto their drum kit – when they'd gone, of course – because they were so annoying and loud. It was a good creative space, but it was bloody freezing. He wouldn't put the heating on. I guess it didn't work, but it was so cold. The acoustics were awful and our equipment was awful, but we managed to write some great songs there.

- 27 August 1979: Open-Air Festival, Leigh

Jon Savage, review of Leigh Festival in *Melody Maker*, **8 September 1979**
Joy Division exorcised the increasing cold with cinematic, metallic blocks of noise.

Kevin Cummins: We drove in and parked about fifty yards from the stage, and just left the car there. There was a row of cars, cos there was hardly anybody there. It was quite exposed. I took pictures of Hooky wearing his overcoat onstage, and it's the middle of August. It was just one of those things that was so badly organised. The poster wasn't ready, so nobody knew it was on, then nobody could get there because there was a public-transport strike, so the only people there were the people who could drive.

The whole day there was hardly anybody there, and then it filled up a bit in the evening when Joy Division came on. Being able to shoot onstage with them was quite exciting for me. I was onstage pretty much for the whole gig. I always enjoy that because you get to feel what the band are feeling.

Peter Hook: I remember playing at Leigh Festival. That wasn't a great gig. It didn't feel very good, it was really cold. The highlight was the forty-inch turd in the toilet that Terry found.

Jeremy Kerr: Everyone got busted on the way in. There was more coppers than audience.

Lesley Gilbert: It was like ten people in the field, and that was it. I think there were more police there than there were crowd. They were stopping everybody when they went in, and I'm sure they took Bernard's girlfriend Sue away somewhere and searched her. It didn't faze anybody that there was hardly anybody there, it was good fun. There was loads of stuff like that, gigs where there was hardly anybody there and nobody was bothered.

Stephen Morris: Leigh Festival – what a washout. Factory meets Zoo halfway. It seemed like an awfully big field, and my abiding memory of that was as soon as it started raining, the twenty or thirty people that were there went and got in their cars and turned their lights on. 'Where have they gone? Oh, they're in their cars, that's all right.' It was bound to be a washout. A lot of Factory ideas must have grown out of some late-night conversation, and if they'd just waited a few hours before making these decisions, they probably would have seen the error of their ways, but no, we'll go through hell or high water and damn the consequences.

- 8 September 1979: Futurama Festival, Leeds

Terry Mason: A major gig, of course, was Futurama. We were on there same night as Public Image, Johnny Rotten's new band, and we were the slot right before them.

Kevin Cummins: For them, it was great, but the whole event was awful. It was everything that punk was against – a huge festival in a draughty hall in Leeds, the Queen's Hall. They hadn't even cleaned it out, it was sparsely attended, and all the rubbish that was stored in there they just swept to the back of the hall and put a bit of fencing in front. It was a firetrap, to be honest. There was an arena-style stage and rig. It was very cold and it was grim.

It was relentless, band after band after band. Until Joy Division came on, it was fairly awful. It worked for them, without being clichéd, that almost Eastern European feel. I don't think it was even what they intended it to be, it just worked like that. As a photographer, Ian's dancing was quite tricky. There were different ways of doing it: you could shoot at a lower shutter speed and get some movement, or you could use a bit of fill-in flash and get him, but still get some movement coming off his arms.

I just wanted to capture the intensity of his performance. It was mesmerising. It always felt dangerous, because you always felt he was slightly out of control, and I'd not really experienced that with any other band. I'd seen the Clash and the Jam and all these bands, and I never felt that they were more than the sum of their parts. But with Ian, it was dangerous. The only other person who was that dangerous onstage was Iggy Pop.

Dave Simpson: It was the first gig I ever went to. It was a place called the Queen's Hall, which is not there any more. It was on Swinegate, they flattened it in the mid-eighties. I remember it vividly because I used to go to flea markets there. The sound was very distinctive. I've got a couple of tapes of it, and as soon as I hear those tapes, I'm instantly back there. At the time I was fifteen or sixteen, never been to a gig before, had nothing to compare it to.

The first thing I remember was the size of the speakers. I'd never seen a proper PA system. I was used to music coming out of a transistor radio, or at best a home stereo. So to be confronted by these speakers that were probably about fifteen feet high, it was like going into another world. I was blown away. It was a really weird echoey sound, but if you listen to the tape, I think it actually enhances it. The way the drums sound, with this massive, giant, reverb-soaked pounding, it just sounds incredible. To me as a kid, it just sounded spookier.

Before Joy Division came on, there were other bands that were using strobes, which, again, I'd never seen before. Hawkwind had lent their laser system to Punishment of Luxury, who I also thought were fantastic that day. It all felt quite futuristic, which it was sup-posed to be. It was billed as the 'world's first science-fiction music festival', which was a grand idea, to put all these forward-looking bands on, with a few special effects, like lasers. There was a couple of people walking around dressed as robots. A very rudimentary vision of the future.

I'd seen their name. On the bus route to my school, there used to be a lot of posters for a venue called the Roots Club in Chapeltown, and I'd seen their name, they played there. I think they'd also played the Fan Club in Brannigan's. That was outside the city centre, more in the West Indian area, as it was then. They had reggae on there and Pink Military or Pink Industry, Cabaret Voltaire – I suppose the esoteric end of the post-punk era. So they had played in Leeds, but I don't think people really knew who they were.

When A Certain Ratio were on, I remember someone turning to me and asking, 'Who's this?' And I said I didn't know, I thought it might be Joy Division. I'd never heard of either of them, they were just names on a poster. No idea what they looked like or sounded like. I realised my faux pas when Tony Wilson came on, an hour or two later, and introduced Joy Division as 'the awesome Joy Division'. Two things crossed my mind: one, that this was going to be great; and two, 'Oh, the other band wasn't Joy Division then, so who were they?'

Joy Division absolutely mesmerised me. It was like seeing the future. They started with 'Dead Souls', which was another weird thing, because I was used to songs having ten-second intros, then the verse comes in, then the chorus. You don't expect a song that begins with about a minute and a half of bass and drums, a tiny bit of guitar and nothing else. The singer not singing at all, just dancing. 'What is this, an instrumental? Who's this bloke dancing?' Then the dancer starts singing, and it starts to fall into place.

I remember Peter Hook putting his boot on the monitor to play 'Transmission'. They played 'Wilderness' and 'I Remember Nothing', and it sounded amazing because of the reverb on the drums. Ian wore a shiny kind of two-tone shirt, looked fantastic under the lights. I don't remember him really saying anything. He might have said, 'Good evening, we're Joy Division.' They just came on and played the music. I loved the mystery of it. These four reasonably young guys playing the music and taking you to all manner of emotions, and yet nothing was explained.

It completely changed my life. Virtually everything I've ever done since that gig has been because of it. Another thing: you had to have your photo taken to get an ID card to get in. So before we went in, me and my mate Bruce had to go to Woolworths and get these photos done, and in this photo-booth picture of me I've got this iron-on Sid Vicious T-shirt, a very crap Vapors/Members-type spiky haircut, and Bruce's arm is coming in through the curtain. I'm looking up, laughing at this arm coming in, and the camera goes off.

I look at that picture now and I think, 'Within a couple of hours of that picture, you were never the same again.' The T-shirt went on Monday morning – it literally changed everything. I remember getting rid of loads of records. Suddenly I wasn't going to listen to Sham 69 or the UK Subs any more, I was going to listen to Joy Division, the Bunnymen, that John Peel kind of thing.

> ### Damaged Goods fanzine, no. 4
> Well, on to the two song wonders, Factory Records artists (actors–?) Joy Division. Why does everyone love Joy Division? Who knows, certainly not I, but it's like one BIG HYPE. 'Shadowplay' and 'She's Lost Control' are the only two songs in their set that I've any time for at all, the rest just being a monotonous drone! Come on you modern boys, look through the Gothic air of intrigue, the nazi name connections, the stylised 'Kentucky-fried' dancing and what do you see – NOTHING, IT'S ALL A POSE! Finito. PS. Is Tony Wilson this year's McClaren?

- 13 September 1979: *No City Fun: The Factory Flick* (Factory FAC 9), 8mm film, premiered at the Scala Cinema, London, with words from 'No City Fun' by Liz Naylor and a soundtrack of *Unknown Pleasures*

Liz Naylor: 'No City Fun', *City Fun* magazine, issue 3, December 1978
manchester where are you? I NEED. I walk around and try real hard to look like a famous writer, with a cigarette dangling beautifully from my lip, dylan thomas has the edge. no one is impressed. no one is convinced . . . . . me neither . . . . right where are people? virgin at the time of writing is closed – THANK GOD, (wish they'd stay closed for good). due to moving (CERTAINLY NOT MOVEMENT, CERTAINLY NOT PROGRESSION.) I mooch down to the underground – HORROR MOVIE, girls with dyed hair and split skirts hate me, fifteen year old schoolboys buy overpriced Clash singles and say 'fab' ejaculate over blondie albums (now you know why they have plastic covers on them!) I swing out, last years [*sic*] thing etc etc etc etc

Liz Naylor: I was so amazed that this thing I'd written had become this other thing, and it felt like a life-saving moment. I don't know what I thought would happen – I'd be signed up by Hollywood. For so long, I'd lived at home, I'd been an utter freak, I'd been queer and on my own, and it's like having no presence in the world or no voice, so suddenly not only had this thing been published but it had been made into a film, and it felt like my vision of Manchester made real.

Looking back at it now, I realise that it's not just my vision. I believe that was the ambience of Manchester, which is why I think Charles Salem chose Joy Division's music, because he recognised something of similarity there. We were talking about the same thing, experiencing the same place at the same time. Looking at it now, I do think it's a psychogeographical film, it feels very situationist, all the stuff with shop fronts, and it looks like a crude piece of English situationism – which is fantastic.

[*Looks at film*] Oh, we're in the Arndale now. Okay. Oh, there's Paperchase – I can't even remember that. Underground market. Watching it now, I can kind of identify most shots where they were, and it is like being pulled back into that journey again, and it really picks up on the moods of the city in that period. It's such an unconscious piece of film-making and it was a rather self-conscious piece of writing, but with a piece of unconscious film-making it creates something quite strange.

- 15 September 1979: *Something Else*, BBC TV

 (Interview as transmitted)
 Tony Wilson: Do you think they will ever play your records?
 Stephen Morris: Doubtful, doubtful.
 Paul Burnett: Is there an automatic right that you have when you bring a record out that it should get played on Radio 1?
 Tony Wilson: If it's a brilliant record, if it's better than most of the dross that's around, and there are records which are better than most of the dross which is around that don't get played because they are slightly unsettling – for the simple reason that they come from somewhere slightly deeper in the soul than the level of a pure hit factory – and those things don't get played.

Stephen Morris: *Something Else* was good. That was where we discovered you could get your hair cut by the make-up ladies. If you went, you could get free haircuts; you could also go into the canteen and get ridiculously subsidised food – it was very, very cheap. Also, I got to say something on television, just the once. We did it with the Jam, which is where Paul Weller noticed us. After that, the Jam did 'Start', and Ian always said they nicked that off us.

Tony Wilson: If you compare the first television, which is 'Shadowplay' for Granada, to the BBC stuff from a year later, there's a real difference, because they really go for it. I think the performance on the BBC *Something Else* show is phenomenal. It's wonderful to have 'Shadowplay' there, and to have the first television visuals of Joy Division, but to have the BBC footage, that is so intense.

Jon Wozencroft: It was in September '79. I had to go back into hospital for a bone-graft operation because I broke my collarbone very badly and had to be stitched up with bone material. I was just recovering from that, and I went into the television room on a Saturday afternoon and there was this programme on called *Something Else.* All the other people in the room were watching *Grandstand* and football results and all of that, and I thought, 'This is obviously something interesting,' so I persuaded them to let me turn it over.

So we turned over to BBC2, and I've never seen a TV musical performance like it. We all know how difficult it is to get good music captured by a television studio. In this case, I don't know what happened, but Ian Curtis's performance and the band's performance totally broke through the plastic of the medium. I think it was just the focusing of a really strong energy and catching the band on a good day, and then realising that this was a nationwide opportunity for them to get their ideas and their music across.

The extraordinary thing was, it was prime-time Saturday afternoon. I think it was about five thirty, five forty-five on a Saturday evening, so anybody could have been watching that, and anybody did in this room that I was in. All these old men who'd got cranky legs and hips suddenly were watching Joy Division instead of *Dad's Army.* It was extraordinary, the effect that it had: there was none of the usual stuff – 'Turn that rubbish over.' I mean, people could obviously recognise that this was something quite unusual.

The way they chose to use their opportunity by starting off with 'Transmission' was quite significant, because the way that song builds is very modular and shows you the development that Joy Division had achieved in such a short period of time. Going from musicians who couldn't even play their instruments, suddenly they were a supergroup. Steve's drumming, Hooky's bass guitar and Bernard's guitar-playing were just extraordinary. It was the counterpoint.

Instead of wrapping themselves around the same melodies and configurations, each of them was reversing certain paradigms, so that Hooky, for example, becomes the lead guitarist. Bernard is then freed up to put all kinds of different shades on what a guitar could do, and he was using a lot of distortion and noise in quite a melodic way. The only other person I could think of who was doing that then was John McKay from Siouxsie and the Banshees. It was a very, very concentrated, focused ten minutes' worth of TV time.

- 28 September 1979: the Factory I, Manchester

Deborah Curtis (from *Touching from a Distance*): As autumn approached they played The Factory for the last time before it closed down for an indefinite period, as the Russell Club's licence had expired. It had been 'our place' for sixteen months and there was a feeling that we were about to begin the next chapter.

Paul Barrowford, joydiv.org: The lights were dim – Joy Division take to the stage and open with a new song called Atmosphere. The piece is slow, gothic, and features Ian Curtis on guitar. Four or five other songs are played the best being Colony, old favourites like Interzone, Wilderness and especially She's Lost Control get the audience bopping frantically. 45 minutes later and a superb, controlled set is finished. The band return for Transmission, a false start, try again. At this point an incident occurs which spoils the whole evening.

Someone must have been having a go at bass player Peter Hook as halfway thru Transmission he starts attacking this unknown person with his bass. The incident continues with Hook chasing the person thru the audience and ends in a scuffle near the cloakroom. Hook returns to the stage and disappears into the dressing room. The band (minus Hook) continue with Step Inside and finish.

Ian Curtis outside the Factory, September 1979 (Phil Alderson)

Peter Hook: Me and Twinny took Bernard's mate out to get him drunk – Dr Silk, he was a magician. And we took him out to get him drunk for a laugh, that's what you did then. And he didn't get drunk, so he must have rumbled what we were doing, putting vodkas in his tomato juice. He must have been doing it to us, because me and Twinny ended up legless. We got back to the Factory and we were just pissed, and when we played I was shouting at Steve all the time to play faster and faster, cos I was drunk.

We had a load of fans at the front; they'd be there at every gig. I remember this kid ran up to one of the fans, covered in badges, and grabbed him by the hair and nutted him on the back of the head. And I thought, 'Oh, that's not on.' So I took me bass off and wielded it like Spartacus, and then the momentum – waaaaaaah – took me right offstage and I went right in the middle of them, and they fucking kicked the shit out of me basically, and then Twinny jumped in and grabbed me by the collar and pulled me to the back.

We grabbed this kid who we presumed was one of the protagonists, and me and Twinny were leathering him, and then we looked up and it was the kid with the badges on – we picked the wrong kid. The rest of the band played on, and it was my first example of when the band plays on really. So they didn't help, the three of them, they just left me and Twinny to it. I remember afterwards I went fucking mad because they didn't help me, they didn't stop playing.

Bob Dickinson: You'd go to see a good band at that time, who would include Joy Division. You'd go because you had to get out of the house, because the house wasn't usually a very nice place to stay. You'd go out because you'd see your mates, you'd go out because in the size of venues that we're talking about that were in use at that time – like Rafters, Band on the Wall, the Russell Club, the Mayflower – there was a sense of intimacy with audiences, you could be very close to the band. It was more than intimacy; it was a sense of dialogue as well.

If you saw these bands, you could change them, and they could change you. You were there to echo what they would do, and they were there to echo what you were doing or saying. There was a lot more shouting: people shouted at the bands, and the bands would shout back at the audiences. I loved the way that there was always this dialogue. That said a lot about what the Manchester music scene was like: it was democratic because you were all involved.

Mary Harron, 'Factory Records: Food for Thought',
Melody Maker, **29 September 1979**
The songs are a series of disconnected images; Ian Curtis says he writes the lyrics to an imaginary film. The purpose of this surrealistic montage is not to convey a message, but to arouse strange feelings. One clue to Joy Division lies in their album's title. Another is the description given by Martin Hannett, who calls them 'dancing music, with gothic overtones'. Unintentionally, Bernard Albrecht gave an excellent description of 'gothic' in our interview, when describing his favourite film, *Nosferatu*. 'The atmosphere is really evil, but you feel comfortable inside it.'

Mary Harron: Tony called me originally, and sent me a bunch of early Factory stuff. I still have the entire package. He'd read the stuff I'd written in *Melody Maker* about the Gang of Four and the Mekons, and that's what sparked his interest. I think he had no idea that I was not British; he'd just read this stuff and was very taken with it, I guess because of the politics, and he was into the sixties radicalism. Anyway, he thought that I would appreciate Factory.

I went up with Steve Taylor from *The Face*, and Tony took us all around Manchester, and I did the interview with Joy Division. I think it was in a Chinese restaurant. Empty. And Tony is driving us around, talking a mile a minute – it was basically a Tony monologue. Then we went to see the producer, Martin Hannett. We saw Orchestral Manoeuvres and interviewed those two guys, and they played me something, I think on a cassette: this electronic pop music, which was new, and which I loved.

I don't think I met Peter Saville then, I met him later. Or maybe I did, and then later met him again at a show in London and got to be friends with him. He had tons of interesting ideas. We talked for about six hours the first time, all about what was happening after punk. Obviously I was very into the Warhol Factory, but I think what I loved most about Factory at that point was the incredible visuals, the style and the theory. The ideas behind it.

It was the most original idea for a record company I think I'd ever seen. I was into the idea of it being a little label with a complete identity, every aspect of it being designed and created within an overall aesthetic. I thought it was incredible, the idea of creating in a non-corporate way. It was not major-label, but they were into manufacturing. And there was nothing as beautiful as what Peter was making.

I was still hungover from punk. And the one new thing I'd got into was Gang of Four and the Mekons. Musically, I did not appreciate Joy Division as much as I did later. I don't know why I wasn't more overwhelmed, because I think they're great now. I don't know why I didn't think more of them, but when I first saw *Eraserhead*, I didn't like it. I think it was too new, I needed more time to appreciate it. The music was very different. What did it relate to? I think I was still into a punk aesthetic that was very tight and disciplined.

I saw them in London, at one of those weird west London pub things; it might have been the Nashville. When I did the interview, they were so nice and smart and innocent. Very bright, I guess working-class Manchester kids, and yet they were serious and innocent and modest, but they had all their ideas about having this life making music. I didn't see any disharmony in them. There were bands that were aggressive towards me, and I didn't get any of that from them. They were not shy exactly, but introspective. Very thoughtful. They were lovely.

Mary Harron, 'Factory Records: Food for Thought',
Melody Maker, **29 September 1979**

History never repeats exactly. But there is one important parallel here: apart from the Distractions, all the Factory groups have turned away from daily life, towards what in the Sixties would have been termed 'inner space'. What the Sixties groups achieved was no more than what Joy Division achieve – a series of thrilling sensations. But because this exploration was done through drugs, they thought they were discovering cosmic truths. Without drugs, today's explorations are private and bewildered, which at least is honest.

Mary Harron: I think I got a lot of it wrong in that article. I felt that I should have listened harder. The other thing was, Tony was pushing them so hard, I resisted. I felt I was being a bit steamrolled, and I was going to be more critical. We were trying to preserve our integrity as outside voices, which nowadays I don't take so seriously. That was the error of rock journalism: that no one should sway my opinion.

But Tony was pushing so hard about giving acid to everybody, a psychedelic revolution in consciousness. As I was anti-hippie in that sense, I thought it was a really bad idea. He was going a mile a minute – it was linked in with Marxism, and with anarchy, and psychedelic revolution – and when he got into giving out acid, I was thinking, 'That's going to be terrible.' And I guess in the end drugs did bring it all down, but it wasn't acid.

At the time, I'd never met somebody with such a total vision – for a place, for creating a social revolution. He had a great description of Malcolm and the Sex Pistols. He said nobody realised that what Malcolm was trying to create when he made the Sex Pistols was the Bay City Rollers of outrage. He didn't intend for the music to be serious. At the time, what he was saying about what he was going to do in Manchester – in a way, he kind of did do it. I think he thought he could create more of a change in consciousness, a psychic revolution.

Tony Wilson: I remember Mary Harron, the reviewer and writer, came to Manchester one night. I think we were in a restaurant, about three or four in the morning. I remember she was saying, 'But are you sure there's more?' And I said, 'I believe there is.' If you look at the lyrics to 'Shadowplay' – 'I let them do everything they wanted to' – there was a complexity in those lyrics which, I said to her, 'I believe that points the way to more complexity of emotion and of expression.' And I was right.

I give Bernard the credit for this thought, which is that punk enabled you to say 'Fuck you', but somehow it couldn't go any further. It was just a single, venomous, two-syllable phrase of anger which was necessary to reignite rock'n'roll, but sooner or later someone was going to want to say more than 'Fuck you'. Someone was going to want to say 'I'm fucked', and it was Joy Division who were the first band to do that, to use the energy and simplicity of punk to express more complex emotions.

9

OCTOBER – NOVEMBER 1979

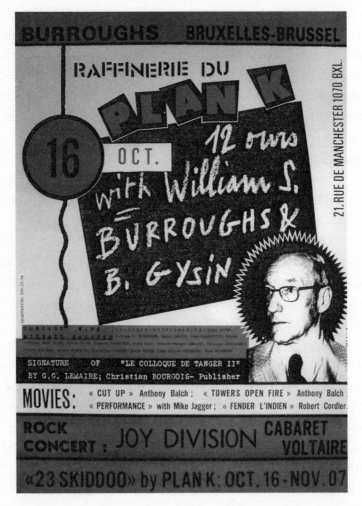

Poster for opening night of the Raffinerie Plan K venue in Brussels,
Belgium, 16 October 1979 (Designed by Marc Borgers)

- 2 October 1979: Mountford Hall, Liverpool University,
opening date of Buzzcocks tour, with Joy Division as support

Pete Shelley: It was in October '79, and we'd just released our
third album, *A Different Kind of Tension*. We were looking for
a support band, and Joy Division were now actually making
records, and so I think it was probably Richard Boon's idea that
here's another band who we know and get on with, let's take them
on a nationwide tour.

I don't think we really got to see all that much of Joy Division
playing at the gigs. Normally, we'd be at the hotel having a huge
slap-up meal before we went onstage, and then we'd arrive just as
they were finishing, and then afterwards we'd all meet up in the
hotel bar, so there was lots of drunken evenings and the bar would
stay open.

Richard Boon: Once Buzzcocks had some major-label funding,
there we were, stupidly passing on this torch, so we toured with the
Slits and Subway Sect, we'd have gigs with the Fall, Gang of Four
and Cabaret Voltaire, and here were Joy Division with their impres-
sively received album, needing to promote it. We invited them; it
was just like, they were mates. They got paid, they had their own
sound guy, but they were very self-sufficient, and of course their
crew and the Buzzcocks' crew got up to stupid roadie mischief, as
did members of both groups.

Pete Shelley: And then, of course, as well as the members of Joy
Division there was also their support crew, people like Terry, who
was always a barrel of laughs. There was a roadie called Twinny,
who would collect pounds – now a pound was still a lot in those
days – and then he would show you his tattoo. He'd take down
his trousers and bend over, and coming out of his backside were
two hands which had been tattooed on, so that's how he'd get his
drink money.

Bernard Sumner: The Buzzcocks tour was our first real experience of proper rock'n'roll and roadies and all that. I remember one of the Buzzcocks' roadies playing an awful trick on me and giving me a big lump of draw, and then about four o'clock in the morning said, 'There you are, eat that.' I was young and naive and I thought my head had fallen off, didn't know where I was. And I know we were young and naive, but it was an adventure for us really and it didn't feel like work, it just felt like fun. So as long as it was fun, we'd do it.

I don't think I was actually married then, I was just cohabiting. It was difficult when we had jobs. I worked in the animation place, Ian worked in a disability rehabilitation centre, Steve worked for his dad, Hooky worked at the dock office in Salford. We finished our jobs at five thirty at night and we'd have a gig in London at nine o'clock, so we had to bomb down to London or finish early, do the gig in London and then drive back and go straight to work the next day.

When we became fully professional we chucked in our jobs and went on the dole, which was quite daunting, but it gave us the freedom to just concentrate on the group. It was daunting because my job was pretty good, and it was quite a big step, having rent to pay and what have you, but it worked out.

Peter Hook: We weren't earning any money and it was becoming a real problem, and in between that the Buzzcocks tour emerged and it gave us our chance to go full-time. But the problem was that for all of us, really it meant a cut in wages, because I think we were only on £11 or £13 a week. Barney was actually on a really good wage with what he was doing at Cosgrove Hall; the rest of us were quite normal. I was on about £23 a week or something, so it meant taking a cut.

I'd moved out from home as well because my mother wouldn't allow it, to be honest. She was embarrassed that I was going to go off and work with a group. I actually lied to the bank manager and got a loan before I left to buy my house, which I bought with Iris, my girlfriend. So it was quite a stressful time for me because I was leaving work, me mam was going to kill me, and then all of a sudden I ended up in this house. We'd no money. I was on £13 a week, and we had no carpets, no chairs, no bed, nothing. I think we had two deckchairs that somebody gave us, and so it was great.

Kevin Cummins: When it was booked, Richard Boon thought he was giving Joy Division a break, but by the time that tour came round, everybody was going to see Joy Division rather than Buzzcocks. A lot of people left at the interval. I think the opening night was at Liverpool University. I shot that for the *NME*. Even then, the *NME* wanted it to be a Buzzcocks review rather than a Joy Division review. Paul and I argued in vain that nobody was interested in Buzzcocks by then, and the people who were going wanted to see Joy Division.

- 4 October 1979: Newcastle City Hall

Jon Wozencroft: Joy Division didn't play that much up in the northeast. I think they played one gig at Middlesbrough Rock Garden, which was a bit of a misnomer because it was anything but like a rock garden: it was a very, very difficult venue to get to underneath a flyover, and quite a violent and alienating place. So everyone was waiting for them to play in Newcastle.

The anticipation by that time was fever-pitch. I'm sure at least half of the audience were there for Joy Division. What is quite extraordinary is that they were playing every night of the week at that point: before Newcastle they'd been to Liverpool, Leeds, then after Newcastle they were going up to Glasgow, to Edinburgh, Dundee, Aberdeen – it was an extraordinarily hectic schedule. Newcastle City Hall's a big space. To jump from the Factory to a place like City Hall must have been quite scary for them.

Joy Division came on that night quite early because they were a support band, and normally what would happen is that people have had a good two or three hours in the bar. Joy Division were on at ten to eight or something crazy like that, and they came across rather nervous. They were quite tight in the middle, but the other thing that's obviously very distracting for them, and especially for Ian, would be that all the Buzzcocks gear would be there and they'd have to work within what the main band had configured for their set. There wasn't much room for movement.

They seemed a bit tired, which is obvious if you consider what their schedule was at that point. They hurried through their set, but they played 'Atrocity Exhibition' at the end, which was like, 'Uh?' There was quite a strange mixture between the *Unknown Pleasures* aspect of it and the tracks that weren't properly digestible because they hadn't been in the public domain – 'Colony', for example, or 'Atrocity Exhibition'. There was a feeling of 'That was a bit quick, wasn't it?' – like going in a flash – but after Joy Division had finished playing at least a third of the audience just left.

- 16 October 1979: Plan K, Brussels

Annik Honoré: Frédéric Flamand was the director of Plan K and he was really into the avant-garde. He was a choreographer. He had this idea that Brussels was the perfect centre to have a cosmopolitan venue where all arts could happen – music, dance, cinema, video. They had used the place to rehearse as a dancing troupe, and by that time already Tuxedo Moon was using the place for rehearsals. He knew a lot about literature and a lot about dance, but nothing about music, and certainly not rock music.

He knew of Michel Duval, and Michel was writing in the *En Attendant* fanzine. Michel knew that everything was happening in London, and I was already living there then, so he said, 'Well, you have to go and find a group,' and we all agreed that Joy Division would suit the mood for the type of evenings that Frédéric had in mind. I was living in London, and it was a time when it was so easy to meet the groups, just to go backstage and talk with them, and if you were a foreigner, you would just go and ask, 'Would you be interested to go abroad to Brussels?' It wasn't very far.

I had seen Joy Division. They played the Nashville Rooms in July. They sounded like no one else, very, very powerful onstage. They sounded really good because the sound was deep and big, and Ian on the stage was fascinating. He sang and he danced in a unique way. At the same time, they looked a bit provincial, nothing like London fashion, but they looked very smart with the nice shirts and trousers. They really impressed me: everybody who was at the Nashville Rooms was thrilled, and there was something exciting going on, something different.

We got there early to make sure we had a ticket, and the room was absolutely packed. Because I was writing a few articles for *En Attendant*, it was easy to go and see who was at the mixing desk. Rob was there, and I went to ask him to do a small interview and have an article for a Belgian magazine, which was funny for him: something foreign, but Belgium – I'm not sure he knew exactly where it was. That's how I got to know them.

They appeared as four very simple lads, very easy-going, nothing sophisticated, but the music was very, very strong. It was hard to believe that these four guys, making jokes and really young, could have such a deep, heavy sound. When Ian was onstage he was coming out of himself, he was a different person. He was kind of possessed by some very strong power, and he looked like he was in another world. At the same time, he looked very strong and very fragile, very vulnerable. At the time, I didn't know he was sick or anything. I think he was very brave to sing and dance like he was doing.

The way he talked with me, he was very much of a gentleman. He was very soft and nice. We stayed up all night talking: he had a lot to say and he didn't seem shy at all then. There was something. The chemistry was there. We both agreed on David Bowie and on Iggy and the Velvet Underground, so that night we listened to *Low*. The books, I think we mentioned Kafka. It went on and on all night, our discussion, and then we came to talk about personal things: more about his life, his married life, his child and the family, and he asked me about my family. I was surprised that he was so young and he was the only one to be married, so it was obviously not so easy for him to go on tour.

When Joy Division realised that they could go with Cabaret Voltaire and that it would be a special evening, with William Burroughs doing a lecture, and dance and films being shown, they agreed immediately to come and perform. Ian was a fan of Burroughs. I think we mentioned it in the conversation; everybody knew who William Burroughs was and everybody was interested. I had read one book, *The Wild Boys*, and Ian had read more because it's not so easy to understand when you're not perfectly bilingual. He was thrilled to meet the man in the flesh.

Richard Kirk: We always seemed to be in Manchester, and we did become friends and we ended up playing together on the same bill. Quite frequently, in fact. Initially, Joy Division would open for us because they weren't at a certain time as well known as Cabaret Voltaire, but obviously that situation changed once they'd got *Unknown Pleasures* out there and they became a lot more popular. They had a bit more of a commercial edge, so they could potentially reach a bigger audience, even though it was along the same lines: it was very dark and almost monochrome in its feel.

I got into William Burroughs in the mid-seventies, when the *NME* was quite counter-cultural. You would read about things like Burroughs in magazines like *NME* because obviously they never taught it on the English Lit curriculum at school. When I first found out about Burroughs, I'd already been doing cut-ups, because I'd been very interested in the Dadaist movement. I remember reading about Tristan Tzara, who used to make poetry by putting a load of words into a paper bag and then pulling them out at random and making a poem.

Then finding out about Burroughs, it was like all the bits of the jigsaw now fitted into place. You can see the appeal to a teenager, where it's just full of filthy language and pornographic imagery and basically anti-Establishment. That's what it said to me. I always thought the job of an artist was to challenge the status quo, and then when you read it in print, you read what Burroughs was saying and his understanding of how things work on this planet politically and in terms of things being controlled – you've hit pay dirt there.

It was Brion Gysin who first started to use cut-ups. He said that writing was fifty years behind painting, and I thought the idea of applying that to music might make it jump forward in the way that Burroughs had done with words. To do it with sounds and noises is what Cabaret Voltaire started to do originally. We were aware of that approach through knowledge of the Dada movement, but it came into focus with reading *The Naked Lunch* and *The Electronic Revolution*.

We went over to Brussels to do a gig at this converted sugar refinery called Plan K, to launch this arts venue. We'd been approached by people there to go and play alongside Joy Division, but the big attraction was that they actually had William Burroughs as part of this event, and Brion Gysin as well. There were various readings given by Burroughs and Gysin, and they were also showing some of the films that Antony Balch made, like *Towers Open Fire* and *The Cut-Ups*.

There were four floors to this venue: the ground floor was where the bands would play, the concert space, and then on the other floors there was performance art and one room where they just showed movies, and that was the first time we'd actually seen the Burroughs movies. They were also showing *Performance*, which is one of my all-time favourite films. It just seemed too perfect, a dream engagement.

Stephen Morris: Ian had met Annik then, and she suggested that we play this place in Brussels called Plan K. We got there and we were in the YMCA, or the Brussels equivalent. Apparently, the YMCA in Belgium operates on a two-tier system: there's the lodge for uncouth youths downstairs, and upstairs was a sort of sauna and a television. 'That's the singer's room, the singer and Cabaret Voltaire are in there, you lot are in here, and yeah, that's your bed over there, Steve' – and it didn't actually have any springs, you went through it.

Peter Hook: I was driving, you see, so I was sober and I remember it all. Plan K was the first time we'd been abroad, which was really exciting. We had loads of problems with Terry. He couldn't seem to get the van above 40 miles an hour, so I ended up driving the van because we were going to be late, we were going to miss the ferry. Terry was a real miserable bastard then. I think he'd finally given up all chance of being in the group and realised he was only going to be a roadie or a tour manager, so it made him really miserable, and Twinny was revelling in it.

Terry Mason: When we went over to Brussels for the first gig outside the UK, again we thought it's a major milestone. You're leaving home turf for the first time. We were playing a gig at a sugar refinery. William Burroughs was on the bill, and Cabaret Voltaire. We thought, 'Right, we're big-time Charlies.' We got sent to this hostel to stay in. It was very central for Brussels, but all of a sudden we get shown this room that's got six beds in it. There was six single beds in one room. I don't think it had a window to the outside world, but it had a window into the corridor.

Stephen Morris: One of my abiding memories of schmoozing Ian was at the Plan K. William Burroughs and Brion Gysin were promoting *The Third Mind*, which had just come out. I always remember Ian going up to Burroughs or Gysin, 'Excuse me, do you have any of those books in English?' He got the bum's rush off William Burroughs, but he had a go.

Peter Hook: Ian decided he was going to get a free book off William Burroughs because he'd read all Burroughs's books and bought them. Bernard and I were most amused. Burroughs was reading first and then he was doing the signing, and Ian went over, and me and Bernard were pissing ourselves behind the pillar. I can't remember what he said, we weren't near enough, and all we heard was Burroughs: 'Oh, fuck off, kid.' We didn't stop laughing for hours. Ian was so embarrassed.

Richard Kirk: The thing I remember most vividly is in one of the upper floors of Plan K there was myself and the other two members of Cabaret Voltaire, Ian and William Burroughs sat round a table drinking. I remember Ian asking Burroughs what he thought about suicide, and I'm 100 per cent certain Ian was talking about the American band Suicide, and William thought he meant the act of suicide, so it all got a bit confusing. I was that in awe of someone like Burroughs, I didn't really know what to say to him, but I was just happy to be sat there around a table with him.

> **Martin X. Ruffian, review in *NMX* fanzine**
> I spent the interval ligging backstage and giving away copies of 'NMX' No. 7. I forgot that this was the issue in which I called Ian Curtis, Joy Division's singer, a 'right prat' or words to that effect but he took it quite well considering, and even promised to put me on that Sunday's guest list for the Buzzcocks/Joy Division gig at the Top Rank. I'm still not convinced that they're brilliant enough to justify all the good press they've had – I can think of unknown groups I rate higher – but there's no denying they are very good.
>
> The music varies from punky fast and simple to doomy slow and weird, always emotional and compelling, though not half as depressing as has been made out. I was compelled but entertained as well. Cabaret Voltaire are Ian Curtis' favourite group, or were on the night, and Joy Division are a bit like Cabaret Voltaire without the synthesizers and drum machine. Experience this for yourself. The Phlegms went wild about it and they were called back for several encores.

Stephen Morris: We did the gig and then we experienced Duvels beer, and, 'Oh, it's quite nice this, isn't it? Let's get a case of this,' and everything from walking offstage is tinged with some sort of hallucinogenic flashbacks because we had about twenty of them. We went back to the quarters quite merry, and then we didn't realise that not only is it shared, it's like a submarine: if you're not in your bed, somebody else is in your bed, and there were other people sleeping in our bleeding room.

Peter Hook: Twinny stole forty-eight Duvels. When we came to do the gear, we were loading out through the bar in Plan K, which was quite funny because it was such an arty do. Everyone was so arty, wandering round – 'Oh God, Joy Division, they're so wonderfully sublime, darling,' in French or Belgian, as they do – and I said, 'Fucking get the gear loaded, you drunken bastard.' Twinny got up onstage, showed his arse for two quid, showed his tattoos to the audience, oh my God, everyone else was pissed. I was driving with Terry, so I was sober, so I said, 'Get the fucking gear out, will you?'

I said, 'Is the gear in the van?' Twinny said, 'Yeah, gear's in the van, yeah.' So I said, 'I'll just check.' And I opened the thing up, and it was full of beer. He'd robbed the bar, left the gear outside and fucking filled the van up with beer. I was going, 'You daft bastard,' and the barman came out with about five bouncers – we had to put all the beer back in.

Terry had a face like a slapped arse. We had a load of drinks from the dressing room, and I had a bottle of tomato juice, and he was sat there with a face like that, and I thought, 'I'll show this cunt.' So anyway, I dived out of the car, went round with the tomato juice and put it over the windscreen of the van just to annoy him. It's amazing, the things you did. And I remember this great face, he just sat there and put the windscreen wipers on, and it was flicking tomato juice all over the street, and I thought, 'Oh, man, you miserable twat.'

So we get back to the hostel, and then Barney picked Twinny's bed up and upended it, so Twinny fell out of bed, and then Twinny went over and picked Barney's bed up, so he fell out of bed, but he fell and banged his head on the radiator. So he went fucking mad and tipped Twinny up again, so Twinny got a bottle of orange juice and poured it in Barney's bed, and then Ian came down. It was just all going off. It was like proper kids abroad for the first time. Fucking madness, it was, it was great, and then Ian was caught pissing in the ashtray.

Terry Mason: Ian needed to pee, and he peed in this flip-top litter bin, sort of waist high, and one of the people managing the hostel is looking through the internal window at Ian peeing and he comes rushing through. English wasn't his first language, and he was screaming at Ian; the rest of us are just falling over for him getting caught. Ian's there: 'You tell me what to do, and I will do it,' moving into that English that English people say when they're talking to foreigners – you say everything louder and slowly. And he said, 'Do you want me to move this?'

So we were still a bunch of lads having fun. By the time we got to Brussels we're already on the Buzzcocks tour. We were still a bunch of daft lads going about the country doing stupid stuff. We had great toys, we had flight cases – you'd put someone in a flight case and push them down a few steps. You know, anyone thinking of joining a band, do it. Touring is good, don't believe what people say.

- 27/28 October 1979: Manchester Apollo

Peter Hook: The strangest thing about after the Buzzcocks tour was that you were playing the same music you were playing before the Buzzcocks tour to nobody, and then all of a sudden there was thousands of the buggers. One minute there's nobody there, the next minute there's thousands, and you're playing the same music. It was quite odd, but we did start getting busier and busier.

Richard Boon: During that tour they improved. This was an opportunity for them to play much more regularly than they had before, and they had to put up with the whole daily grind of show last night, get up, travel, soundcheck, show again, and they got more disciplined as a result, it started to work. They were actually working as a band. I'm sure that they'd probably all taken leave from the dole office or their day job to do it. I think it gave them an instinct for more professionalism.

In terms of presentation, it was guitar, singer, bass, drums at the back – very classic. As the gigs got more regular, Hooky started to loosen up and he would get a bit more lively, but in terms of holding the audience's attention and delivering a performance, Ian carried a particular live performance burden, which was something that he'd obviously wanted but I'm not sure he was happy with. I think the initial forced mannerism of his recorded vocals fed into how he was onstage, and he initially thought, 'This is how I either want to be presented or want to be seen.'

But then he would lose himself in that – that being some kind of euphoria, which was probably private. I think his internal emotions weren't presented to the audience, there was no heart-rending thing. A lot of the audience may have thought so, but I don't. He'd achieved some kind of ambition and was enjoying it, but once there's a commercial envelope broken, people want more and more from you. He just wanted something from himself initially.

It was all very good-natured, and I filmed one of those gigs. There were two independent video facilities in Manchester in the late seventies: there was Granada Television, and there was the Manchester Film and Video Workshop, which was the tail end of some post-hippie community project that boiled down to being Bob Jones, who had a video camera. I think Rob Gretton said, 'The band would like to see what they look like onstage.' It's very important for bands to see what they look like onstage: Are they throwing the right shapes, are they making the right moves?

So Bob and I filmed them in the Manchester Apollo from a box, and constantly argued about focus-pulling and where to move the camera. There was some number which for me was fantastic, where Ian went right out into the wings and did his dancing. I wanted to keep the camera on the microphone, knowing that after a few bars he'd be back, and Bob was like, 'No, he's over there.' And I won: I kept the camera on the microphone, the music builds and then suddenly he's in. I just knew he'd be over there, but the song was building and building, so the tension is on the microphone.

Paul Morley: On the Buzzcocks tour they played the Manchester Apollo, and they seemed to belong but they also seemed a bit adrift.

They seemed to belong on a big stage and in big circumstances, so to speak, but they seemed a little adrift too, like it wasn't quite their time yet. It always seemed better to see them in a smaller space, when the energy became ... well, literally psychedelic at times because of the way everything was moving.

I was talking to them recently about that self-consciousness they must have had very quickly, that they'd done something that was special, and how that infected and impacted upon them. The naivety and the underdog thing had been removed quite quickly, because suddenly they were being heralded and hailed, not just by the locals but by the biggies. There were other people now taking it very seriously, and obviously they must have had a sense within the unit that they'd done something special.

That could have ruined them in a way, it could have given them a kind of London hubris. It could have really spoiled them, but each member of the group had their own ambition. Ian's ambition obviously was the one that ultimately created the great catastrophe, but I think the others had their own ambition within that, even if it was just to be the greatest bass player on the planet or to make a really great guitar sound. All of that was important technically and was still going on, and supported Ian's wider ambition.

I got the feeling that each instrument was not dealt with in a way that a normal group would use, so it wasn't so much a lead guitar, it was almost a side guitar and a lead bass, and the drums were almost used in a jazz way, funnily enough, where they weren't really just a banal pulse but were jittery and edgy, and Stephen's eccentricity, his own nerdiness, was coming through, in a way. Live and on record, it was different, but both were unorthodox in terms of the way the dynamics were used.

Sometimes you got the feeling they were in completely different spaces and almost weren't hearing each other, and other times you got the feeling they were completely connected. Then the voice was interesting, because for a while there was the Jim Morrison thing, and then there was Ian finding his own place. Then, towards the end, the disconcerting crooning started to happen, so as his lyrics got more and more desolate and desperate and deranged, the voice got suaver, which was also part of the distraction that we all fell for at the time.

Jon Wozencroft: Once Joy Division really found their seam, they almost always started with 'Dead Souls'. That track has a very, very progressive, intense build-up; it's nearly three minutes before the vocal comes in. This gives Ian a chance both to calibrate – to position himself to start to read the atmosphere, to feel how the band behind him are locking in with each other on that particular evening – and to decide how far he wants to travel. Once he was able to position or balance himself to go out of his body, he would use performance as a way of projecting himself, channelling.

I saw it with my own eyes and ears. There were some very powerful things happening, but there's also an interesting feature in that there was no real light show in Joy Division performances; everything was quite stark, quite monumental. Just by that physical necessity, because of his epilepsy, which I didn't know about at the time, Ian would be the point of focus, so he could take that aspect of himself as a point of focus and amplify it and project it, so that there was this incredible movement going on that you can't quantify. It was very ritualistic.

Terry Mason: The Buzzcocks tour was the traditional UK twenty-five-, thirty-day tour, playing places that were two and a half thousand capacity and the like. A lot of people say it was exhausting. It's what bands did, you know; it's not like you were doing a thirty-state tour of America in five weeks. The distances are not that big: you're going from Sheffield to Birmingham. We were the support band, so the band could get to a venue early, but there was nothing for them to do until Buzzcocks had finished their soundcheck.

But Ian's seizures were becoming more and more frequent and they were much larger. At that point, you've got Ian in a situation whereby everything that boys join a band to do – the drink, the drugs, the women – all of that is written out of Ian's script. He's won the keys to Willy Wonka's chocolate factory, but all of a sudden he's told if you taste any chocolate, you will die. Ian's there and he has to moderate his drink, the only drugs he's seeing are the collection of barbs that are prescribed to him to control his seizures, and women are out of the question due to the effects of said barbs.

On the Buzzcocks tour we were always conscious. After Ian had the first seizure, we always watched out for him. A lot of the time we'd have to watch for Ian showing the signs that he was having a seizure. Now of course the signs of having a seizure were very much like Ian's dance style; some of the eye movements he had, he'd sort of built into his stage persona, so to speak. So some of the time you're thinking, 'Is he or isn't he?' And you'd be ready to go, and he'd just look at you and smile, he'd say, 'Got you.'

Deborah Curtis: He danced like that before he got epilepsy. I think he was looking for an original energy to express. I told myself at first that it was all part of the act, you know? Part of being in the band, but it was all wrong. There wasn't an Ian at home and an Ian in the world; it became like that all the time. People admired him for the things that were destroying him. I don't think people understood that he would still be like that when he came home. It wasn't just a show.

Richard Boon: I was very upset at one gig where Ian had a fit. Rob said nothing about Ian's condition, that he was epileptic, and all the road crew who were actually working and paying attention didn't know what to do, apart from taking him offstage. I was very cross. I said, 'Rob, you should have told us what the procedures were.' So that was a bit alarming.

Bernard Sumner: When the illness came, at first we thought, 'Well, he's never had it before, so it will go away. It's just a bit of stress or something.' We just thought it would be temporary, but it wasn't, and we thought, 'Shit, there's no solution to this. We'll carry on, but we'll just have to tone everything down. We won't have any flashing lights, we'll try and make sure he gets to bed early, and try and tone it down as much as we can and see how we go on.'

We didn't know anything about epilepsy neither. I did a little bit because I used to work with a lad that had it, but he had petit mal, where he used to just fall on the floor and go to sleep, but Ian had full fits. I guess we were in a bit of a state of shock. We didn't really know what to do. We thought, 'Well, they'll be able to medicate him to calm it all down,' but we didn't really know about the side effects of the drugs. We didn't know enough about it, and I don't think medical science at that time knew enough about it neither. We didn't have a solution.

Stephen Morris: The one that I remember being most shocked by was Eric's. The dressing room was right at the side of the stage, and Terry caught him and took him off, and you could see him having the fit off the side of the stage. That was the good thing about 'Interzone', because Hooky could sing it. If Ian had a fit, we could drag him offstage and do 'Interzone'.

Peter Hook: Rob had had more fights with the lighting guy cos he'd always start flashing, and that was what would send Ian into a fit. That was his worst one, at Bournemouth: I had to sit on him for an hour and a half holding his tongue in the dressing room. Then he just wouldn't come round, so I said to Rob, 'We're going to have to take him to hospital.' Everyone was pissed and they'd all fucked off, and it was only me and Rob in the dressing room, so me and Rob had to pick him up and put him in the car and take him to hospital in Bournemouth, and they brought him out of it.

Then it was really funny, because I came back and them lot were in the dressing room having a drink, the bastards. I said, 'Where's Twinny?' They went, 'Oh, we've not seen him. We've not seen him since you went.' I thought, 'Where the fucking hell is he?' He'd disappeared. Anyway, I found him in a cupboard at the back of the stage. I went, 'What are you doing?' And he went, 'He's possessed by the devil, that bastard.' What a nightmare: the lead singer's off, he's off. I was like, 'Oh fuck, everyone else is pissed.'

Annik Honoré: I witnessed a few of his fits. It was really, really frightening, it was like he was possessed by the devil. He was literally rising from the ground, that's how I remember it. Ian was mostly embarrassed that he felt like he couldn't be like everybody else because – it could happen at any time – he couldn't drive, because he couldn't be as responsible as the others, and that was really annoying him, that he was being looked after. I wouldn't say that the others saw him as a sick man, because everybody was young and innocent.

Nobody realised how serious this was. They didn't treat him any differently, and they should have paid more attention to his disease and made sure that there was not so much light and noise, and not so much late nights and more sleep, but it's almost impossible in a rock band. I think he felt diminished, and from knowing and having met other epileptic people he knew exactly what could happen and how bad it could get, and that was frightening him. He was also frightened that it would make people frightened of getting to know him better, like myself.

He knew it's not much fun to be with a sick person, because it can be very dangerous. I mean, he could die from a fit, from falling on his head or from swallowing his tongue. It was extremely violent.

Bernard Sumner: We played in Bournemouth once. His mate who he'd always gone on about, who was this performance artist who used to chain himself to cars and do all that weird shit, didn't turn up at the gig, and Ian was really upset about it. Really pissed off. It was on the Buzzcocks tour.

He went real fuckin' weird after it. We were staying in this shitty boarding house, and the Buzzcocks were staying in this shitty hotel, and we walked along to their hotel for a drink, and coming back along the beach Ian starting walking out towards the sea. It was pitch black, about one in the morning, and he went walking out into the sea, and we had to go and get him. He had a shadow on his personality that was so dark that I don't think even he could see into it.

Stephen Morris: Ian would say he was all right even when he wasn't all right. He was his own worst enemy in a number of departments, and that was one of them. He should really have said, 'I can't do it,' but he did. He wanted to do it, we wanted to do it, and it was kind of, 'Well, it'll be all right,' when it was obviously clearly never going to be all right because he was just going to get worse.

The drugs didn't help, the treatment that he was on, because it was very hit and miss, and they'd give you a load of these psycho-tropic drugs: 'They might make you feel a bit ill, but see if they work, then we'll give you another lot and see what they do.' So in a way, as soon as you're diagnosed with epilepsy, it's automatically bound to get a lot worse once you start taking the pills to make you get better.

Peter Hook: It was always a problem. We just had to look after him. Once he found out he was ill, he was the worst: he just didn't want to do it, he wanted to be a rock'n'roll superstar. The doctors told him to be quiet and to try and lead a quiet life and not to drink, and he just went berserk. We were always trying to stop him. He did not want to admit that he was ill, without a shadow of a doubt, and what we were doing was really bad for his illness. I think, if anything, Ian felt worse about that, because he felt that he was holding us back.

Probably one of the reasons why he drove himself so hard was because he knew we all wanted it so badly and we were all enjoy-ing it so much. Part of his problem was that he didn't want to let anybody down. He was a people-pleaser, he wanted everyone to be happy round him, and sometimes he'd say things to people just to make them happy, and worry about the consequences later, which is what I would imagine happened with Debbie quite a lot.

He was a bit of a yes-man, I suppose. He was a nice guy; he'd always agree with you, he was very difficult to have a fight with, Ian. I never had a fight with him, ever. I never fell out with Ian, or Steve for that matter, but Ian used to always fall out with Rob. They really did clash, and it was generally about money, which I think was because Debbie was in his ear.

Deborah Curtis: It was like a family. I heard Iris, Hooky's girlfriend, saying, 'They're a family, we can't get into it.' They were close, they'd protect each other. They'll exclude anyone who isn't quite what they're looking for, you know? I remember when I was expecting Natalie and standing at the door of the Factory, and Tony looking me up and down, and it was written all over his face what he was thinking: 'How can we have a rock star with a six-months-pregnant wife standing by the stage?' It wasn't quite the thing.

Lesley Gilbert: To start with, the group were quite happy to have girlfriends and wives there, and then as they started doing more gigs and being away more, certain situations got a bit dodgy. It was very much a lads' thing, it was a little gang, and girls don't fit into boys' gangs, do they? Certainly not then, because it was a while ago. Factory was very male-dominated as well, that was another little gang, so it was all boys together. I think in certain situations they suffered, the girlfriends, being there. The longer that went on, then the more difficult it got for the girlfriends to be there.

And, of course, I had a nine-to-five job, and I know Bernard's girlfriend did, so we couldn't be going all over the place anyway. We had jobs to hold down to support them. I mean, I supported Rob for a few years, so I couldn't be following them around, and also, God, I mean, where's the fun in that? You've got your own things to do. It's just the way things turned out. I don't think it was anything like, 'Right, this is how it's going to be: girlfriends, wives not allowed.' It's just the way things happened.

Stephen Morris: Girlfriends didn't go to the gigs.

Gillian Gilbert: Only in Manchester. I used to come to some of the others, but it caused ructions. Debbie used to drive Ian to some of the gigs, didn't she?

Stephen Morris: But Ian had tried to persuade her not to.

Deborah Curtis: Then this glamorous Belgian turned up. She was attractive and she was free, and she had a nice accent. I don't blame Ian. I think most people need a partner, and if you exclude that partner you have to find somebody else. It's only natural. He must have been very lonely.

Tony Wilson: I wasn't aware of Ian's relationship with Deborah going wrong. I was aware of Ian's relationship with Annik going right, I suppose, and brutally it never seemed surprising somehow that people move on. I mean, the great surprise in all of our lives was the rock-hard relationship between Rob and Lesley, whereas most of us grow and change, and things change from our teen-age sweethearts. So to me as someone who's grown through several relationships, it was not a surprise that Ian had found this new girl-friend, but I liked Annik and I liked Deborah as well.

Bernard Sumner: At the end of the Buzzcocks tour we heard that they were going to set us up for some jolly japes, so I thought, 'Well, we're the experts at that, we'll get them first.' So we went to get a big bucket of maggots, and one of the roadies distracted their lighting guy's attention and we poured the maggots over his lighting desk, and when he came back he was like, 'What the fucking hell?'

They had all their girlfriends and wives with them, the Buzzcocks, and they all turned up in a minibus. They left one of the windows open, so we bought a load of mice and put live mice in the minibus. So at the end of the night, when they got in the minibus, all the girls started screaming their heads off, they come running out of the minibus. Of course, we were waiting outside in Steve's Cortina with a load of eggs and just pelted them. It was fun. I think they got us back, though. I seem to recall that Steve had a sunroof on his car, left it open, so they got a huge trifle at the gig and dropped it straight through. See, you didn't need drugs in those days.

- 9/10 November 1979: Rainbow Theatre, London, Buzzcocks tour ends

Anton Corbijn: I moved to England in October '79, and I met them within two weeks of moving to London. I went to see them at a show in the Rainbow, in London, and I must have had a magazine in Holland that I worked for, so I could meet Rob Gretton backstage. I suggested a photograph the next day – they were in London – and they said yes. We did it at Lancaster Gate tube station. My idea was unknown pleasures, people walking away on their way to unknown pleasures. In the end, my trip to England was unknown pleasures in my eyes.

> **James Brown, sabotagetimes.com**
> Bernard Sumner: There's a famous photograph taken by Anton Corbijn. I think it was the first time we met Anton, it was his first photo session in the UK, and it was at Lancaster Gate tube station. And on it we've all got this really short hair. We were supporting the Buzzcocks. We were sitting round bored in a boarding house in Leeds, somewhere like that. I'd just got a cut, but I had a little bit of hair stuck up at the back and it was annoying me, so I got a pair of scissors and I said to Rob, 'Can you cut that little bit of hair, it's annoying me?' So he cut it, but he cut a big lump out the back of my hair.
> Stephen Morris: The problem with Rob's barbering techniques was the scissors he used – they were massive.

Instead of using nice, normal barbering scissors, he used to use massive ones: they were tailor-scissors: big, clunking great rusty brown things. I think he was using the wrong things, but it did result in that rather odd angular style. Bernard Sumner: With me, he cut this little bit off, cut a big chunk out of my hair, so I said, 'That's no good, you've made a right balls of it,' so he ended up cutting all me hair short, and then they were like, 'That looks daft because he's got dead short hair. You're gonna have to cut everyone else's [laughs].' So it started with Rob cutting that little bit of stuck-up hair off, then he worked his way through the whole group, and that's why we've all got that haircut on that photograph.

Anton Corbijn: So we went to this tunnel, and when they all looked away it wasn't as strong as when somebody looked back, so I think I have a few pictures of Bernard looking back, and then I asked Ian to look back, and that became the image in the end. When I did that photograph I showed it to a few people, but nobody was interested. People just want to see faces, so that picture wasn't really published until Ian died, and then suddenly it looked like a prophecy, which of course it wasn't at all for me.

Almost all the imagery of Joy Division was quasi-documentary – people come and take a few pictures, they walk around or they stand somewhere – but this was with an idea in mind, it was slightly more conceptual. That's maybe why it lasted so long, but it wasn't a big shoot, it was just a few minutes, and I remember very much, me being Dutch, I arrived and I want to shake their hands, they're going to shake my hand. After I'd done the picture, they actually shook my hand. I always remember that very vividly because I of course felt like quite a lonely boy in London.

I came over with my girlfriend, but my English was bad, and you try to build up something in England and it was my first proper shoot. It was just four young guys who were standing there smoking, shaking, like this – 'Are we okay?' – underdressed, malnourished.

That's what I always thought of the north of England. It was quite a shock if you came from Holland, where socially everybody was sort of taken care of. You come to England, and there's extreme poverty and people drinking and smoking and having just a little shirt on and a thin coat and they stand outside in the winter.

10

NOVEMBER 1979 – FEBRUARY 1980

Ian Curtis at Pennine Sound Studios, Oldham, 8 January 1980 (Daniel Meadows)

Bernard Sumner: I was into . . . I suppose nowadays you'd call it slacking, but in those days I called it being a lazy twat. I couldn't believe that I was now a professional musician. My whole ambition was to do something that I enjoyed, but not actually work hard at it. Just let the ether flow through me – ha! – and I'd be this medium for this music from the spirits that came through me. I'd just lie there and the music would come through my fingers, because I'd imagined that's what art was.

It's difficult to speak for everyone, but one of the funny things was that we never talked about the music. We had an understanding which we never felt the need to vocalise. I felt that there was an otherworldliness to the music, that we were plucking it out of the air. We felt that talking about the music would stop that inspiration. In the same way, we never talked about Ian's lyrics or performance. I felt that if I thought about what he did, then it would stop. I thought, 'If something great is happening, don't look at the sun, don't look at the sun.'

Peter Hook: Rob had the foresight that it was better to keep control, and he had the vision. We made as much money on ten thousand copies of *Unknown Pleasures* as Siouxsie and the Banshees or any band – the Cure – did on ten million. We were making a lot of money on very few record sales, and that also governed the way you acted as a group: you could be fussy about what you did, you could do wacky things where you weren't doing them just for the money, because you were earning on your records.

It meant that you could do things differently because you had this great deal with Factory. There's no doubt about that; it gave us the freedom to not have to work ourselves to death. We could pick and choose because we had a bedrock. It was definitely Rob and Tony who gave us that.

Jon Wozencroft: You take some of those tracks that are part of the interregnum between *Unknown Pleasures* and *Closer*, and many groups could form whole careers around them. Tracks like 'The

Only Mistake', 'Something Must Break' – I mean, they're amazing, and yet Joy Division were spoiled for choice. My feeling is that the band were getting songs recorded for posterity and moving quickly on to the next phase.

This next phase is, of course, the Sordide Sentimental recordings: 'Atmosphere' and 'Dead Souls'. Rob gives them away to a little company in Rouen, in France, and they come out in an edition of 1,578. That is extraordinary: it's acts of generosity like that that keep DIY underground fanzines – small publishers – living in hope that they can compete with major companies, because they're supported by the bands that are in pole position at the time, which Joy Division were.

- 12 October 1979: release of *Earcom 2* twelve-inch, Fast Records
- October/November 1979: Cargo Studios, recording of 'Atmosphere', 'Dead Souls', 'Ice Age'
- 16 November 1979: release of 'Transmission' seven-inch, Factory Records

Stephen Morris: We'd recorded 'Transmission', *Unknown Pleasures* was out and we'd gone on a tour of the Highlands, and kids would come up to you and say, 'When is "Transmission" coming out?' How do they know 'Transmission''s coming out? Who's told them? And you suddenly realised that people were very interested in you, and the audience was growing and people wanted to buy your records.

They wanted to buy 'Transmission' before it was out, which I identify with because I was a bit like that with bands. You'd go to the record shop and say, 'Have you got it yet? Have you got it yet?' *Ziggy Stardust and the Spiders from Mars*, when that came out, I used to badger the hell out of the record shop: 'Have you got it yet? Have you got it yet?' – 'No, it's not out.' I could understand cos I felt passionate about that, but the fact that you could see other people were feeling the same way about you, that was good.

When 'Transmission' came out, I thought it was Joy Division's first pop record because it mentioned the radio, and that's got to get played on the radio – they like that. It did take on a life of its own, and it's all about being pop; but it wasn't pop really, it was a million miles away from popular music. There's this lot of music that straight people listen to, and then there's other music over here which you've got to work at to like and you've got to be a little bit odd to like.

Peter Hook: With Joy Division it never stopped, we never had a dry period writing-wise. It was very easy to write because basically you had the whole world in front of you. Every time you write a song, it narrows down, doesn't it? Till it becomes really difficult, but then everything was wide open, so it was dead easy. We used to write two songs a month. We were really prolific as a group and we always worked; there was no arsing about, we used to go and rehearse, bang, bang, bang. With Joy Division we always worked really hard.

Ian Curtis (Radio Lancashire interview): When we started playing we played a few dates with the Rezillos. Bob Last was their manager at the time and he talked then about setting up a record label. And he wanted us to do a single for them. But due to Factory coming along and other things – he did things with Gang of Four and the Human League first and got tied in in a sort of management way with the Human League, I think he manages another one – it never came about.

When we were doing the album we had quite a few tracks left over. We recorded sixteen in all and just cut ten, and our manager, Rob Gretton, had talked to him about certain things and we'd always kept in touch. He mentioned his idea for *Earcom*, and we just offered him the two tracks to put out on that. Cos we like to get everything we record out one way or another, like we've done the *Earcom*, we're doing the Sordide Sentimental thing, which are a French limited edition magazine-cum-record thing.

There are two tracks on that that will be coming out that won't be on an album or a single. It's just that we like getting as much stuff out as we can really, in some form or another. You know, it's often hard with Factory because obviously they're limited financially. I mean, you can't just put out a record, you know, when you've got other things planned. So with no room on the LP, we tend to look for other outlets for them.

Stephen Morris: 'Auto-Suggestion' we made up on the spot. It was just me and Hooky soundchecking, and we were just waiting for Martin to do whatever he was doing. I think 'Candidate' was made up in the same way. We were just playing, and it is basically just me and Hooky and then a bit of backwards guitar, stick on some lyrics, and it was literally that quick, but still good. That was how we wrote; in fact, it was easier doing it like that. It's strange to think that for the largest extent, Joy Division just existed in our heads.

> *The Story So Far* **fanzine, issue 3, October 1979**
> I ask them how heavily they intend to rely on synthesisers in future.
> Ian – 'If we think that the keyboards fit in, we'll use them. There is no conscious decision to write a song featuring synthesiser.'
> So how about a full time keyboard player?
> Ian – 'I don't think so . . . it would have to be someone who couldn't really play, so that (they) could learn to play like us.'
> In fact, Joy Division have just recorded a single for the Sordide Sentimental label. It features Bernard's synthesiser on a very moody song called 'Atmosphere'. According to their manager and hairdresser Rob Gretton ('It's going into the realms of stupidity, in my opinion!' – Stephen Morris) it's probably one of the best things they've put on vinyl. Rob has hopes of getting the band into the studio soon to cut the second album, but before that they have dates in Holland,

Belgium, Germany and, tentatively, America. People are beginning to take notice.

Bernard Sumner: 'Atmosphere' is my favourite Joy Division song. I just think it's incredibly emotive and brooding and powerful, and I like the production. I like 'Transmission' as well because that's really exciting, but only the live recording.

Peter Hook: 'Dead Souls' was done in Cargo much quicker than any of the others. Compared to nowadays the whole thing was done unbelievably quickly. 'Dead Souls' was more or less recorded just as a good record of the group, and its ebb and flow. What I love about Joy Division is the quieten-downs and the build-ups, and 'Dead Souls' to me is the perfect ebb-and-flow record, it really is. It's more a group recording than anything else, that one particular tune.

Bernard Sumner: I always wanted to make music that did something new. I didn't like people who always looked at the past. When I was a kid, people in the family used to go on about, ooh, the fifties and the old rock'n'roll bands, and I hated it. I thought, 'Well, that was then, and this is now.' Until I was in the group I never thought about synthesizers or electronic instruments, but then Ian introduced me to Kraftwerk. He used to play *Trans-Europe Express* before we went onstage, and I loved it. I'd never heard it before. I'd heard *Autobahn*, but *Trans-Europe Express* had these beats in it that instinctively felt like dance music to me, and these massive keyboards, and I was thinking, 'Wow, that's really interesting, what they're doing.' I decided to learn a bit about the technology. I was quite technically-minded anyway: I was good with my hands, and my grandfather was an engineer. We didn't have any money. I wanted a synthesizer, couldn't afford one, so I decided to build one from electronic components. I got one in a kit basically. From the very early days of Joy Division I was basically an insomniac, and I used to sit up half the night watching films like *2001: A Space Odyssey* and *Clockwork Orange*, and watch them over and over again because there was no late-night TV. I used to get this magazine called *Electronics Today*, and in it was this synthesizer. So I thought, 'This is really cheap, only like £200, how difficult can it be to build it?' It was like soldering components by hand. It took about two months of doing that, and it didn't work incredibly well.

With that first synthesizer, it had all these knobs on that I didn't know what they meant, like LFO, filter resonance and sample-and-hold waveforms, and I just thought, 'That sounds great, that sounds really interesting – what does it do?' Then I learned about synthesizers and started using it within Joy Division. In fact, if you've got any of the footage from the Apollo when we played with the Buzzcocks, you can hear me using that synthesizer. I really got into it and found that you could make really abstract noises with it.

'Atmosphere' was on a sixteen-track, and it was the first polyphonic synthesizer that I got, which was a Solina string synth, and a Bontempi organ from Woolworths, and I used to play both of them together, and I couldn't believe you could get a synthesizer that could play more than one note. That was a real turn-on for me. We had a limited period of time to do it in, and me and Hooky always felt that Martin did his best stuff when he did it quick and didn't have too much time to think about it.

Peter Hook: The transition from working to not working was purely for the Buzzcocks tour, and then after that we had nothing, so what happened was that you went from giving up your job, the excitement of your rehearsals, going on the Buzzcocks tour, and then just appearing at home, jobless, wondering when your next gigs were going to be. Rob was out getting us a few gigs, and basically I remember a lot of time just sitting about doing nothing after the Buzzcocks tour, until we started getting a few more gigs and started getting bigger as a group.

Daniel Meadows: The first time I got involved was, I think, November 1979. Tony knew I was a photographer. I'd been working as a photographer in residence in north-east Lancashire – Burnley,

Nelson and Colne. One of my sponsors was Mid-Pennine Arts, but they didn't pay me much money, so I'd started working freelance for newspapers and magazines, and one of the stories that I put up to the *Observer* Sunday supplement magazine was the treatment of long-term schizophrenics in particular, but patients at a place called Clayton Ward, at Prestwich Psychiatric Hospital.

I went to live with these patients for two weeks in difficult circumstances, and made these photographs, and it turned out that I scooped *World in Action*, who'd been trying to do the same story. So they hauled me in and interviewed me at Granada, and they offered me a researcher's job. My artist-in-residence contract had come to an end and I was looking to stretch myself a bit. In those days they had about three thousand applications for every researcher's job, and you had to take it seriously if you were offered that kind of thing. There weren't many entry points into big media.

I'd come out of the art-school counter-cultural thing at the end of the sixties. I'd spent fourteen months living in a double-decker bus, offering free pictures to people in pop-up studio sessions in cities. I'd written a book about that. So all of these things were in the background, but I think it was when I peed on their doorstep, as it were, by messing up their story that they wanted to do that they hauled me in. I was working on *Granada Reports* first, then I moved on to *What's On*, and these had quite large audiences locally and they were programmes that I watched myself.

Granada was actually quite cool in those days. I've no idea what it's like now, but the BBC was always rather boring, particularly local television. Granada had a bit of spunk about it. I think it was leftish, and the city was small enough for the presenters to be recognised. As you went around researching and making little films with the reporters, they were known, and people would say hello to them, like they were cousins or something. Bob Greaves was the daddy figure of the news room: local man, on the screen every night. His sidekick was Tony Wilson, this foppish Cambridge graduate who used lots of clever words in his links from item to item and did lots of ridiculous things in a kind of *flâneur* style, which would be very unfamiliar to working-class northerners, but was also, I think, rather engaging. I'd been up there for almost ten years, and whenever you saw Tony Wilson out doing one of his TV reports, everyone would roll down their car windows and shout 'Wanker!' at him. It seemed sort of appropriate really.

When I went to work at Granada, they had these huge open-plan offices, and the desks would be grouped together with maybe fifteen people sitting around them, and at the end Tony Wilson would sit, like a king, and I got to like him a lot. He would come in late, wearing a shirt that would look like a blouse, maybe under a leather jacket or a nice coat, and he would fling off his scarf and shake his hair, and over his shoulder would be a pair of Harley-Davidson leather motorbike panniers, and he'd pull them open and start pulling things out, putting money into envelopes in between the two panniers, and I'd ask him what on earth he was doing, and he'd say, 'This is the entire Factory office.'

So I got to hear about Factory Records, and the Russell Club gigs they'd put on. I'd joined Granada after *So It Goes*, his music programme, and *What's On*, the programme I worked on, was the one that took over. He'd moved on from talking about other people's pop music to making his own. Tony invited me down to Alan Erasmus's flat in south Manchester to photograph Vini Reilly, who was making an album called *The Return of the Durutti Column*. Vini was very gentle, sweet-natured, introverted. Tony drove me down there in his large maroon-red Peugeot estate car, which was filthy and had a broken windscreen, but it was still quite a cool vehicle for someone of his age to be driving.

I did ask him, 'How are you doing this? You seem to be funding a whole record label.' Did he earn that sort of money at Granada? 'No,' he said, 'I keep it separate. This is from £10,000 that my mother left me. Where other people would have bought a house' – you could easily buy a house for that in those days – 'I decided I'd set up a record company with it and see how long the money would last, and to put on gigs and have my own bands.' And he began to explain that Factory was this loose arrangement of him and Alan

Erasmus and Martin Hannett, the producer, and Rob Gretton, who was managing Joy Division.

Anyway, we're going to Alan Erasmus's flat, which he said was 'the best chance we have of having an office, and you're going to meet Vini Reilly and photograph him, cos we need to promote his new album'. I don't know if Vini or the other people around understood how Tony was possessed by the situationists, and he had nicked from Guy Debord this idea that you could make a record – in Debord's case it was a book, *Mémoires* – that had a sandpaper cover, the idea being that this cultural item would destroy the cultural items next to it.

So he made this album that was this sweet guitar music, mixed with sounds of birdsong and stuff, put together by Martin Hannett, but called it *The Return of the Durutti Column* and put it in this sandpaper cover. But he hadn't worked out yet how to make the sandpaper cover. As I was saying hello to Vini, who was such a shy character, and sitting with him having a coffee, trying to get to see him a bit before we took the pictures, all these young blokes were sitting around, and they were in fact Joy Division, and they were helping put together this sandpaper album. They'd been given these square album-sized sheets of sandpaper which they were gluing together, and they had this silver spray paint and stencils with 'Return of the Durutti Column' and 'FACT14', which was the number of the album, and they were assembling these things, sitting on the floor. And I joined in. They said, 'Make your own album cover for Vini's album, Daniel!' So I did, and then went off to photograph Vini, and when we came back, they'd finished the album that I'd sprayed on, and they gave it to me. So that was my first meeting with them.

They were just a bunch of young blokes sitting around joshing with each other. They were five years younger than me. At that age, that is quite a gap. At least, it felt like it for me. Also, they were working-class northern boys, and I was a middle-class southern bloke. So even though I'd lived in the north for ten years by then, there was a certain social gap there that takes a while to cross. They were very friendly, but I didn't think these were going to be my chums or anything.

But I was intrigued. It was Tony's world, and he'd let me into it. It was fun. I think the picture was used in *Sounds* when the album was released: job done. And Tony paid me. He just said, 'Give me an invoice,' and I'd give him an invoice and he'd pay me. So I always liked working for him. Then it was back to Granada, and then another invitation would come.

- 18 December 1979: Joy Division live concert at Les Bains Douches, broadcast on *Feedback*, with Bernard Lenoir, French Inter radio

Commentary:
['Shadowplay'] . . . 'Joy Division live from Les Bains Douches, with an old ghost of Jim Morrison, who drags himself around there.'
['Transmission'] . . . '"Transmission" by Joy Division, the title of their last single. "Dance to the radio", and if one day you start dancing like the singer of Joy Division, be careful not to be taken away by the two nurses from the psychiatric hospital.'

Bernard Sumner (interviewed by Alan Hempsall, 'A Day Out with Joy Division', *Extro* magazine, 1980): We played this really select club where people queue outside in the street but you only get past the doors if you're famous or if you look 'right', like Studio 54. After the gig they laid on a special meal for us upstairs and there were all these select people milling around and believe it or not, the club even had a swimming pool that you could actually use.

Tony Wilson: My great memory was walking down some very large flight of stairs at some big club in Paris one night, and suddenly Rob shouting out, 'Where's your Belgian boiler, Ian?' And Annik going, 'I'm right behind you, Rob.' I remember enjoying that enormously.

Stephen Morris at Pennine Sound Studios, Oldham, 8 January 1980 (Daniel Meadows)

- 8 January 1980: recording 'Love Will Tear Us Apart' (v.1), 'These Days' and 'Sound of Music' at Pennine Sound Studios, Oldham

Daniel Meadows: The next one was more serious, in a way. Tony asked me to go and photograph Joy Division at Pennine Sound Studios, with Martin Hannett. This was in Oldham, in January, so a couple of months after that first meeting in Alan Erasmus's flat. That was when I first met Martin Hannett. I liked Martin. He was nearer to my age. I had cut my hair by then, but my hair had been pretty much like his – a great bush of hippie hair. He didn't care.

He was very monk-like. He was sitting there behind the mixing desk, and he didn't have manners, in the sense that he wasn't saying 'please' and 'thank you', but you could see that he was deeply into some creative process, and it was very much his little kingdom. At that stage I'd never seen a proper recording session going on, so I was interested to witness what was happening, trying not to get in the way, trying not to click at times when they were actually recording, but watching and trying to get some pictures of the band in rehearsal.

It was a handful of pictures: you've got Martin Hannett in his studio; you've got Stephen Morris chilling in the overstuffed chairs, and you can see Hannett through the glass; Bernard playing guitar; then there's Bernard and Ian Curtis separately. It was a weird studio; it looked like somewhere you might have your wedding pictures taken. There were these inappropriate-looking velour curtains at the windows and then this stone fireplace that looked like it had come off a Derbyshire hillside.

It was a proper studio, but I couldn't imagine who had put it together for what purpose, and here was this rock band that seemed to not fit in the setting. It seemed to me that they were all incredibly obedient to Martin. It felt like it was Martin Hannett's event, and they were doing what he told them to do. That's how it felt at the time. I also felt that Bernard was a link in the collaboration. He seemed to be the one who was most in communication with Martin, and relaying to the others what he wanted.

I don't think I saw Stephen play the drums all evening. All I saw was some guitar-playing, a bit of singing and a lot of mucking about with the synthesizer. And that was it, one short session. But I did get a very nice picture of Martin Hannett that night, and I did like Martin. I felt that he was from a generation and a musical tradition that I understood. And here were these other people making a completely different sort of sound. And although I was very excited by the punks, musically they were a generation behind me.

I remember talking to Wilson about this. I was saying, 'You're promoting all this stuff that's new, but what do you listen to when you go home?' – 'Buffalo Springfield!' I remember going out and buying a Buffalo Springfield album that he'd told me to buy, *Expecting to Fly*. It fascinated me that he had this passion for new music and went to endless gigs, spent a lot of time listening to young musicians, and yet the music he listened to for pleasure was not the music he was promoting. At that time, anyway.

I can't tell you I was enamoured of the music that night, because you know what recording sessions are like: they're just in bits. If you walk in on one, you have no idea what the big picture is. But

I felt absolutely that Martin did know what the big picture was; he was trying very hard, and repeatedly, and in a rather bossy determined manner, and they got on with it. It was very much work. Getting it done.

Alan Hempsall, 'A Day Out with Joy Division', *Extro* magazine, 1980

Sitting down to drink I ask Ian about his liking for the work of J. G. Ballard and William Burroughs. I discover that he has read a good deal of both authors' works including 'Crash' (my personal favourite), 'Terminal Beach', 'Atrocity Exhibition', and 'High Rise' by Ballard and 'Soft Machine', 'Naked Lunch' and 'Wild Boys' by William Burroughs. He also has a small booklet by Burroughs called 'APO-33' which he happens to have with him. I glanced through it and found it very interesting. I wonder if any of the books have influenced Ian's lyrics.

Bernard Sumner and Martin Hannett at Pennine Sound Studios, Oldham, 8 January 1980 (Daniel Meadows)

'Well, subconsciously I suppose some things must stick but I'm not influenced consciously by them.'

What about that song the band perform called 'Welcome to the Atrocity Exhibition', surely that was influenced by Ballard?

'Actually no, I'd written the lyrics way before I read "Atrocity Exhibition" and I was looking for a title because sometimes I just can't think up a good title. Anyway I just saw this title at the beginning of one of his books and I thought that it just fitted with the ideas in the lyrics. Sometime after I wrote the lyrics and the song had been established in our set, I read the book and it is by pure coincidence that some of the ideas in the book are similar to some of the ideas in the lyrics.'

Jon Wozencroft: If you were at this time of an inquisitive nature, Joy Division was like an advent calendar: you'd open up a window and you'd see a gateway to another place, there'd be all of these routes out into parallel worlds. It was an education in itself. The obvious example is 'Atrocity Exhibition': you want to know what atrocity exhibition, and then you find out it's a book by J. G. Ballard. You take some of the references: for example, 'Colony', which is Franz Kafka, or obscure tracks like 'The Kill', and see the references to Dostoevsky. Ian was an incredibly cultured young man.

Why they're such an important band for the moment is because they were dealing with a lot of digital paradigms, as it turns out: alienation, loneliness, space, materiality, the cityscapes, this is all digital aesthetics basically, twenty-five, thirty years before we find ourselves in these conditions. I mean, just the ability to place J. G. Ballard within a musical context – amazing. Same with the understanding of various ideas behind Burroughs's and Gysin's work, the 'Dream Machine', and the whole cultural moment that we were in in '78, '79, '80 and even '81.

All of a sudden the avant-garde got a little bit of air space in the culture. It happens. Well, we know now it happens very rarely, but at that time everything sort of combined in this quite beautiful moment where what was good was also popular. You would hear it on the radio, and you would see Joy Division records in suburban record shops that normally wouldn't stock that kind of thing.

Alan Hempsall: I'd picked up the early Burroughs and Ballard books, and I'd even written one or two reviews for a sci-fi magazine called *Extro*. I wrote a review for *The Unlimited Dream Company* when it came out around that time, and that was how I got to do an interview with Joy Division for *Extro*. When I first met Ian, there was obviously some common ground with what we were reading. One of my first novels when I got into reading some serious stuff was *Crash* by Ballard, and that in turn got me into *Naked Lunch*.

They were a bit other-worldly, they were a bit different from what your English Literature master might have recommended for you, and there was something obviously that would appeal to someone in their late teens who's fascinated by something a bit dark, the darker side of human nature, pushing the envelope a little bit, deciding to read things that might be deemed socially unacceptable, that push the boundary a little bit.

Certainly, Ballard was always using common reference points that you could relate to. There was none of that Isaac Asimov and Michael Moorcock fantasy; these were real buildings – a lot of Ballard's stuff was Shepperton. William Burroughs was the same: a lot of easy reference points but very, very strange things going on in there that made the work more threatening in a way by virtue of the apparent familiarity.

They were recording one of the 'Love Will Tear Us Apart' sessions at Pennine, somewhere up on the Oldham Road. It was in the shell of a disused church. Ian pulled out this leaflet that he picked up from William Burroughs at Plan K, called *APO-33*. He certainly came up with some stuff that I'd never come across before, so that was good. I got the impression that Ballard and Burroughs were two of his most favourite writers. I can't recall him mentioning anybody else to me particularly.

It was funny because obviously I had no journalistic background, and I think that was one of the reasons why they allowed
me to do it, because at that time they weren't giving interviews to
the press full stop. They'd stopped the year previously and decided
they weren't going to bother with journalists any more. So I said,
'Well, why don't you do it with me, and I'll do it as is?' And they
were, 'Okay.'

So anyway, I got picked up and I turned up with a tape recorder,
and Rob said, 'You can forget about the tape recorder straight away.'
– 'What do you mean?' – 'We don't want to be taped, just write
down an article if you like of experiences, and if you misquote us,
you misquote us.' And at that point Steve Morris turned round and
said, 'Oh, they all make it up anyway, it doesn't really matter, does
it?' So fair enough: I wrote it up the following day so as to remember everything as clearly as possible.

I followed them round for the day and didn't really make notes.
I decided at that point the best thing to do was just relax and treat
it like a day out. They did allow me to take photographs, and it was
really just watching them record, getting quotes off them, we went
down the pub for a couple of hours, and I spent the day out with
them. I think I even called it 'A Day Out with Joy Division', because
fundamentally that's what it was in the end.

There was a lot of laughing and joking. They were always into
winding one another up, that was the big thing, always looking for
the next way to wind one another up – the jape. They were living
for that: getting the roadie stitched up for something or another,
and if you managed to do that, you could bet your bottom dol-
lar they'd be turning round and doing likewise to you the following day. It wouldn't be long before they had something horrendous
done to them, so there was a lot of horseplay or larking around.

Martin was always more hands-on at the production stage.
When they were recording – and it was the same when he worked
with Crispy Ambulance – he let the engineer do his stuff, and he
just used to sit there and listen, and it was only when we got to
the producing stage that he used to come alive and throw all the

musicians out: 'You're not allowed in. This is my time, you've had your say.' He was very, very passive at the actual recording stage. The engineer would be busier than he was.

He was a lovely bloke, always: a bit more laid-back than the others, not so into the high jinks as them. He'd just let them get on with it, thought it was all a bit beneath him really. He was the guy who was going to pull it all together, and that was his art. He always had a very dry sense of humour, very ready with a laugh and a joke – at the musicians' expense normally – but a lovely, friendly bloke.

They did some overdubs on 'These Days', and I remember being very struck by the sequence at the beginning, which I thought was a sequencer, and it turned out in fact to be Bernard's guitar fed through a very extreme, very fast gate that was opening and closing very quickly. That wrong-footed me completely, but Bernard and Martin explained that to me in some detail, which was unusual for them. 'Love Will Tear Us Apart' seemed more typical to me, whereas 'These Days' was the one that I really thought, 'Wow, they've got a winner with that one.'

Alan Hempsall, 'A Day Out with Joy Division', *Extro* magazine, 1980
Ian leads me away to show me his guitar which he has recently acquired. It's a Vox, a fairly antiquated one too with push-button effects which are built into the body and are battery powered. He tells me he is learning to play and attempts to illustrate vocally some of the weird and wonderful sounds he can create with the effects on the Vox.

Soon Martin is ready to record the vocal tracks and we all move into the control room. Ian begins to sing. While Martin is busy at the mixing desk, Rob, Hooky and Steve busy themselves, criticising one another's idea of mixing and producing which invariably subsides into a lighthearted, but nevertheless crushing, hurling of insults. Rob appears to be the instigator of these mock slanging matches and piss-takes and through the day the conversation is to be peppered with them.

At last Bernard arrives and, while Rob tells Ian how badly he is singing today, I ask Bernard what he thinks of working in studios. 'I don't mind doing the overdubs but the backing tracks can be tedious. I'm quite pleased with this, it's sounding o.k. Two of these three tracks we're working on today will be on the new single, the first one will be the "A" side then it's a choice of the other two for the "B" side, probably the last one. I'd like Factory records to put it out as a 12" single but whether that will be possible or not, I don't know.'

Well it certainly deserves to go out as a 12". Although it is already being recorded, it won't be released for a couple of months. The 'A' side is called 'Love Will Tear Us Apart', a bouncy number that treads new ground for Joy Division with its keyboard dominated sound. Then there's a song called 'The Sound of Music' which is a little more than what we are used to from the band but none the worse for it. The last song on the tape, and this is the one Bernard tells me will probably be the 'B' side, is called 'These Days' and I thought this one was really something to write home about, this song would really benefit for being spread across twelve inches of plastic. It has a powerful beat and a good bassline strung together by a Moroder-esque rhythm created by what I thought to be a synth.

'Actually,' said Bernard, 'it's a guitar fed through a synth and that rhythm is created by passing the guitar's signal through a passage in the synth that only lets part of the signal through. So, in effect what the synth is doing with the signal is this . . .' (illustrates by tapping ends of his forefinger and thumb together).

When the vocal tracks are complete Ian goes to his mum's for tea while Bernard does some keyboards and acoustic guitar overdubs on 'Love Will Tear Us Apart'.

Terry Mason: There were 999 Ians. He could be talking to me, maybe we'd be talking about something being on BBC2, next conversation he'd be talking to Barney about 'Did you see Hill's Angels on *The Benny Hill Show* last night?' He talks to Tony Wilson, he has a different persona, he talks to Jon Savage, he's different again, and not many people see the exact same slice of Ian. You only got the bit that he wanted you to have. Ian's conversations were very much one-to-one all the time, even if they were just moving a few degrees and the one-to-one was someone three foot to one side of you.

Paul Morley: My sense is that when you're putting together stories and images and ideas that are so unique and original, it's coming from somewhere, and I think he was an antenna among other people. One of the things that was hard for Ian was being in the middle of that bunch of people, being so sensitive, because Hooky's a fucker in a way, in a nice way, Bernard's a git, in a nice way, Steve's beautifully batty, there's Gretton, there's Wilson, there's Erasmus, there's Deborah, there's Annik. That's challenging stuff. I couldn't cope with any of that, to be honest. I wouldn't have lasted a day. I would have been out of there like a shot, because it's scary. In a way, the scariness of the music sometimes is simply reinterpreting being in this weird situation with this weird set of people moving fucking fast through stuff in a pop group, which wasn't quite what it was cracked up to be, and then turning that into these great myths about existence.

I think it must have been tough for him to be in the middle of all that. In a way, we've not thought of the idea of suddenly committing yourself to something: 'We all went along to see the Sex Pistols, yeah, it's great. Oh, let's form a group.' That sounds like a good idea, and then suddenly it's a matter of life or death, really quickly, and that's probably not good for his health.

- 11 January 1980: Paradiso, Amsterdam, start of ten-date European tour

Peter Hook, Berlin, January 1980 (Mark Reeder)

Deborah Curtis (from *Touching from a Distance*): As I came out of the shop I saw the car coming down the road towards me. The driver slowed down as if he was going to stop to allow Ian to say goodbye (as they were going to the Continent for about ten days), but Ian's stony face turned the other way and the car carried on, just as though we had fallen out and weren't speaking. Unknown to me he was setting the scene for taking Annik on tour with him.

Peter Hook: It was fucking hell, it was like being locked up with a load of farting, pissed-up bastards for two weeks. It was the first time I've ever wanted to come home from being on tour. It was awful. We were just locked up. Twinny was being a real arsehole, and so was Barney, from what I can remember. I'm sure he'd say the same about me. That was the first time when you were too close: you never got a bleeding minute from each other. Everywhere we stayed we were all together. It was a fucking nightmare, there was no space at all.

Ian was with Annik, which made it difficult because we were all taking the piss out of him and we were fucked off because she was there. It was a difficult time. It was freezing, we were locked in the Transit all the time, it was really difficult. We always played good shows, it never affected the show. Don't know why.

Stephen Morris: Annik was Annik. I don't blame her for any of it, but she had Ian written on her forehead as if she'd been clutching some unreleased version of *The Atrocity Exhibition* or some rare J. G. Ballard books. She was sophistication to someone from Macclesfield, someone who used to ride pigs for entertainment, to be confronted with someone who works in the Belgian embassy. I don't think any of us really knew where Belgium was at that time. Annik refined his intellectualism. When he was with her he'd change again. She made him think he was an artist.

Annik Honoré: They never travelled much as teenagers, and when they first went to Europe I think something happened for them. Ian was more interested in some cities, like Berlin, because they had a strong history, and I think it appealed to him. But suddenly when you travel you grow up, you see so much more than your own little city, and you really start becoming more open to other cultures, and Ian was a lot into that. He was not so much a local lad; he had a lot more to discover.

He was fascinated by seeing all the old buildings. Even Brussels and Paris and Amsterdam, they have these wonderful buildings and architecture, and he liked that, so travelling in the van he got to see all these places and meet all the foreigners. That's exciting. A lot more than just meeting the people down the road.

Bernard Sumner: I remember playing Belgium. Michel Duval – who was then the boss of Crepuscule Records, which was a branch of Factory – was finding it incredibly funny to shove us in the shittiest hotels that he could possibly find. I remember staying in one room that he put us in, and when we got there the whole room was at an angle, so when you went in the shower, the shower was at an angle and the water would actually run down the wall.

The next time he actually put us in a brothel, a proper brothel with ultraviolet lights, and we had to wait until eleven o'clock at night before we could get in our rooms. It was UV lights and speakers under the bed playing romantic music, and me and Steve were sharing the room, and he was like, 'I'll sleep on the floor.' I tend to remember the hotels more than the gigs really. Gigs were just a bit of fun and a bit of work, not like earth-shattering moments for me, I must admit. We tried to do our best at them.

- 15 January 1980: Kant Kino, Berlin

Mark Reeder: In July 1978 I'd left Manchester to live in Berlin. We kept in touch. As soon as I got to Germany, Rob was like, 'Right, now we're going to re-release *An Ideal for Living* as a twelve-inch' – because it was fashionable, and because the sound on the seven-inch was shit. The idea was, I was going to promote the twelve-inch in Germany to all the radio stations, so then they might get some gigs in Germany. That was my job, basically: Rob said, 'Can you promote this twelve-inch?' and I did.

Then, 'We've got a new single coming out, "Transmission".' And Tony created Factory Records, and suddenly I was their man in Berlin. I got paid. My rent was eighty marks a month, and they gave me something like a third of that, and I got my phone bill paid as well, which I was really surprised about. And I'd send Rob the receipts for postage, for sending records out. He was good like that, Rob; he didn't want me to be out of pocket from promoting the band.

It was just Joy Division at that point, it wasn't any other band really, until they released the first *Factory Sample*, and then it would be another band – Durutti Column or someone like that. I was always hoping that Vini would get over and do a gig, but he never

Joy Division live at the Kant Kino, Berlin, 21 January 1980 (Mark Reeder)

did. We had A Certain Ratio, people like that, coming over. Tony liked the idea of having somebody in Berlin. He told me years later that in reality they wanted me to do Factory Germany – Factory Deutschland – but they weren't prepared to pay for it.

He asked me to send him some cassettes of the things I was listening to, which I would release on Factory Deutschland, and it was things like P/1E and Mania D, before they were Malaria, Gudrun Gut's band. But Tony's like, 'I can't sell this, it's fucking rubbish.' He wasn't prepared to put the money in to have the record label. He told me later he liked the idea, it would look really great on letterheads. But that was all it was ever going to be.

I realised that no one in Berlin really got the Joy Division records. I was getting no reaction off the radio stations at all. Also, they'd read in the music press about this right-wing image that they had. So the Germans were a bit cold when it came to Joy Division. I said, 'You've got to see them play live. Once you've seen them play, you'll know that it's brilliant.' It's the best band in the world, they've got to understand. I said to Rob, 'You've got to come and play Berlin.' – 'It's fucking miles away, what do we want to play Berlin for? No one plays there.'

So I said to Ian, 'You've got to convince Rob to play Berlin.' Ian definitely wanted to, because it was going to Berlin and seeing the Brandenburg Gate and all the history. Eventually, I heard that they were doing a tour of Holland, and they had a gig in Cologne. So I said, 'Rob, if you're playing Cologne, it's not that far from Cologne to Berlin. It's a couple of hours' drive.' So he said, 'Okay, if you sort us something out, we'll come.' So I went to the Kant Kino, which was this cinema that had gigs on.

I spoke to Conny Konzack. I said, 'I've got this fantastic band, they really want to play here. They're playing in Cologne.' And he's like, 'Never heard of them.' But in the end he said, 'Okay, we'll do this gig.' He'd read a bit about them in the papers, and he said he'd put them on. So Rob got in touch with the people who were doing the promotion in Holland, and they expanded the tour, and so they came to Berlin.

It was a fucking mess. The sound was totally rubbish. They'd got this dead cheap PA guy who was a bit of a hippie, and he didn't care. They had no real sound system of any kind. And the Kant Kino being a cinema, it didn't hold very many people. It wasn't a stand-up venue, there were seats, and in the middle of the seats they had this mixing desk. You couldn't hear Ian's voice: every time they turned the vocals up, they'd be feeding back. It wasn't happening.

Maybe fifty people turned up at this gig. The poster was shit. I think Conny got someone in the office to try and draw the *Unknown Pleasures* cover, and they put about ten photocopies of this outside the Kant Kino, so obviously no one's going to come to this gig. I saw this poster and I thought, 'They're going to kill me.' I knew Peter Saville had taken such care over the artwork, and look at this shitty poster! Anyway, someone at the front is going, 'Turn the vocals up!' And Bernard, with real venom, goes, 'Speak fucking English, you German bastard!' And that was it really, the gig was over.

The audience was already a bit hostile, and a bit sceptical about this band from the UK who have this right-wing Nazi imagery.

And then for this to come out of someone who they thought actually spoke German, cos Bernard had presented himself as Bernard Albrecht on the records, and they all thought he was German. And then he spits this back, and I'm thinking, 'The gig's over.' But they finished the set, and the band were completely elated by this concert. They thought it had gone down really well.

They'd done loads of gigs like that, and they'd had quite a few 'incidents' in the meantime. I think Ian's dancing took off that edge. There was Hooky's legs akimbo, down the front with his back to the audience, and Bernard just stood there chopping at his guitar. And Stephen was like a machine on the drums. Brilliant. That was the beauty of both the Buzzcocks and Joy Division: they had drummers that were a bit like Ian Paice of Deep Purple, who had a very distinctive style, and you couldn't compare it to anything else. Steve's machine-like drumming was awesome.

Joy Division in Berlin, January 1980 (Hermann Vaske)

Then they wanted me to show them around Berlin. Ian wanted to see the Brandenburg Gate – from both sides of the wall, of course – and stick his fingers in the bullet holes from the Second World War. That was awesome for them. We didn't go to any gigs, or any clubs at all. They didn't want to do that, they just wanted to absorb the city, and it was freezing cold – it was January and there was snow everywhere.

I took them to East Berlin. We had a *Schweinshaxe* [pork knuckle] in this very old restaurant. They couldn't believe it, that you could get what looked like half a baby's leg, crispy-baked in the oven, for like 3p or something. They thought it was the most delicious thing that they'd ever eaten. They wanted to have it everywhere. I think for them it was just a really interesting trip.

And then Bernard and Ian were going, 'Come back with us!' I hadn't planned on going back to Manchester at all. 'If you come back with us, you can come back in the van.' So I get into this Ford Transit, and we drove back from Berlin to Manchester. A mad dash to Hook of Holland to catch the ferry, which we actually missed. Ian had an epileptic fit when we were in the van going back. I hadn't known it was that bad.

Bernard Sumner: Berlin, we played a place called the Kant Kino. Mark Reeder put the concert on. We used to get titles from anywhere. Everyone chipped in: 'I've got an idea, I've got an idea.' We got a lot from an old film poster that we took from the Kant Kino. It was an art-house cinema, and it had this big poster with all the forthcoming films on it, so we stole it and took it to our rehearsal room and put it up there, and if we wanted a title, we used to go and just get one word from one film and one word from another.

For us, titles didn't have to be related to the song really. It was more interesting if they weren't. The titles were just handles with which to pick the songs up, and we didn't really connect the titles with the lyrics. That's not what you're supposed to do, but that's just the way we wanted it to be.

Deborah Curtis (from *Touching from a Distance*): When Ian came home we practically passed on the doorstep, as I was on my way to work. I had already dropped Natalie off at my parents' and whenever she was there Ian never made the effort to go and see her, even if he had been away on tour. I returned after midnight and found the house strangely quiet, but eventually located Ian lying on the floor of the blue room. He had consumed most of a bottle of duty-free Pernod and so was difficult to rouse.

I was annoyed to find him incoherent and when he gained consciousness he spewed all over the carpet. He didn't raise any objections when I insisted he clean it up himself, then he sloped off to bed. I noticed weals on his body, but could not be sure if they were recent or not. After he had gone I picked up the Bible and the knife which were lying on the floor. The Bible was still open. Chapter two of The Book of Revelation of St John the Divine was gouged from top to bottom. I read the still-legible words referring to Jezebel and flattered myself into thinking he had been worried about my fidelity while he was away.

Stephen Morris: He said he didn't remember anything about it, that he had a blackout, which I can believe to a certain extent. But it's more likely that he just got pissed and vented his frustration. The stuff he was taking anyway was pretty heavy. He was on Largactil. It must have been horrible. He was having more and more fits.

The more successful we got, or the more you could see success beckoning you, the worse Ian's condition became. It's bleeding obvious really: if you're going to carry on doing something that involves staying up all night, drinking, running about and acting like an idiot when you've got epilepsy, you're not going to make it any better. The only way we could have sorted it out was just to say, 'Right, that's it, it's over, let's forget about it. We can't carry on because he's ill.' But we very naively ignored that and went along with it.

With Annik, it was part and parcel of the same thing, because you're knocking about with the extra. He got himself in a situation. He was never a person who would say no; he would say whatever you wanted to hear. So he'd got himself into a situation where he was saying something that would make Debbie happy, and he'd met this other person who wasn't one of the one-night-standers, and they're saying, 'What are you going to do?' He'd say, 'Well, whatever you want me to do.' He'd got epilepsy as well, and you can see it's a disaster happening in very slow motion.

Bernard Sumner: When you get married very young, perhaps too young, and you live in a restricted environment like I did in Salford and Ian did in Macclesfield, and then you start travelling the wider world, it changes you. Also, growing older changes you, and people fall in and out of love as you get older, and unfortunately that's just human nature and it happens sometimes. We thought it was very dangerous, what he was doing, and I suppose there was a bit of resentment from the group, but ultimately we thought, 'Well, that's his personal business.'

Peter Hook: You were so carried away with it and so glad to have it, the trajectory, that we'd just say, 'Ian, are you all right? Are you going to be able to do this?' And he'd go, 'Oh yes. Ha ha. Just give us a fag and I'll be fine.' And we thought, 'All right, that's okay then.' We didn't know any better, we weren't very responsible, we were his age, and if he said to you he was okay and the doctors had let him out, then you thought, 'Well, he must be okay.' Now, with hindsight and experience, you'd just say, 'No, you're not doing that, it's obvious that you're going to suffer.'

There were no adults. Tony wasn't really an adult because he was enjoying it so much. One of the things I've learned about Tony is that he doesn't have any adult outlook to anything; he just carries on like a kid with everything. Nobody said, 'Stop it.' I think Alan Erasmus was the only one that might have said, 'Hey, fucking hell, hang on a minute.' Martin Hannett was completely off it, and the rest of us were just so happy. The thing was, we listened to Ian, Ian told us he was all right, and we believed him. I don't know what else you're supposed to do at twenty-one.

Terry Mason: We were like children. We were twenty, twenty-one as this is coming up, which nowadays makes us seem as if we were quite mature, but we acted like children. The whole set-up seemed without any adult leadership: we thought there'd be some adult leadership from Rob, we expected some from Tony, but there was none of that. The nearest to an adult in our organisation as such was Tony, and when you've got Tony as the adult, you don't have much hope.

Lindsay Reade: We were kids, all of us were kids, there was nobody over the age of thirty around. I think the two relative grown-ups were Martin Hannett and Tony Wilson. I know it sounds stupid considering the amount of drugs Martin took, but they were taking charge of things – but that was more the music side of things. Ian was a grown-up actually: he was very old for his age. He wasn't like a young kid. I mean, you can tell it in his lyrics: those are grown-up writings, aren't they? It's not kids' stuff.

Bernard Sumner: Generally, Ian was incredibly pleasant, polite and really nice, but sometimes in life if you don't have teeth, people take advantage of that. Ian's response to that was to become totally explosive. That's the way he would get things done if someone opposed him, but never for no reason, always for good reason. I liked Ian and I think very highly of him, not just because he's my mate and because of old times, but because I genuinely think that he was what people say he was: he was really extremely talented.

You couldn't take your eyes off him as a performer, and he was the real deal. It wasn't some front or some image or anything, he was the real McCoy, and like all of us, we've all got our personality flaws. I suppose his worst flaw was trying to be positive and trying to tell you what you wanted to hear, when really you just want: 'Just tell me the truth, Ian, what do you really think? It might upset me, but just tell me what you really think.' And I think he found that a little bit difficult to do. I tell you, that was his worst fault.

- 7 February 1980: the Factory II, the New Osborne Club

Mick Middles, review of the New Osborne Club show in
***Record Mirror*, 1 March 1980**
The set is 90 per cent new material. Without doubt, this
is a favourable sign and I'm relieved to find that the new
songs steer carefully clear of that threatening area of solid
self-indulgence. However, despite a couple of moments of
pure nostalgic magic, Joy Division are unable to capture the
essence of their passion.

Liz Naylor: One of the last Joy Division gigs in Manchester was
a benefit for *City Fun* set up by Factory, sarcastically. We did not
ask them to do that benefit at the Osborne Club, it was a hostile
gesture, but the interesting thing – and perhaps Rob Gretton is the
important person here – is that Joy Division always crossed that
divide. They felt very much like a people's band. It makes them
sound rather dour, but there was a certain accessibility there, and
perhaps that was through Rob.

Daniel Meadows: Tony said to me, 'Thanks for the pictures so
far. I need some pictures of Ian Curtis blurred – you know, the
spastic dancing? Don't give me any more sharp pictures, Daniel,
I want blurred. Come to the Osborne Club.' And that was the
first time I really heard them play. I'd been to a Factory night at
the Russell Club back in April 1979, and I'd got a feel for what
Factory was all about, and Granada was a cultural centre, so
these bands would be coming in and out all the time. You'd hear
the music and have an appreciation of what the next generation
were doing.

But the New Osborne was the first time I heard them play. It was
unimposing, in a pretty grim part of Manchester: old cotton mills,
which at that time had closed down. There was a newish housing
estate which was a tough place. I remember it being large and dark
and barn-like. A low ceiling, a small stage, a couple of spotlights. In

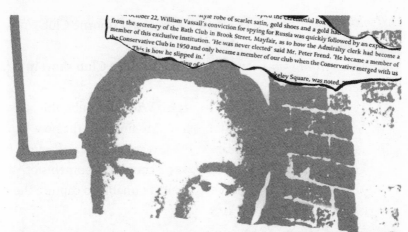

KIM·PHILBY·REAPPEARS
JOY DIVISION - A CERT
AIN RATIO - SECTION25
NEW OSBOURNE — FEB 7
FAC FOR CITY FUNDS !
(£1¼)

'Kim Philby Reappears': poster for Joy Division at the New Osborne Club, February
1980 (Courtesy of Jon Savage)

the pictures you can see some light at the back, which was a bar, the
usual crowd of stalwart post-punks standing at the front, probably
not contributing much to the music of the evening, but certainly
entering into the spirit of it.

Bernard Sumner and Ian Curtis: Joy Division, the New Osborne Club, 7 February
1980 (Daniel Meadows)

I subsequently realised it wasn't the greatest gig. It was very
near the end of Curtis's life, maybe things were falling apart a bit,
I don't know, but I just remember the intensity of that music. I'm
pretty much on the stage to photograph them, alongside them,
I'm not down in a pit, and being a tall bloke I'm pretty much eye
to eye with them in those photographs. I deliberately did some
blurred pictures. It wasn't hard: the light is never very good. It
was also incredibly loud, being right there in it. I was between
the speakers and the stage a lot of the time, and being completely
deafened by it. Hooky's bass was thumping into me, but it wasn't
the loudness that made it intense. Curtis had this incredibly mesmeric . . . you couldn't take your eyes off him. I'd been to gigs
and seen all kinds of bands, but I'd never seen a performer, a
singer, where you had to keep watching him. You couldn't not
look. He wore these cool dark clothes, but he was completely
sweated through, very quickly, doing this extraordinary dance.
You weren't looking at anybody else.

When Rod Stewart or somebody was playing, all the girls would be waiting for him to wriggle or throw his mike up in the air, and there was something sexual going on between the performer and the crowd, but with him it wasn't like that. There were a lot of blokes in that audience, and they were quite aggressive, punching the air, jumping up and down. It was strange, because it wasn't homo-sexual, either. It was unlike anything I'd ever seen. It was strangely private. He was doing something I suppose a lot of young men sort of do in front of a mirror.

It had that private feel to it, made public, and there was a real tension in that. He wasn't playing air guitar – a lot of lead singers do – he was pumping his arms up and down as though he was a runner, but it was like a dance move, and at the same time it was very intimate. He was doing it to this noise, and it was a very differ-ent kind of noise. By this time I had *Unknown Pleasures*, and what

Peter Hook and Ian Curtis: Joy Division, the New Osborne Club, 7 February 1980
(Daniel Meadows)

I loved about it was the incredible tunes playing in the bass, using the bass guitar to play a tune. I'd never heard a band that played in that way.

The two things that really got into my head was the tuneful bass thing and this mesmeric performance that matched the singing. It was a visual version of the noise he was making. He had a lovely voice. He didn't have a fantastic range, but he had a deep baritone. I was right there on the stage with them. Something I've always loved about being a photographer is how close you can get to things that are happening. It's extraordinarily intense when you're right in the middle of the music like that. There isn't a better ticket in the house.

Mark Reeder: That was when I first met Annik. Hooky said, 'That girl there is Ian's bit on the side, his Belgian boiler. Can you make sure they don't run into each other?' Because Bernard's wife and Debbie had come out together, they just wanted to get Annik. And that was how I got to know her. She seemed very pleasant and very intelligent. She was totally different to what I knew, which was Manchester girls.

Annik was the secretary to the Belgian ambassador in London. She wasn't just *a* secretary. Her father was the chief of police of south Belgium. She went to a dead good school, a Belgian version of public school. She knew about fine wine and good food, she knew how to make nice cakes, she knew about Dostoevsky and she knew about films, and they were things that he couldn't get from Debbie. He could talk about things with Annik that he couldn't talk about with Debbie.

With Debbie it was always like, 'When are you coming home? Your tea's on the table. When are you going to get a proper job?' I remember one night Debbie took us home, with Ian, in their car. I think they had a Morris Countryman. Arguing all the way. I just thought it was a typical northern English relationship. They got married early, and it was like *Coronation Street*. And when I got to know Annik well, I realised that she was in love with his lyricism, the fact that he was a poet, the music and everything. Maybe later on it might have become something else.

But Ian's epilepsy was brought on by the stress of being in this relationship with Debbie, and wanting to maintain that relationship. He loved the baby, he wanted to be in the relationship, but he also wanted the relationship with Annik at the same time, and as it wasn't going anywhere, the home relationship was falling apart. And then the band and the pressure – all these things were manifesting in the epilepsy. I don't think it was any other reason than being under extreme stress. In his young mind, he couldn't deal with that.

- 8 February 1980: University of London Union

Jon Wozencroft: This was promoted by Final Solution, so it was publicised quite well in advance. They came on and they played 'Dead Souls', and I turned around and looked to my left and there was this guy taping it, and I thought, 'That's good, I can concentrate on just really taking in every moment of this.' So I was just totally enraptured, and they were really up for it that evening because it was a showcase for them: all the music press people were there, they were not on tour, so they hadn't been victims of a punishing schedule.

They had yet to record the new material in Britannia Row Studios, so they weren't quite sure of how to focus it, so it was still the sense of something quite embryonic. If you look at that set list, it's a marvellous combination between tracks like 'Glass', which very rarely got played, and 'The Eternal', as the first encore. Can you imagine? You've never heard this thing before. They go offstage – 'More!' Whaaaa! They come on and they play 'The Eternal', and people are like, 'What the fuck is that?'

Because it was extraordinary. It's like a piece of classical music for its time, set to this amazingly evocative lyric, and it's like an oration. It's not dark in the sense of being depressing or anything, but it's like this childlike dream sequence orchestrated with this beautiful use of synthesizer and the counterpoint from Hooky's bass guitar, and Steve's percussion on it is great. They often cite Kraftwerk as a major influence, but what they do with the electronic aspect is very unusual and, I think, unique.

When I saw Ian's performance that particular night, there was the sense that you might be able to use this energy in a very powerful way – in a very powerful, progressive and expansive way – to have a very strong emotional effect upon an audience. So this was a very strong disclosure to me that there's actually a lot of white light happening here, it's not all about death, doom and destruction.

Joy Division's music is very uplifting. It's got nothing to do with sitting in a bedsit being depressed, chewing your fingernails and wondering if you're going to throw yourself out the window. It's about transforming normal lives into something magical and life-affirming. The cliché of Joy Division has been very dark and depressing. For me, that was not the case at all: they were joy-bringers, and I felt charged as a result of that concert. These things are not understood or recognised in our culture, and it's important to acknowledge where we find them in our own lives.

Peter Saville: I would see them when they played in London, and I was aware of a growing aura. It was nice to be part of that aura. It was probably spoiling and ego massaging to be part of the aura of Joy Division, and I think they grew into their performances. I remember seeing them at London University, and Ian had that strange white guitar, sort of sci-fi guitar, and they played a song called 'Love Will Tear Us Apart'. There's a special experience when you realise they've discovered a song. It's one of the holy grails of the pop industry.

When I heard them play 'Love Will Tear Us Apart', it was obviously a hit. You can't stop songs like that being hits, and that was exciting. I remember standing in the audience at London University and thinking, 'Oh fuck, now they've got a single on top of this myth that's building.' It might have been after that London University concert, I can't remember, but we went for a meal together, about a dozen or twenty people, and Ian was there sitting at another table from everyone else. His mind was elsewhere.

11

FEBRUARY – MARCH 1980

Ian Curtis and Peter Hook: Joy Division, Trinity Hall, Bristol, 5 March 1980
(Andrew Davis)

**Paul Morley, review of University of London Union show,
NME, 16 February 1980**
Joy Division's music is physical and lucid, music about
uncontrollable emotions, impulses, prejudices, fears. The
group have turned inarticulacy and vagueness into concrete,
disturbing impressions of the most degenerate, deepest
desires . . . Joy Division will tear you apart. Still.

Chris Bohn, review of University of London Union show,
Melody Maker, **16 February 1980**
Joy Division are masters of this gothic gloom, and they're
getting even better at it. Since they played London last
November with the Buzzcocks, they've added new songs,
more vigorous than their predecessors. Less colourful now,
they're getting closer to the despair that's been the core of
their work thus far.

- 28 February 1980: the Warehouse, Preston

Ian Curtis (Radio Blackburn interview by Spyda and Steve Barker,
28 February 1980): We've played in Europe already in Holland and
Germany, and we are going to America. I think they wanted us to
go for about three months or so [*laughs*], but we're only going for
about two weeks, three weeks, and Rough Trade will probably be
organising that. I think we're going with Cabaret Voltaire. I like
them, they're a good group [*laughs*].

Yeah, but we tend to do what we want really. We play the music
we want to play and we play the places we want to play. I'd hate to
be on the usual record company, where you get an album out and
you do a tour, and you do all the Odeons and all the this, that and
the others. I couldn't just do that at all. We had experience of that
supporting the Buzzcocks. It was really soul-destroying, you know,
at the end of it. We said we'd never tour . . . and we'll never do a tour,
I don't think – or if we do, it won't be longer than about two weeks.

I just want to carry on the way we are, I think. Basically we want
to play and enjoy what we like playing. I think when we stop doing
that . . . I think, well, that will be the time to pack it in. That'll be
the end.

- 29 February 1980: the Lyceum, London

Dylan Jones: I saw Joy Division twice: once at the Moonlight Club in
West Hampstead, and once at the Lyceum, both in 1980. However,

I can really only remember the Lyceum concert. I've checked online, and it says it was a Friday, although I always remember it as a Sunday. Don't know why. Something to do with the light and the mood on the street outside the concert before we went in.

During that time – 1976 to 1980 – punk and post-punk always seemed incredibly odd in the daylight, and to me it was always meant to be music that you listened to and went to see at night. So often, when I heard the likes of Joy Division or Throbbing Gristle or Wire in the daytime, it seemed completely incongruous, and perhaps even a bit threatening. This is probably why I thought that gig was on a Sunday summer evening, as it felt threatening.

I went to hundreds of punk gigs – literally – but what people rarely mention is how aggressive they were, and often how scary. I remember seeing Generation X at the Nag's Head in High Wycombe, the Jam at the 100 Club, seeing bands at the Red Cow, the Marquee, the Roxy and the Hope and Anchor, and there was always an undercurrent of violence. I saw glasses being thrown around the room, people kicked downstairs at the Rainbow and violence at Clash gigs, Ramones gigs, Banshees gigs, Iggy Pop gigs.

Everyone was on speed, no one ate, everybody looked over each other's shoulders. I loved it, but there was always an edge. Plus, I was a bit of a Neurotic Boy Outsider and didn't smile much at gigs, probably because I was afraid someone would thump me. I remember a girl asked me to cheer up at the Joy Division Lyceum gig, in the way that a builder might shout at a girl, 'Cheer up, luv, it might never happen!' Maybe I was on speed, but I was almost certainly paranoid, which was my default state of mind at the time. Skinny, anxious and pale, in a leather jacket.

Joy Division made a very menacing, disturbing noise, one that was northern, industrial, complicated yet strangely simple. It wasn't always easy to listen to, which in those days was an obvious advantage. And onstage they were mesmeric, what with Ian Curtis doing his epileptic dance and the rest of the band trying as hard as they could to look as hard as they could. Black clothes, grey clothes, sombre lighting, cold, austere and brilliant. I couldn't take my eyes off Curtis, or indeed the rest of the band.

I saw A Certain Ratio, who were already a sign of the times, a band who felt and sounded like the eighties, and, of course, Killing Joke, who I loved for a year in a kind of guilty-pleasure way, the way you might have enjoyed Slade seven or eight years earlier. Killing Joke were the cabaret version of punk, noise merchants who appeared to want to blend Sham 69 with early Banshees. They were great fun, but when Joy Division came on you could see that they had already left bands like Killing Joke well behind. They owned the stage. They owned that year, in fact.

Tony Wilson: There was a strange one, one night. Again I was side stage at the Lyceum. I'd started to recognise how the band began to react when they knew he was going off; you began noticing it. Rob was away back at the main mixing desk, and as usual it was Terry's job, side stage, to try to deal with this. So sure enough, Ian went into a fit and Terry dragged him off, then I helped Terry and we carried Ian, still shaking, up the side stairs, these stone stairs up into the heights above the stage somewhere, away from everywhere.

And I remember us both holding him to stop him banging against the wall, and then suddenly around this corner came John Curd, the most frightening promoter that Britain has ever seen, and to watch Curd's face go white in complete shock and say 'I'll leave you two to it' was something of a moment. I thought Curd was unshockable, but he was shocked. You were just aware that Ian was an epileptic. It was what it was.

Jon Wozencroft: Joy Division's performances from March 1980 onwards get progressively more scrappy, not only because Ian's health was deteriorating, although no one knew much about that at the time, but also because the weight of expectation upon them to come out with the most amazing gig ever, every time they played, was enormous. People started writing about them in February 1980 as if they were the Second Coming. The write-ups of those London gigs – the Lyceum and University of London by Paul Morley, by Chris Bohn – they were: we've just seen the light. Joy Division walk on water, they can do no wrong.

At the end of that month the Sordide Sentimental record came out – 'Dead Souls' and 'Atmosphere' – and it had been widely distributed on cassette, because John Peel played it all the time because he was feeling sorry for all of those who couldn't get hold of a copy. Many people were going through every record shop, every independent shop in the country looking for a copy. When it did come out, Rob was down in London and he was handing them out. Two days later they were gone, disappeared for ever. 'Where can I get *Licht und Blindheit*?' Look at that for a title.

- March 1980: Joy Division at Strawberry Studios, recording 'Love Will Tear Us Apart' and 'She's Lost Control' twelve-inch
- 18–30 March 1980: Joy Division at Britannia Row Studios, recording *Closer*

Tony Wilson: I do look back on my one moment of interference, which was talking to Ian once about singing, about the shape of phrases. I felt that when you extend a syllable over two notes or something, in the space within the syllable is where the emotion comes in. I then went out and bought a Frank Sinatra double album, and I remember turning up at Strawberry one day around that time, and I did find both Sinatra records out of their sleeves on the floor in front of the record player, so they had listened to them.

Certainly, the conversation came between Pennine Studios' 'Love Will Tear Us Apart' and the one we all know. The difference between the two – the fact that Ian does change a bit – I would love to think that I was connected to that. The conversations with Ian – apart from my very first conversation, where he was an obnoxious, violent rat – he was always like this thoughtful schoolkid, and that's how I treated him, and it was how he behaved towards me, and he was lovely.

Bernard Sumner: With 'Love Will Tear Us Apart', we just thought, 'It's good. It would be good to play this live.' We played it live a couple of times and people got into it, and that's as far as it went. We just didn't think about it – it seemed to work that way, you see. It seemed that the more we analysed stuff and the more we thought about it, the less successful the results were. So we have this, we don't know where it's coming from but it's coming, let's not think about it, don't talk about it to each other and just see what happens. That's the way we did it. We never really thought about it; we just did it and thought, 'Mmm.'

We thought, 'Right, it would be good if we had something fast and dancey.' That was the first thing we'd say. We'd go into rehearsals and we'd go, 'Let's write something, but before we write let's get a fast, dancey beat, because we know that works at live gigs, and also they're the hardest tracks to write.' So Steve would come up with a beat, me and Hooky would start jamming to it, and then Ian would go, 'Oh, that bit's good.' So we'd go, 'Right, stop. What was it we were playing? We played this, right? Okay, let's just play that, just repeat that part.' That's as far as it went.

We thought it was a really strong track and that we were going to put an extra effort in on the production. In fact, we recorded it once, and Martin did his usual toned-down production, and we just said, 'Right, we're not having it this time, it sounds like it's been toned down.' So we said, 'No, no, no, we're not having it. It's a good track, this one, it's better, so we've got to record it again.' So he threw a big sulk about that, a big wobbler, probably called us all a bunch of twats.

We went in the studio, and he was sulking. We recorded it and recorded it and recorded it, and did loads – overdubs and that. I think he did a really good job of it – it sounded much better than the first one he did – but he was in a sulk about it. Steve left about midnight, and I was doing some acoustic-guitar overdubs, and it got to about two thirty in the morning, Rob was there, I think Hooky was there, and we just finished the overdubs, and Martin and Rob went, 'Oh, it sounds great now, sounds great.'

And Martin went, 'I'm not quite finished.' We went, 'What do you mean?' He says, 'I need Steve back to double-track the snare drum.' So because we'd made him do the production again, he made Steve get out of bed – he was right across the other side of London, in a flat – and get a taxi or drive over. It took him about three-quarters of an hour to get to the studio, double-track the snare drum, just so Martin could prove a point really. I'm sure he never used the double track, but he could be like that, Martin.

Stephen Morris: 'Love Will Tear Us Apart' I always thought was a pop classic in the making from the word go. Me and Ian used to have a lot of conversations because I had to drive him about and drop him off. One of the conversations that we had was about the Captain and Tennille record, 'Love Will Keep Us Together'. I'd got this bootleg by the Tubes and it's got a weird cover of 'Love Will Keep Us Together', and I said, 'Well wouldn't it be better if they did something really nasty to it, instead of like being a twee pop song? "Love will rip us to shreds," or something like that?' Anyway, it ended up being 'Love Will Tear Us Apart'.

I've got a lot of problems with 'Love Will Tear Us Apart' personally. The A-side version of it is just me in a very bad mood. Every time I listen to it I can hear the bad mood that I was in. That was the one where we'd all done it separately. I'd gone home, back to the flat, and it was two o'clock in the morning and Martin wasn't very happy about the drumming, so he rang me up and said, 'I'm going to do the bass drum again.' So I get up, go all the way back to the studio just to do the sodding bass drum again. I can hear my teeth clenching every time I listen to it. I can almost re-experience it – it's a bit like the madeleines thing. The other side I'm fine with, because he just let me play what I wanted and didn't drag me back at an unearthly hour in the morning, but the A-side just brings back some sort of red mist.

Paul Morley: You would first hear 'Love Will Tear Us Apart' live and you would go, 'Oh my God,' because you did have enough about you to think, 'That is a fucking great pop song.' It was catchy and it had an incredible energy. You knew from the moment you heard that 'Love will tear us apart'. I immediately made it the last line of a review as soon as I heard it – 'Joy Division will tear you apart' – because Ian could use language in a fresh, invigorating way, and that was what was brilliant and that's why they've lasted and transcended the moment.

Peter Hook: Martin's production made it poppy. I was listening to it live, and it sounds a lot different live cos there's no guitar on the verses, apart from Ian playing it, which is very scratchy and very punky, very primitive guitar. It sounds more like Joy Division live than the record. The record's quite a poppy production.

I remember Martin was so fed up with us that he decided to mix 'Love Will Tear Us Apart' at three o'clock in the morning on a Saturday. Rob phoned me up about eleven o'clock and he said, 'Listen, Martin's gone to the studio, you'd better get down there,' cos I was the only one that had a car. And I said, 'Well, I haven't got any money.' And he went, 'Borrow some money and get down there. Don't let him fuck it up, you've got to go down there.'

So I had to get up, and first of all I had to go to me in-laws and borrow three quid so I could put a gallon of petrol in me car and drive to Strawberry. I remember Martin was so fucking annoyed that I'd turned up, because he thought he was going to get away with doing it on his own. So I sat in for the 'Love Will Tear Us Apart' mix in Strawberry, which we didn't actually use. Martin actually mixed 'Love Will Tear Us Apart' with the engineer who did *Closer*, and that was how they met, I think.

Stephen Morris: I remember when we recorded *Closer*, we went back to Martin's thing of recording in hallowed halls, and we went to Pink Floyd's studio in Britannia Row. It was Martin's ideal place, I suppose. It was a bit odd cos we were living then in two flats in Baker Street, and again there was this hoi polloi sort of party flat at one end and intellectual flats at the other. You'd have Annik hanging about, and when Ian was with Annik he'd turn into a vegetarian.

We'd be eating baby lambs from the kebab shop: 'Ugh, how can you? Ooh, I can't eat another baby lamb.'

It was great, but I had no idea that it was going to be the last thing that we did. It was like, 'Oh, this is going up another gear. This is fantastic, a lot more professional. It's better than *Unknown Pleasures*, songs are better and everything.' Ian was playing guitar, and that was something new, but no, no idea that there wasn't going to be any more of it.

Bernard Sumner: *Closer* got closer to the sound that I particularly wanted. I also enjoyed the experience because we were away in London. We stayed in a flat off Baker Street possibly. I enjoyed that as well, being in a flat; it was a bit like the Beatles in *Help!* We got treated well at the studio in Britannia Row. I remember them bringing sandwiches in and tea and stuff like that – wahey! Posh. The studio belonged to Pink Floyd: it's where they've done a lot of their big albums, and it had this sound system that sounded just like the best club you've ever been in.

Britannia Row was a really conducive place to work in. It had a much better sound than Strawberry, which was a seventies kind of design studio where they deaden everything down, take the room out of everything, which scientifically is very sound, but it never worked out because the machines weren't good enough to reproduce the room sounds. The idea with seventies sound was the whole studio would be completely dead and muffled, and you'd add the echo and reverb with machines, but the technology wasn't up to it, and that idea has been ditched.

Most of *Closer* we pumped out through some big speakers, and recorded the speakers to make it sound live. We did more overdubs, and I found that interesting. We actually recorded the instruments separately. Everyone would record together, but then you'd replace your original tape with a better sound. We had a bit more money, so we could work on the sound of the bass, the sound of the guitar. We started doing a lot more keyboard then, a lot of experimentation with Martin. We had more synthesizers.

There was a modular synthesizer in there that we used to make bass-drum sounds with.

The great thing about Martin was that he was truly experimental. It made it really fun in the studio because you weren't just recording it, 'Right, that's it. Off home, lads.' It was, 'What can we do with this sound, how can we change it?' For example, I had a string synthesizer and I said, 'Martin, I want it to sound like an old seventy-eight record.' I think what I really wanted was for it to sound like a Mellotron, but I didn't know what a Mellotron was, so he put it through a graphic equaliser, split all the bands up and put it through this thing called a Marshall Time Modulator and made it 'woooo, woooo', to try and copy what the seventy-eight record did, and stuff like that I found really interesting.

We used to work at night, because Martin was trying desperately to get us into taking drugs. He loved staying up, and I had some sleepers and used to take them during the day. I'd bring my sleeping bag into the studio and I'd just lay there all night. In fact, I did a lot of the keyboards for *Closer* while I was laid down, with this ARP Omni synthesizer. I was so relaxed: I was getting into sleepers, and it's there in the blood. Even though we got up about four o'clock in the afternoon, all evening we'd be super-relaxed, and I enjoyed the whole thing thoroughly, laid down on this couch at the back end of Britannia Row.

A weird thing happened one night. We were doing 'Decades'. We used to record it by direct injection, where you put the synth straight into the board, but we wanted some real-life ambience on it. Britannia Row had a huge games room, so Martin put some big speakers up in there. The track finished and we were just winding on to finish the tape, and there was an eerie, ghostly whistling of one of the tunes out of 'Decades', and there was no one in the room. If you go to those master tapes now, it might still be there. It really freaked us all out.

Stephen Morris: When we did the 'Atrocity Exhibition' on *Closer*, we discovered that if you put the syndrum through this very cheap

Japanese fuzz pedal, it would sound not unlike Jimi Hendrix, that sort of 'Star-Spangled Banner' feedback noise. If you listen to the 'Atrocity Exhibition', there's a sound that goes kind of all the way through it which is like someone slaughtering a pig, and that's me and Martin going mad on the syndrum.

Bernard Sumner: We felt like we were free down there. We didn't have day jobs then, we had a couple of weeks to record it in, and we had fun down in London. We were going out to clubs and restaurants. Living together as a band was quite a lot of fun, especially with Rob. Rob was a bit of a lazy slob, and he would always make us late, he'd never get out of bed. 'Come on, Rob, we've got to go to the studio.' – 'Fuck off, I'm not getting out of bed.'

He had two false teeth in the front and he'd have his teeth in teeth water by the side of the bed, so when you went in to try and get him up, he'd pick the glass up, take his teeth out and throw the teeth water over you. So one night to get our own back we had a roadie there, Ozzie, and he had two false teeth, so in the middle of the night we swapped Ozzie's teeth with Rob's teeth, so when he got up the next day he was like, 'Who's been pissing round with my teeth? They don't fit any more,' and he had these two massive teeth. We had really good laugh, a lot of practical jokes doing down.

Peter Hook: We were there all the time on *Closer*, which we weren't on *Unknown Pleasures* because we were working. So we were a lot more focused. We used to drive Martin mad, Bernard and I, Bernard in one corner, me in the other. He'd go, 'It's your go.' – 'It's my go? It's your go.' – 'I asked him about the hi-hat.' And Martin would go, 'What are you fucking whispering about?' – 'Nothing, Martin, nothing.' It was like that all the time, we drove him fucking berserk, and he used to stop the session and demand that Rob eject us. We used to really annoy him, it was great.

It was better being full-time cos you could concentrate, and we had a laugh cos you didn't have to go home at the end of the night, you went back to the flat. It was a good laugh most of the time. The only thing that was sad about it was Ian's illness, but he hid that so well most of the time. I'm only aware of one bad fit that he had when we were doing *Closer*, which is the one where he banged his head on the sink in Britannia Road and we found him in the toilet with his head cut open. The rest of it, it seemed like it was okay.

It was very interesting watching Ian with Annik. We were just taking the piss out of him all the time, putting cornflakes in the bed and just japes, daft, stupid things, you know, but she used to get so wound up. There was one night I remember: we had a glass pane in the door, and we'd been taking the piss out of him, throwing beer at them while they were in bed or summat daft, and Annik fucking chased us out, and we ran in our flat, held the door shut, and she was fucking kicking the door with her dressing gown on, like a fucking bloke would do. Fucking hell, she used to go mad.

Annik Honoré: Rob just saw women as trouble-makers, and it's true that mostly the rock business is very male, and so they liked to make jokes – more because I was a foreigner than because I was a girl. I just think they thought that if girls are around, they wouldn't concentrate so well on the music and on working. I was the only girl around, but I don't think I was in the way.

I felt very privileged to be able to be close to them when they were recording *Closer*, but I was really trying to make myself as tiny as possible, which is the way I am naturally anyway. I think artists need to be able to create the way they want, and it is such a privilege to see people think or record or act that when they are doing it, they really should be left in peace. When I was watching the recording of *Closer*, it was mainly at night-time. I was working during the day at the embassy and I would come afterwards, and I was staying with them in that apartment.

I was just sitting there watching Ian singing. The image I would have in mind was Ian was very tired and very quiet, and every time he would sing he would turn his back and put his hand on his head or on his eyes and he would stand apart from the others, from

Martin and Rob and the band, just to be in himself. He was look-ing at his shoes and really trying to find something coming from inside, and he was extremely, extremely quiet and very soft-spoken.

Peter Hook: We were only in the studio for three weeks, and we decided to bring our wives and girlfriends down in the middle, which was a complete debacle. Oh my God, what a cock-up that was. I think they all went back the same night. Oh, that was terri-ble, that was a mistake, that one, fucking hell, man. Every one of us had a fight with our respective girlfriend, and they all stormed off on the train, probably because of the guilt of Ian being there with Annik. We had to cover it up, and he was living in the other flat and . . . oh God.

Then, of course, we had Ian's illness and Annik hanging round all the time, which we were really annoyed about because we didn't want her round, we just wanted it to be us. We were going to have a day off and we'd all been out drinking the night before, and Rob was late picking Lesley up from the station. Oh, fucking hell, man, it went off proper. I had a massive row with Iris, and they all went home really fucking annoyed.

Lesley Gilbert: That was awful, another horrible time. It was when that whole Annik thing was going on. I was really sorry I went in the end: it upset mine and Rob's relationship for a short while because there was all this trying to protect Ian, who wasn't very well. He was trying to get Ian and Hooky to calm down, because Ian had Debbie on his case, and Hooky had Iris on his case because Ian had Annik there, and Iris thought that was all wrong. It all felt nasty.

Annik Honoré: The songs I remember were the slow ones, like 'Decades' and 'The Eternal'. He was always recording on his own: the group would be recording the music at a different time. I remember he had one fit during the recording, otherwise he was pretty tired from taking all the drugs, so he was not well. He had lots of them to take – tons of pills which he had in little boxes. He was always very embarrassed about taking all the pills because most of the time it would make him go like drugged-up, so he was very subdued and drowsy.

He had that book where he was writing the lyrics, but he would never discuss them or show them. It was really private. It's afterwards, when I had a tape of *Closer* and I started listening to them, then I understood what it was all about, and it was very sad what he was singing about, very, very sad. I can't say that every song he was singing was about himself. I think he was using his own feelings, but his songs were a lot more than just himself. He could push himself outside because he was not a down-to-earth person. He was writing about thoughts and dreams and feelings he had, just poetry and a bit surreal.

Bernard Sumner: In Macclesfield there was a little Down's syndrome kid that lived in a house with a garden. Ian grew up round there, and the kid would never be able to come out of the house, and the kid's whole universe was the house to the garden wall. Ian said many years later that he moved back to Macclesfield and walked past the house, and by chance he saw the kid. Ian had grown up from being five to twenty, twenty-two years old; the kid still looked exactly the same, and his universe was still the house and the garden, and that's what 'The Eternal' was about.

Martin Hannett: It was bit fraught, from the point of view that Ian was having lots of fits, but basically very workmanlike. All the little bits and pieces were taken care of.

Bernard Sumner: His problems accumulated gradually, one by one, as if some conspiracy had been waged against him. Because of his illness he couldn't have carried on for any more than a year and a half. He did have epilepsy, but he also had it very, very, very strong, big grand mal fits. No messing about. He couldn't pick his daughter up, he couldn't drive a car, he had to be careful at railway stations that he didn't stand too near the edge – a lot of things he couldn't do, and that's very difficult for a young man in his twenties to come to terms with.

I remember talking to him one night, one very late night in the *Closer* sessions. We were working very late with Martin at Britannia Road in Islington, and Ian was saying to me that doing this album felt very strange because he felt that all his words were writing themselves and that he'd always in the past struggled to complete a song. Like he'd have the start, but he'd always struggled to complete it. But now he just had the whole song straight off.

He said that at the same time he had this terrible claustrophobic feeling that he was in a whirlpool and drowning and he was being pulled down, and I don't really know what he meant by that but I've often thought about it. I remember him that night having a fit in Britannia Road and falling down the stairs. I think they had a spiral staircase there, he just fell down the stairs and cut his head open. The worst thing for us was that we felt so helpless; it was like watching someone suffer and knowing there's nothing you can do. Obviously it was worse for him, but we just felt so impotent about it.

Peter Hook: 'Love Will Tear Us Apart', when you analyse the lyric, is so heartfelt and obviously so painful, because I think everybody adult is going to go through a relationship or an episode like that where you feel cut off and a stranger to a lover. I find the lyrics very painful now that I know what Ian was going through, so I view it in a completely different light.

Stephen Morris: I don't think he really knew what he wanted. About a month before his first suicide attempt, he told me on the phone he was packing in the group and him and Debbie were going to go off and live in Holland, and open a bookshop. Which really surprised me.

Deborah Curtis (from *Touching from a Distance*): When Ian told me that the band were going to stop gigging for twelve months, I wasn't pleased. It was a sensible enough decision, but I knew that it would not be carried through and believed it to be a mere pacifier, designed to calm Ian down. Sure enough, an American tour was soon announced – not only that, but a string of British gigs were arranged in preparation.

Paul Morley: With *Closer*, I get the feeling by then it was about his life, and previously he hadn't necessarily been so direct about his life. The reason why we didn't all notice the reality of the situation was because we half thought he was still in that mode of not being direct. Vocally, he seemed to be playing with what we now look upon with vocalists and singers and performers and personalities as playing games with their identity and what they are and how they want to present themselves. By then he was certainly potentially a major rock star and was having fun with that idea, I'm sure, hence the crooning and the suavity.

It was just his life and everything had collapsed in on itself. There was no real separation between theatre and his life, between what he felt and what he was doing onstage. You got the feeling that there was definitely a tip, a switch. Before those last few months, his life fed into the music and his image and his words. Then it turned around and the music was the centre of his existence, and he would walk out of the music into his life. He had to come out of his music to go into his life, and his life was falling apart and he would have preferred to have stayed in the music.

Peter Saville: With Joy Division, a typical kind of pattern was being followed. They were in Britannia Row making their next album. I don't know if they knew what it would be called; they certainly hadn't finished the tracks. At some point while they were there at Britannia Row, Rob had the foresight to think, 'Well, we'd better go and see Peter about a cover. Who knows, it could take him weeks, it could take him months, so let's go and get him on that now.'

I was on Portobello Road, in a division of Virgin, and I had my own studio there, and Rob brought them round and said, 'They're making the album. We need a cover.' And I said, 'Well, do they have anything?' – 'No.' And by this time, through perhaps my other work with Factory, a kind of an understanding had developed between myself and Tony and Rob: that Peter would have something. I had my own things which I wanted to do or draw attention to, and I think Rob expected that I would have something to show to them rather than they give to me.

I was very nervous. I mean, all I had to go off was what they'd given me for *Unknown Pleasures*, and I said, 'Rob, I don't know if I've got anything.' And he was insistent: 'You must have something.' I had great respect for them, there was the growing aura of Joy Division. I was a bit scared. I didn't want to take something from a book or the shelf and say, 'I like this,' and them kind of look at me and think, 'Well, you're just hopeless.'

But Rob pressured me, and there was something I was excited about. There was a photographic expression of neoclassicism by a man called Bernard Pierre Wolff in a French magazine called *Zoom*. Under Rob's pressure, I took the magazine off the shelf and said, 'Well, if you actually want to know what I feel something about today, it's this,' and I opened the magazine and put it on the drawing board and stepped away. And I didn't know what to expect. I kind of expected that they would say, 'Well, yeah, okay, but what else have you got?'

They were all there, and they all crowded around the drawing board and turned the pages, and they were intrigued. The nice thing about Joy Division at that stage was that the natural hierarchies that ultimately crystallise hadn't crystallised yet. They were still four friends in something together; nobody was more important than anyone else. It's nice that stage with groups, when there's just a group of people in something together, each one doing what they can do, and each part being crucial to the whole, and Joy Division were in that state.

So they just looked at the pictures and turned the pages, and they seemed to like them, which was a relief. And I think they pointed at one and said, 'We want this for the cover.' It was still the days of tearing things out of magazines and photocopying them, but by this point I knew that we couldn't do that, and I said, 'Well, let's see if we can get this picture.' It was time to do things properly. I looked at what they'd chosen, and it was fascinating. I probably said, 'Are you sure?' I knew what I wanted to do. I had my own work to do. I was delighted that their interest in the Bernard Pierre Wolff photographs was going to provide the opportunity for me to do something with those pictures. And that was it, and they left.

At some point it came to pass that it was going to be called *Closer*, and all of the same conditions applied. 'Does anybody want the name on the front?' – 'Well, no, not really. If you want to.' – 'Does anybody want "Joy Division" on the front?' – 'No, not really. If you want to.' So I put things where I wanted to put them. I didn't want to put 'Joy Division' on the front, it was vulgar. '*Closer*' was interesting, and it needed it: the composition needed it, the landscape image needed it.

I wanted to touch the feeling of an etching, like a late-eighteenth-, early-nineteenth-century architectural print, which were usually deep-impression prints – gravure or something like that – so I wanted the soft paper that they would use for that kind of print. And it needed an inscription. The font is something I'd found in a reference book by a German professor: he was fairly convinced that these particular letters were the earliest form of serif lettering, second-century lapidary lettering, which means stone-cut, and he'd traced some off a column and then completed the rest of the alphabet for the edification of typographers.

I converted the font into the means by which I could set titling with it. And it needed something, it needed '*Closer*' on the front, and it was interesting. Closer, closer – the ambiguity of the title and the juxtaposition of the title and the image were nice. I seem to remember thinking that the music was a bit heavy. It didn't have that immediacy of *Unknown Pleasures*, it was a move on from that. I don't know if I listened to it that much. I couldn't tell you the track listing. I mean, no one ever put the fucking titles on the covers, you can't know what the tracks are.

Jon Wozencroft: One's a black album, one's a white album. The interesting thing is that until the last minute *Unknown Pleasures* was visually a white album. Peter Saville decided at the last minute that it'd be more powerful if the image was reversed out of black rather than black onto a white background. That's a great design decision, but it turned the record into something else.

There is no doubt that there is something of the end point in *Closer*. I'm sure Ian wasn't planning his escape or anything like that, but he was gifted in a way that he would know this wasn't going to last for ever. Even the contemporary reports that have since been documented say his ambition was actually to move to Europe and open a bookshop and become a studio-based artist rather than a performing band, which might have happened quite organically – a Brian Eno-type figure.

Paul Morley: Ian did get taken over or went through changes, because in some ways *Unknown Pleasures* is still a guy who likes Ballard and Burroughs. It's an album about a young man trying to go out into the world instead of retreating into his world, which is what he did on *Closer*. *Unknown Pleasures* is the 'Wouldn't it be great to be an artist, wouldn't it be great to be like Burroughs and Bowie and Ballard and Iggy?' Then *Closer* was the artist, that was where he joined those ranks and therefore pulled *Unknown Pleasures* with him.

Annik Honoré: They were making this incredible music, also partly thanks to Martin, who was really helping them create a very specific sound. None of them realised how strong and powerful the music was. It was just chemistry. It's just like a love story: each individual is nothing on their own, and when they are together, it's enormous. That's what was Joy Division: the music and Ian, and when they were recording, Martin. The chemistry of these five together was absolutely astounding, so, so strong.

They made it very naturally and candidly, and that's why it's so good, because they were not self-conscious about it. I think it was coming from deep within them, and they so much wanted to do it. I don't know if Ian wanted to make history, I don't think it was like that. I think it's because he had this huge, huge talent and it was coming out when he was singing or when he was onstage. But it was spontaneous, it was not calculated, you know, not artificial; they just had the light, the spirit.

JUDGED PURELY ON MY OWN TERMS, AND NOT TO BE ~~INTER~~ ~~AS~~ INTERPRETED AS AN OPINION OR REFLECTION OF MASS MEDIA OR PUBLIC ~~TASTE~~ TASTE, BUT A CRITICISM OF MY OWN ESOTERIC, ~~AND~~ AND ELITIST MIND OF WHICH THE MYSTERIES ~~ARE~~ ~~~~ OF LIFE ARE VERY FEW AND BESIDE WHICH THE GRACE OF GOD HAS DEEMED TO INDICATE IN A VISION THE TRUE NATURE OF ALL THINGS, PLUS THE FACT THAT EVERYONE ELSE ~~IS~~ ARE A SNEAKY, TAKING LOAD OF TOSSERS, DECREE THAT THIS LP IS A ~~~~ DISASTER. I.K.CURT

Ian Curtis's handwritten note to Rob Gretton after the *Closer* sessions, March/April 1980 (Courtesy of Lesley Gilbert, Benedict Gretton and Laura Gretton)

12

APRIL – MAY 1980

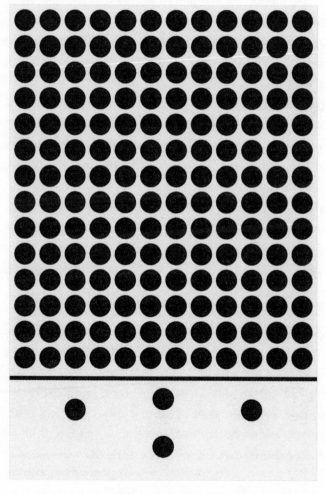

'Joy Division', 1998 screen-print on paper 150 x 100cm (Courtesy
of Herald St, London)

- 2 April 1980: the Moonlight Club, London
- 3 April 1980: the Moonlight Club, London
- 4 April 1980: the Rainbow Theatre, London
- 4 April 1980: the Moonlight Club, London

Paul Morley: You'd see them at the Rainbow, and then at the same time you could see them at the Moonlight on the same day. It was moving incredibly fast, it all seemed to be accelerating incredibly fast.

Bernard Sumner: Ian then started having fits onstage. One gig, we were supporting the Stranglers at the Rainbow. I remember we were doing the 'Atrocity Exhibition'. He always used to dance onstage, but we finished the track and he was still dancing. He just spun round and round till he crashed into the drums, and then ended up on the stage having a fit, and by this time he'd had quite a few.

So we carried him off, and then there were people in the corridors: 'What's going on? Oh, it's that guy that has the fits.' And we put him in the dressing room, and he went, 'Leave me alone, leave me alone.' We left him for a bit to give him a bit of space, and then when we opened the door he was just in tears, and we didn't know what to do. He was our mate, we wanted to help him, but we just didn't have a solution to that particular problem. It was really sad.

Stephen Morris: We did stupid things, like the Stranglers' benefit gig while we were doing three nights at the Moonlight. He had a fit after the Stranglers gig and then carried on to the Moonlight. 'Can we not just . . .' – but we never even thought, and he honestly never said, 'Oh, I'm not up to it.' He wouldn't have said that. He was just, 'No, I'm fine, I'm fine, yeah.' That was the beginning of the end, because he couldn't do without being in a band, and he couldn't pretend. Because of that, he would be drained.

Terry Mason: The Good Friday gig with the Stranglers, Ian had a major seizure there. We then rushed across town over to the

Moonlight Club to do this Factory night. No one in that building really came to see any of the support acts; they were there to
see Joy Division, they were there to see Ian. He's had one seizure
at the Rainbow, but still – his commitment. We went over to the
Moonlight, and Ian just crumpled onstage. At that point there
should have been really large alarm bells going, but no one seemed
to hear any. The world had got out of control.

The film that was one of Ian's favourites at the time was *Eraserhead*,
David Lynch, and it's a very strange, disturbing film. The hero of the
movie stares at a radiator, which opens up and there's this girl with
rather big cheeks who's dancing, doing a little act inside the radiator, and there's stuff falling from the ceiling – the film's in black and
white, so we don't know what the stuff is. And that was like Ian: he
was there in his little show, and like the woman in the radiator, he'd
lost control of what his show was about in the end.

Tony Wilson: Ian's performance was always electric, but it would
suddenly get even more electric. You wouldn't see Ian about to go
off, but you would see Bernard and Hooky and Stephen begin to
look at each other onstage, and I began to recognise it from that.
One of the most profound performances was after they'd supported
the bloody Stranglers at the Rainbow and then come across to do
Factory by Moonlight, which was some crazy idea that we'd had –
which I should apologise for because it did set Ian off.

Lindsay Reade: The more the gigging got intense, the more the fits
were taking place. But this may have a parallel with his private life
as well, because the two things were amplifying together in terms of
stress. The stress of performing, of being on the road: the demands
on his time were getting much bigger with each month or week.
Plus his private life was disintegrating because he'd got the stress of
having a baby, plus the fact that his marriage was in pieces and he
loved another woman. He was an honourable guy, he didn't want to
hurt anyone's feelings and he wanted to do the best for everybody,
so you've got two things literally tearing him apart.

I actually think he couldn't go on with it. He must have felt he couldn't go on with it. It was going to reach a point, and it did that Easter. He'd had the worst fit ever onstage, in front of more people than had ever witnessed anything like that, and he must have privately thought, 'This can't go on.' That was at the Rainbow. That must have been really humiliating, for all those people to see that. People think it's glamorous – rock star falling into drum kit, wow – but he wouldn't have felt like that. He would have felt really ashamed, and not in control.

Bernard Sumner: After that, he had serious doubts about his future. Eventually, he decided he wanted to leave the band. Quite understandably. Who wants that to happen to them onstage? We came to an agreement. He wanted to leave the band, he wanted to buy a corner shop down in Portsmouth, he wanted to go off and write a book. We didn't want him to because we'd put so much work into it, but we understood his predicament. The agreement was that he wouldn't do any gigs for a year, that we'd just write.

But around this time he would agree to anything you told him. Ian was very open to suggestion at this time. He'd made up his mind to leave the band. He was going to do something completely different, and we said, 'No, don't do that. We'll just record, take the pressure off.' And without any change of expression, he'd say, 'Yeah, okay.' If we'd have told him to go and cut three of his fingers off, I think he would have done it. He was so suggestible. He really wanted one of us to come up and tell him what to do, and that would have been his way out.

Paul Morley: The whole point of Ian is that after a while it seems that he was always on the edge of life. There were obviously moments when you just assumed it was part of the choreography, as anarchic as that choreography had become, and then selfishly you enjoyed it because it was an event, it was a happening, it was a thing, and he'd given it. He was really laying his life on the line for this music, and it elevated everything and there seemed to be a kind of sacrifice.

You felt that he was really entering into what Iggy Pop would do – it seemed to be his equivalent of slashing his chest – really giving you something, giving you a heck of a performance. Selfishly you'd deem it a kind of extreme entertainment. At that time there'd be Public Image, there'd be Throbbing Gristle, there'd be Gang of Four: that tearing apart of clichés suddenly seemed to have ideological fervour and purpose, and Joy Division seemed to be part of that. There was a real reason for this, and it went beyond just fashion and style and music.

Because everything had happened so suddenly through punk. A new band would appear – it would be Siouxsie, it would be the Pistols, it would be the Clash, it would be Wire, it would be constant unbelievable novelty – and I guess you felt that within that you had to keep beating that, sustaining that, otherwise people might lose interest.

- 8 April 1980: Derby Hall, Bury

Stephen Morris: After the first suicide attempt, before that gig in Bury, I remember saying to Rob – cos it was a Saturday and the gig was on a Monday – that we ought to pull it, and Rob got really angry about it. I was really shocked when we did that gig. Also, when he said he wanted to go and live in Holland and do a bookshop, it was us that persuaded him not to. Again, he'd been very pliable. If he'd stuck to what he wanted, he'd probably still be alive today.

Bernard Sumner: Ian had just tried to commit suicide for the first time. He took a drug overdose and he told me afterwards that he'd not gone through with it: he panicked and phoned the ambulance only because he'd heard that if you don't take enough of them, then it can cause brain damage. I didn't really believe him, I thought, 'Oh, it's just a cry for help.' They put him under the care of a psychiatrist: I think he was actually in hospital. We already had a gig booked. If we booked a gig, it never got cancelled, so we had to do it.

Tony brought Ian down to the gig. He was in no fit state to play, and he should have still been in hospital. We went onstage, and it was Simon Topping and Alan Hempsall, and we had to blag them or bribe them to go up and sing a few songs with us, because we were like, 'Shit, we shouldn't be here, but the audience are here. Let's just go on and play. Ian can sing a couple and then come off, Alan can go on, sing a couple, then Ian can sing a couple.' But it didn't go down too well with the audience, because they didn't know that he'd just come out of hospital.

Peter Hook: Rob didn't want to pull it, so we decided to get the other singers in, which we thought was quite exciting. I mean, no one really thought about how Ian would feel about that. I can imagine he was decimated really, because if they'd carried on with another bass player, I'd have fucking battered them. I'd have said, 'No, you don't, piss off,' but Ian was so nice that he seemed to let Rob think it was a good idea to let the others play so we could do it, so we went ahead, and it was stupid.

Alan Hempsall: I'd been out for the afternoon and got a phone call, and it was Bernard, and he just said, 'Oh, Ian's ill, and we've got a gig tonight. We were wondering if you'd like to stand in for him.' So I was like, 'Well, sure, yeah, why not? It sounds great to me.' So I got picked up and driven over to what was the Derby Hall in Bury, and I'd been told Ian was ill, but I turned up to find him there. I thought, 'Well, that's a little bit strange.' He seemed okay, but I said, 'Well, they've asked me up here to sing a little bit, so let's go for it.'

It was quite unusual, because we had the Minny Pops on the bill with us from Holland and they came on and did a full set. Now this gig had been sold out some way in advance and there were tickets exchanging hands outside for about £5 each, and that was a lot of money at the time. Section 25 were due on next and did four numbers, and then they did 'Girls Don't Count', which was their big single at the time and was our cue to come onstage and join them.

So as 'Girls Don't Count' starts up, Hooky comes onstage with Steve and Bernard to join the three members of Section 25, so at this point we've got two bass players, two drummers, a guitarist with a keyboard. Larry, the singer, did the words to 'Girls Don't Count', while me and Simon Topping from A Certain Ratio came on and did some kind of weird backing-vocal thing to it, but then that was their signal. At the end of that, Section 25 walked off with Simon, leaving me and the other three remaining members of Joy Division.

We then launch into 'Digital' and 'Love Will Tear Us Apart'. Ian had said in the dressing room before we went on, 'I'll come on and do two slow numbers because I feel okay enough just to do a couple of slow ones, and that'll be it.' So once I'd done 'Love Will Tear Us Apart', that was my cue to walk off the stage and Ian's cue to walk on, and I believe it was 'The Eternal' and 'Decades' – he did those two. And then he walked off, I walked back on with Simon Topping and the rest of Section 25, and we did a cover version of 'Sister Ray' by the Velvet Underground.

So there's a certain amount of confusion by this stage, and the whole thing from Section 25 going on to us coming off had been about forty minutes, but the audience, I think, felt a little bit cheated or certainly didn't realise what had been going on. There was a big Victorian glass chandelier suspended above the stage and somebody threw a bottle or a glass and it hit the chandelier square on, and as we were walking off we just got covered in shards of broken glass that showered down from the ceiling.

Lindsay Reade: I have very clear memories of standing higher up than the floor and watching this crowd, who were obviously beginning to get more and more uneasy, not to say unhappy. Then I saw the first bottle being thrown, which didn't particularly worry me because I'd been to the Electric Circus and thought this is par for the course. But then my attention went to Rob Gretton's face, and he looked really angry, like it was an eruption – Mount Vesuvius. Without a moment's hesitation he jumped off the stage straight into the crowd and then it just erupted.

Alan Hempsall: Everybody just started throwing things, and we got bundled into the dressing room. Tony and Alan Erasmus were there barring our exit because Hooky fancied a bit of a fight. Nobody else did, of course, but I think Hooky was trying to rouse everybody, going, 'Come on, there's enough of us, we can take them.' But I decided that discretion was the better part of valour, as did most of the other people in the dressing room.

We just got covered in broken glass and there was broken bottles being smashed against the dressing-room door. The roadies, Terry and Twinny, waded in, Rob waded in as well. Twinny got clocked over the back of the head with a pint pot and had to get taken to the local accident and emergency. Lindsay, Tony's wife at the time, drove him there and he had to have his head stitched up. It all ended in trial and tribulation, and so I think a lesson was learned then: it was like, 'We won't do that again in a hurry.'

Peter Hook: The people that caused the trouble at Bury couldn't get in because they didn't have any money, but Rob let them in – Mr Philanthropist Gretton. Ian was too ill to do it really; we just decided or he just decided that he'd come on for two numbers, and that was the worst I'd ever seen him then. We did the gig and he just went off, and it turned into a riot. Ian was really upset about it, and I remember catching me then girlfriend at the time pissed, giving Ian a load of shit, and I had to grab hold of her and tell her to fuck off, so it was really bad.

Bernard Sumner: The whole thing just kicked off. It turned into a complete fiasco, a riot. It was horrible, and of course it wasn't great for Ian because he immediately thought, 'All this is my fault,' and burst out in tears, he just took all the blame himself. Really it shouldn't have been happening in the first place – you've got to draw the line somewhere. He just broke down again, went back to hospital. He was in a complete state. We should never have got him out of the hospital, it was a totally fucking idiotic thing to do.

Lindsay Reade: Twinny and I had to sit in casualty, and the instigators of this thing, the other side, were in casualty as well. So it was like the Christmas Day truce, when the cigarettes were shared between the opposing sides. What these two were saying was that they'd had enough: they'd only seen A Certain Ratio last week, and they hadn't paid good money for a bloody Joy Division gig to have to watch Ratio again – because of course Simon Topping was singing at that point when they chucked the bottle.

The worst thing was that it really upset Ian, but I don't think any of us realised how upsetting it was to Ian that this happened. My other clear memory of that night is what Ian told me a day or two later. He said he was standing in the wings of the stage watching the band play without him, and he just had this feeling that he was looking down and they were carrying on without him, and that they were going to keep carrying on without him.

- 11 April 1980: the Factory I, Manchester

Deborah Curtis (from *Touching from a Distance*): When Joy Division played the reopened Factory Club, it was the first time I'd seen Ian since he had gone to live with Tony Wilson. The atmosphere was strained, but Ian did make an effort. All the same, nothing was said about what had happened or how long he intended to stay at Tony's. It was crowded in the bar and I had hoped for a more intimate meeting, but after a short while it was time for him to join the rest of the band.

When he left I went to talk to the other girls. No one had rung me to see how I was – I suppose because they were embarrassed. Yet now they began to tell me what had happened in London while *Closer* was being recorded. It was then I found out that while Ian allowed me to worry about money and accommodation, two flats had been booked. The majority had been squashed into one flat, while Ian and Annik enjoyed the luxury of space for themselves. I was told he behaved in an obsequious manner to her and she in turn ordered him about like an obedient little dog.

I had a few more drinks and by the end of the set I was beside myself with jealousy, humiliation and anger. To say I was miserable is to put it mildly. Ian was already downstairs. I followed him down and tried to attract his attention. I don't know if he knew what was coming or he had already decided to ignore me, but I played right into his hands and threw my handbag at him in a temper. He carried on talking. Someone whispered to me that Ian had intended to come home with me that night but had consequently changed his mind.

The frustration was intolerable. I was desperate for any kind of communication, I was still too much in love to think about ending the marriage for myself. Tony was heard to tell Ian to 'rise above it'. I drove away from the club alone.

Bob Dickinson: The thing about Ian was that he was the focal point for the band, and his vocals and his lyrics are incredibly vulnerable. I was always interested in the way that he wanted to use this very strange American accent and pitched his voice very low, and it sounded to me very ethereal, like a character from a film, something that floats in front of you and isn't quite there.

And at the same time he's got this charisma. Hooky has charisma, Barney has charisma, the whole band has a joint charisma, but Ian's charisma was unnerving and unsettling because of the physical things that he did onstage. Once you'd seen him, once he'd done that thing where he shook himself into a frenzy, into a kind of dance that was not a dance, it was a disturbing kind of fit, once he'd done that and you'd seen it, you knew that the next number you saw or the next occasion where you saw them, he was going to take you in that direction. You didn't know where you were going to end up, you didn't know what was going to happen to him. It was unsettling to watch him do it, it was thrilling to watch him do it, but you just didn't know where it was going to take you. I think that kind of charismatic power was what really captured my attention. It still grabs me when I see them on film, I still find that really unsettling to watch. Every show was a unique journey.

Iggy cut himself up with bits of glass, didn't he? Deliberately. Ian must have known about that. Watching Ian was a bit like watching someone like Marina Abramović or Ron Athey, performance artists who deliberately lacerate themselves, cut themselves, bleed for an audience, except with Ian he didn't bleed, but he sacrificed something of himself for you, whether you liked it or not. You didn't know whether it would happen; it often did happen, and occasionally it went wrong.

I saw Joy Division at the Russell Club later on, and Ian was drinking beer – a lot of beer – onstage, and he went into one of these dance routines, these fits, and he knocked himself out, he collapsed, he just blacked out and fell over onstage. I'd never seen him do that before, I never saw that happen, but I thought, 'Well, I can understand why that's happened: he's worked himself up into a frenzy and he's gone beyond the point where his body, his mind can stand it.'

The interesting thing was that the band kept playing, and Ian just woke up, and I was quite concerned about him because when he fell down he fell off the stage, he fell off and he bumped his head, and I thought he could have seriously injured himself. But he just got up, got back onstage and went on with the next number, and so there was always this worry that you'd be witnessing a show where he might go beyond the beyond, because it was going beyond what anyone else was doing at the time, but even he had limits.

There was that kind of awareness of performance art, and I suppose it came from an art-school sensibility among some bands (not all of them). It was something that went through punk rock, in the sense that singers especially or performers knew that in order to shock audiences, they could do something shocking: they dressed up in a shocking way, they could behave in a shocking way.

I'm not sure whether Ian knew about it, I just think he sensed it, and it's something that he did because of this character that he became when he was onstage, and this character which didn't have a name was the storyteller in the songs, the narrator, the dancer. He was like his own puppet, because he moved like a puppet, and you felt his vulnerability in that puppet-like movement, and the sense you got that he was potentially hurting himself and potentially going to suffer was something that you were really aware of.

Excerpt from hypnotism tape:
Bernard: You hire your services. What as? What services?
Ian: Trained . . . soldier.
Bernard: How do you feel?
Ian: Very weak?
Bernard: Why do you feel weak?
Ian: Feverish, very, very hot. Very . . . resigned to it.
Bernard: You're resigned to it? What?
Ian: The end of it. It's easy . . . I suppose.
Bernard: The end of your life? Would you say you've had a good life?
Ian: That's not for me to . . . to judge.

Bernard Sumner: Ian had fallen out with Debbie and just needed somewhere to stay, so he stayed with me for a week, which wasn't great for him because I was still an insomniac and I was staying up till five in the morning. I remember coming back from rehearsals one day and we took a short-cut through the graveyard, and I said to him, 'You're lucky, your name could be on one of those stones if you'd succeeded the other week.' I said, 'You really, really want to think about it. It's not worth ending up like that, you know.'

And he was like, 'Yeah, right, yeah' – no sort of connection in the response. He'd made his mind up, I think. I don't know, because he kept those thoughts hermetically sealed off from those around him. He had his public agenda and he had his private agenda. I'm not saying he was a secretive person – he wasn't – but he was a very determined person, and if he was going to do something, he was going to do it, and if he was going to do it, he certainly wouldn't discuss it with you.

I was interested in hypnotism. I read a book on hypnotic regression: that sometimes if you've got problems in your present, then regression could unlock problems that had occurred either in your childhood or – if you believed in it – in your previous lives. And we were just talking about it one day at rehearsals, and Ian was like, 'Oh, that sounds interesting, I'd really like to try that.' So I said, 'Why don't we try it now?' So we tried it, and he went under very, very easy, and we came up with these experiences. He told me about when he was a kid in his cot, and he could describe the wallpaper, and then he went back further to previous lives. We just did it for a laugh, but that was months before. And then when he stayed at my house, I said, 'You know what we did at rehearsal?' He said, 'Well, you've told me what happened, but I can't remember anything about it.' And I said, 'Well, do you think it might help you in any way if, you know, you experienced some of the things?' He said, 'Yeah, I'd like to try it.' 'Well, what I'll do this time is, I'll record it on a cassette.'

I hypnotised him again, and he went back to exactly the same experiences that he'd had at the rehearsal room. One was a kind of pagan battlefield, which was just pure horror, bodies and limbs everywhere, horror flashing past his eyes. Then there was blackness. One I distinctly remember was about the Hundred Years War between Britain and France, and he'd been captured and was kept in a jail in Spain, of all places, and spent his days there, locked up. And the other was in Victorian times, where he was in a library of some sort surrounded by books.

What struck me was, it was so easy to put him in a trance. One of his solutions to a problem was rage, but not in a horrible macho kind of way. It was fire, he was a human blowtorch, and he'd burn you out of his way with his rage. Now his other solution was that someone would come along and play God, tell him what to do. And you can't do that with a person's life. Just before he died, we were loath to advise him, because whatever we said, he would have just done it, and you can't be responsible for another person's future, and their past as well.

Tony Wilson: It got weirder because of Ian's epilepsy, and then Ian took the first overdose. Everyone tried to help; he even went to stay with Barney for a while. He stayed with me and Lindsay for a week. I'm not sure how much help that was because I think Lindsay was as barmy as bloody Ian. In fact, I've still got my one effort to help that week: I still have a little blue piece of paper I put into my collected Yeats for Ian to look at some particular Yeats poems and stuff.

Lindsay Reade: I said to Tony, 'Maybe you should suggest that he come and stay at our house,' because we lived in Charlesworth, a very small village in the country near Glossop. I thought if his problem is two women, then the best thing is to remove yourself from both women and have some time out. I didn't think that Ian would accept because I didn't really know Ian that well then. He'd never even been to our house, I think, but he accepted.

It felt as though we were just like brother and sister. It felt as though we were members of a family who weren't normally accustomed to being together. He was chain-smoking all the time. Now, I wouldn't be able to tolerate that, but then it didn't bother me at all. So there was this comfortable kind of familiarity: we didn't speak all that much, we just played records and hung out, ate meals and spent the day together, not doing anything very much.

We didn't go out. We should have done. We just sat in the lounge, listening to music: Lou Reed, Iggy Pop, those kinds of things. I felt he was very depressed. It began to get to me, because I've always operated on a kind of low-grade depression myself. If I'm with someone who is, then I can quite rapidly go along with them, and as the week progressed that's what started to happen, that I started to feel depressed as well. We were both depressed by the end of the week.

Tony Wilson: We tried to help but we didn't. Yeah, we didn't see it coming, we didn't see it coming. The fact that I left poor Ian and poor Lindsay at home for the entire week while I went to work because I had a day job, and they drove each other nuts, in the sweetest possible way, I suppose, that was hardly very sensible of me, was it? If you look back and you think how stupid, the fact that none of us really saw it coming, the fact that we were, you know, it's twenty-four hours from Tulsa, isn't it? Twenty-four hours from the plane to America.

Annik Honoré: He tried to commit suicide, so it was obvious then that he wasn't well, and he was saying so in the lyrics. He appeared very depressed during the recording of *Closer*, although in a letter he said how much he loved those three weeks of London because we could see each other regularly. But otherwise he appeared so very tired and depressed from his disease more than anything else. There's no way out, there's no escape. That's probably what was depressing him the most. I had that tape of *Closer*, I had a Walkman and I was listening to it all the time and trying to understand, because I never saw any written lyrics. I could only understand from my hearing 'I like watching the leaves as they fall.' The 'Atrocity Exhibition' and all the lyrics on the LP are really depressing and sad, and it's surprising nobody would pay attention. Maybe for the others it was more like literature, which it was in a way, but it was also coming from his depression.

Tony Wilson: I was getting the train to London from Piccadilly for Granada, and as I drove to the station I saw Ian and Annik hand-in-hand traipsing the side streets near the station, and I said hello to them, and it was obvious they were walking the streets all night together. They got on the train, and I let them be together till Macclesfield, and then after we left Macclesfield and Ian had got off I went to join Annik.

We got into conversation, and Annik expressed how worried she was, how fearful she was. And I'm all kind of, 'No, no, it's just art, it's just an album, for God's sake. It's wonderful, I know, but it's nothing to be frightened of.' And she said, 'Don't you understand, Tony? When he says, "I take the blame," he means it.' And I went, 'No, no, no, no, it's just art.' How fucking stupid can you get?

Annik Honoré: I was really worried about his health and about his mood. I told Tony, but there were not so many people I could tell really. I was surprised he didn't realise, and they probably would think, 'Oh, this girl, she's taking things too dramatically.' But the thing is, I went on holiday abroad with the tape of the record, and I was reading *The Idiot* at the time, Dostoevsky. I was in Egypt, and it really made sense that this record was tragic.

Listening over and over and trying to understand everything he was saying, then I was absolutely sure this record was just tragic and dramatic. I was crying; even now if I listen to it I cry. I don't know if it's me or the mood of the record, but I kept crying listening to his songs, because you can tell he's suffering, he's taking it too seriously, he's really putting himself into those songs. But they were a rock band, and so you just carry on, and when you're so young I don't think you realise how serious it is.

Terry Mason: The lyrics weren't published. They were very ambiguous, and particularly helped by the band saying you can read your own interpretations into it. If people would have seen them, I think there would have been alarm bells going about Ian. You look at them now and you think the man had serious demons inside his head. They're not right, they're Stephen King's darkest moments. It's all done with hindsight, of course, but you think, 'God, what on earth was he thinking, what was going through his mind?'

I wouldn't have seen Ian in the music business for that much longer. I would have seen him as a writer of prose, and I think that's what he possibly would have wanted, to get away from it. He'd got the stepping stone by being in the band and he was an incredibly talented writer.

Iain Gray: I used to see Ian at gigs, and the last time I ever saw him was in the Beach Club that April. He was always very polite. The Pop Group were on, and he was there with Debbie. I went, 'Hi, Ian, do you mind if I have a quick word with you?' He went, 'No.' I just went, 'I haven't seen you for a while. *Unknown Pleasures* is great.' He said he'd been recording in London, and he mentioned about going to America.

I said, 'I saw you at the New Osborne club, and that track you open with ...' He'd just stood there, the first three minutes of instrumental, just doing the dance. I'd seen them loads of times by then, and even then it was still messianic. I said, 'What is it called?' – '"Dead Souls".' – 'Oh, it's brilliant.' He went, 'Oh, ta.' He wasn't big-headed. He was just having a nice quiet drink with his wife, watching the Pop Group. They seemed very happy together.

I knew him quite closely for a period of time, but I never equated what he was singing about with what he did. When you talked to him, he was such a sweet guy, laughed, joked, but there was always something of the night about him, even when I knew him, moments when he was keeping things back. Maybe he was a very good actor – it was all a facade.

I think the Ian that Ian became he must have hated, because it wasn't him. The real Ian was this kind of *Waltons* guy, a really loving, caring individual. But the lyrics he's singing are of a guy who's going through the heart of darkness. He's there, soulless and bent on destruction. It is black and white, and I think Ian always wanted to get back to the white, and he couldn't. He talked about opening a bookshop and desperate things, wanting the old Ian, but it had gone.

I think the Ian Ian became was always there. He was just fighting it and he was a very good actor, but there were moments of strange-ness where you would think, 'What's that about?' On the train jour-ney to London in late 1976, he talked about, 'Have you ever thought of dying, Iain?' I just started laughing: 'What are you on about?' And he went, 'I sometimes think, is there anything else?' It was just a throwaway remark, but I thought afterwards it was a really strange thing for someone to say who is picture-postcard happy.

Since then I've worked in mental health for many years, and I've seen people like him who, people would say, 'What a shock, they killed themselves.' But Ian was doing it onstage. I think we all have demons inside, and the demon inside Ian must have been an awful one. He was obviously fighting that when I spoke to him in April. We were talking about Werner Herzog, and he was saying he was really into that. I mentioned *Stroszek*, and he said, 'Oh, I'd like to see that, that's supposed to be really good.' And then it was on television three weeks later.

- 28 April 1980: T. J. Davidson's Rehearsal Rooms, Manchester, 'Love Will Tear Us Apart' video shoot

Bernard Sumner: That video for 'Love Will Tear Us Apart' was shot just after Ian had tried to commit suicide, so it was a really trying time for us. There are some very famous photographs. Anton Corbijn took them. Me and Ian are carrying a flight case, and Ian's sat down, like this, and he looks quite depressed. He wasn't normally like that, but that was quite near to the end. We felt, 'Well, what can we try to do to cheer him up? We'll write a couple of songs.' And we wrote 'In a Lonely Place' and 'Ceremony' in a week, we shot the video, but it was all hopeless really.

Anton Corbijn: Rob Gretton had contacted me: could I send them some contact sheets from the previous session? And they used it on this Sordide Sentimental release in Belgium, with 'Dead Souls' and 'Atmosphere' on the other side. I used the horizontal picture in there, which was quite different. And that's also the reason they asked me to come up to Manchester a couple of months later, because they actually liked the pictures – nobody else did – and they asked me to come up for the video shooting of 'Love Will Tear Us Apart' as a fly-on-the-wall kind of thing.

They said, 'We won't pose for you, but we'd love you to take some pictures.' So that's what I did, and then I got the picture of Ian where he sits on a speaker or an amplifier, staring into the abyss, in a way, with a cigarette. That was the second good picture I took. I think I only took two good pictures, but they've lasted all those years. I guess there was something in there that everybody can relate to. I assumed he was tired, but I didn't realise it was maybe he was tired of life. How many things went through his mind . . .

I have the feeling everyone was in a good mood actually; there was nothing that I would have thought was like doom or gloom. I just thought Ian was tired and they had to do this video, but that was all a whole new world to me as well – it was the first time I was at the making of a video. There's another shot of the same place where Ian was sitting, which is a different atmosphere, the light is different and how he looks is different. The other is more intense.

Stephen Morris: 'Ceremony' and 'In a Lonely Place' were the last two songs that we did. God knows if they're the right lyrics. We couldn't make them out. All we had was a really naff rehearsal tape of it.

- 2 May 1980: High Hall, Birmingham University

Jeremy Kerr: He was not well, Ian. I remember the mixing desk – it was Pink Floyd's mixing desk, all fluorescent lights – that's the only thing I can remember about that gig, and it was a nice room. They were good, but he was ill.

Tony Wilson: The last conversation we had, which was at the Birmingham gig, which was the last gig ever, was about how interested I was in his and Simon Topping's use of archaic language. Now I can't quite remember which: there's a line from A Certain Ratio and a line from Joy Division around that time which interested me. I think one of them is 'When all's said and done'. It's an archaic use of language, and that interested me that they both used it.

Lesley Gilbert: We went and stayed with him for a couple of nights while Lindsay and Tony were away. I thought he seemed okay then, he seemed as if he'd decided what he was going to do. Now whether that meant he was going to commit suicide . . . That's not what I thought. I thought it meant he'd decided which way he was going to go, Debbie or Annik. He didn't say which way, but the overall feeling that I got was that he'd come to some sort of decision and felt quite relieved about it.

Annik Honoré: In the last letter he writes, he does say that he's looking forward to going, especially . . . I can't remember which city, but there's a city in particular he'd like to go to, because there they would have a few days off, so it would give him a chance to rest and visit. Maybe it was New York. So he was looking forward to that, but he was mentioning that it was a long time not to see each other and that he wished I was going with them. Everybody thought he was happy to go there, to the States – another adventure.

Peter Hook: It was horrible, the pain you felt witnessing Ian. He was obviously ill, he was obviously really struggling, but he never gave up, he never stopped, he didn't want to stop. I never read Ian's letters, but I found them recently and I was reading Ian's letter to Annik just before we were supposed to go to America, and it was just really weird to read the letter and him looking forward to it, and then for him to commit suicide. I still haven't come to terms with it. It just seems really weird.

Terry Mason: The minder role was to have started the first day on the US tour. My job would have been to make sure Ian takes his medication, get him back to the hotel, try to have him go to bed, make sure that he ate properly, because quite obviously, once we were on tour in America, the band would be playing places where fans would want to have their ten minutes of fame with the new Jim Morrison. It would have been a fantastic job to have done as well: it would have given me more time with Ian. Also, we could talk about owning dogs.

The tour was never in doubt. Ian's position inside the band and Factory was such that if Ian really didn't want to go, I'm sure he could have turned round and said, 'No, I don't want to do it now.' No one would have had any complaints if he'd said, 'Look, I just want to sort out me life, get me health on a better track than it is now.' I was round at Ian's house on the Thursday before we were supposed to go, and he'd gone out and got his passport photos done for the American embassy. As far as I'm concerned, Ian wanted to go.

In his letters to Annik he was saying how he was looking forward to doing it. He was a bit apprehensive, but I think Ian probably felt he was carrying the weight of the world. At that point all of Factory and the people involved in Factory were basically on Ian's shoulders. If he'd said no, there would certainly have been repercussions for an awful lot of people by him not carrying on. Ian was a very honourable person, and I always got the impression that he would do it to keep up his side of the agreement in being with Factory and being with the band.

By the Thursday Ian seemed to have got his head sorted out: he was going to get divorced from Debbie, he was still going to see Natalie, and at the end of the US tour he'd got to have six months off. All he had to do was the US tour, and then there would be six months' complete break. At that point he could have walked away, if he wanted to. You have to think that something happened, something snapped on the Saturday night, because Ian showed no signs of not wanting to go to America.

Lesley Gilbert: I bumped into them on the Friday. Ian was with Rob and Hooky. I worked on Deansgate and I just bumped into them in my lunch hour, and they'd been shopping for clothes to go to America because they were going on the Monday, so it was, well, the day before he died. They were so excited and showing me what they'd bought, and Ian was really looking forward to it.

Rob Gretton Notebook
14/5/80 Rehearsals
15/5/80 Bought clothes

Harry Fenton	£0.85 Polish
" "	£45.49 Shoes
" "	£12.99 Jacket
Jonathan Silver	£6.99 T/Shirt
" "	£17.99 Trousers
Last Picture Show	£10.00 Shirt
Ray Alan	£12.97 "

Top Man	£49.94 Shirts/Trs
Ray Alan	£2.00 T/Shirts
Wakefield	£6.00 T/Shirts
	£165.22

Peter Hook: We rehearsed on the Friday night and I drove Ian home in me Mark 10 420G, the red one with the gold flash at the side, KFR 666F. I drove him home cos I lived in Moston and he was staying with his parents in Moston, and we were laughing and screaming in the car because we were going to America on the Monday morning. We were over the moon, we really were. I dropped him off at his parents', and he said he was going back tomorrow to see Natalie before he went. He said, 'I'll see you at the airport,' and that was the last time I saw him.

Kevin Cummins: It was the night of Mick Middles's wedding, and Rob and Lesley and me and a girl I was seeing at the time went to the wedding, then to the reception and back to Rob's afterwards, and we were up virtually all night. I was going to go to America with them. We were just talking about the tour, and how things had moved on so brilliantly, and how exciting it was going to the States. We were all looking forward to it. It was everybody's first trip to America, and you're not going to say no to that.

When you're playing local gigs around Manchester, Huddersfield and everywhere within a twenty-mile radius, the first time you played the Marquee or wherever in London was always so exciting. It was a landmark gig. When Buzzcocks played the Marquee, we organised a coach trip from Manchester to go and see it. The whole idea of it was so exciting. And this was a step up. 'We've got to go to this.' And with America, you're not going to turn it down, you're just not.

Bernard Sumner: He had been staying at my house, and we used to stay up late talking about various things. He always used to talk about Nietzsche and a lot of books that he'd read, a lot of philosophers and stuff. We used to go out into Manchester and play pool in a couple of bars. We used to go out with this strange guy that I worked with at the animation place, a guy called Paul Dawson. He was very odd. He was into magic tricks and used to call himself the Amazing Noswad.

Well, Noswad is Dawson backwards, and me and Ian and Paul used to go out, but he was very strange, very, very strange. He used to collect stuffed animals – like the guy out of *Psycho*. I remember he got made redundant and he spent all his redundancy money on buying stuffed animals, and his ambition was to buy a stuffed human being. Ian found him fascinating, and so we were due to go out with him for a drink on the Saturday night.

We were going to America on the Monday. Ian had gone back to live with his mum and dad on the Thursday or something, and he phoned me on the Friday night and said, 'I can't come out tomorrow, I'm going to go and see Debbie before we go away.' You kind of think 'Oh-oh' a little bit, 'It's going to end in tears.' I just thought they were going to have an argument, so I said, 'Are you sure? Why don't you just come out and have a drink? We'll have a laugh.' But no: 'I've got to see her.'

It was on the Saturday night that we were supposed to be going out. I said, 'Well, I'm actually going over to Blackpool tomorrow to see Section 25,' which was another group that was on the Factory label, good friends of mine over near Blackpool. I said, 'So I won't see you on the Sunday, I'll just see you at the airport on Monday.' I did have trepidations, I was a little bit worried, but he seemed quite calm and rational, because he always did. That was the last time I spoke to him.

Annik Honoré: I returned from my holiday in Egypt during the week before Ian died, so we managed to call each other a few times. I was probably in Belgium for about five days before I was due to go back to England, and we managed to speak three times. He was desperate to find out if I was okay after this holiday. It appeared like a dangerous place to go and very far away, so he really wanted to know how I was.

The conversations we had later were always about the trip to America and how we could arrange to meet before, because I was due back on the Sunday and they were due to fly to America on the Monday. The last time we spoke was on the Saturday night, when I was at Plan K, backstage with Digital Dance, and it was a short conversation where basically he said that I have to call him, that he would call me on the Sunday when I'm back home in England, in London.

I always thought I was the last one to talk to him, but apparently so many things happened on that Saturday night. He saw Debbie after that, late, because it's an hour earlier where he was, so maybe it was like nine or ten at Plan K, but it was only eight or nine in Macclesfield. But it was very short and I couldn't hear him very well – I was backstage with lots of people around – and basically we just agreed that he should call me at home the following day, and he told me he was listening to a record and was going to watch a film and he was alone. But I could feel he wasn't well.

I'd spoken with him a couple of days before, and he was impatient for me to come back – it had been such a long time. He hadn't seen me for more than three weeks now, and he said that it's imperative that we meet before they go to America, because otherwise it would be like seven or eight weeks without seeing each other. So that's what we were saying on the phone: he was trying to give me the latest news about the arrangements to the airport and the flight and things like that, but we had only very short conversations in those days from abroad.

Deborah Curtis (from *Touching from a Distance*): I'd had enough. I was working so hard, and all these money problems. My mum was looking after Natalie. Having a baby makes you grow up. It didn't make him grow up. I could have stayed with him that night, but he made it clear that he didn't want me there. I would have fallen asleep, I was dead on my feet, and I could have woken up the next day and he'd have done it while I was asleep. I think he'd decided, he was just trying to pick his moment. I don't think he had any intention of going to America, he was frightened of flying, and he possibly didn't want to die in America. Maybe the American thing hurried it up.

Richard Boon: I basically think he couldn't cope with success. All the psychic and physical places, the degree of success they'd already had was disrupting his family life, making him travel, having a lot of uncertainty about what he was doing. Maybe he wasn't happy necessarily with what they were doing. Did he want more of it? He just said no.

13

MAY 1980

Peter Hook: The police phoned me up. They couldn't get in touch with Rob, they couldn't get in touch with anybody. I was the first one that they told. It was really weird because I was sitting down just about to have me Sunday lunch, me and Iris, and the phone rang. I went on the phone, and they said, 'We're trying to get in touch with Rob Gretton.' And I said, 'He should be at home.' They said, 'We phoned him at home, he's not there.' I said, 'Why, what's the problem?' And they said, 'Oh, I'm sorry to tell you this, but Ian Curtis has committed suicide.'

And I went, 'Right, okay.' And they went, 'Right, okay. Well, if you speak to Mr Gretton, could you get him to call us?' And I went, 'Yeah, right, okay,' and put the phone down, and went and sat back and had me dinner. And then Iris said to me, 'Who was on the phone, by the way?' And I went, 'Oh, Ian's killed himself,' and that was it then, that was the shock of it. It was really weird, horrible, and then everything seems a blur after that. I must have tried to get in touch with Rob, or driven probably to see him – I can't remember, to be honest.

Lesley Gilbert: We'd been out because it was a really nice day, and we'd gone for a walk in the park, and there was an athletics meeting on, so we'd stayed to watch that. Then when we got back – we hadn't been back very long – Hooky and Iris came round and obviously told us. They'd been trying to find us, because they lived really close to my mum and dad's, and they'd even been round there looking for us. So that was Sunday teatime-ish, I suppose.

It was numbness more than shock. I had no inkling, I had no thoughts in my mind that maybe that's what he'd do, but I still don't remember feeling shocked, just a bit puzzled, I suppose, and a bit numb. I can't remember how Rob reacted. When you spend that much time with somebody and they do something like that without anybody having an inkling about it . . . I think everybody was just a bit, 'Well, what was that for then?'

Bernard Sumner: The original idea was that Ian would meet me the next day, cos we were going to go over to a friend's house near Blackpool. We were going to go water skiing. But he never turned up, and I went water skiing anyway. I came back to my friend's house and I was drying myself off with a towel, and the phone rang, and it was Rob. It was Larry's house or Paul's house, out of Section 25. He said, 'I've got a bit of bad news for you. I'm afraid Ian's committed suicide.' – 'You mean, he's tried to kill himself?' – 'No, he's done it.'

And it was like the cymbals at that gig. The whole room just turned upside down. I put the phone down, went and washed my face with cold water. It was just the biggest shock I'd ever had in my life. I found it quite difficult to accept at first that he had actually done it. But yeah, that was it, no tour of America. Everything just collapsed, no more future. And I'm sure it was the same for everyone else involved.

I was just in a state of shock, because apart from everything else, it's quite an incredible act of violence to kill yourself. I sometimes wonder whether Ian's explosive personality actually gave him the bollocks to go through with it. People say that people who commit suicide are cowards, but I think the opposite is true. I think it takes a great deal of courage to kill yourself – not that I'm advocating it, obviously – but certainly in my darkest moments I would never have the courage to do anything like that, or the desire.

I guess it was just a great feeling of anger at Ian for doing it, on behalf of his family and his parents. It's an act of violence against his parents, who had done so much for him to bring him up, so I felt really sorry for them, but angry on behalf of the group. Although I didn't think it was an act of cowardice, I did think it was a terribly selfish thing to do, but there again, it was easy for me to sit there and think that because I was looking at it from my perspective as a human being.

I didn't have any of the problems that he had, so what I think is pretty irrelevant really, because I wasn't him. So in the end I dropped the anger and forgave him personally, but you just scan over: Was there any way I could have stopped him? Was there anything I could have done? But apart from putting a twenty-four-hour watch on him, no, there wasn't, but it's a terrible thing to do to those around you, because if not completely, it partially destroys their lives as well.

Stephen Morris: I was shocked when I first heard, but then I thought it was probably an accident, knowing him. Maybe he didn't mean to do it, but I think he did. I think he was a bit worried cos someone had told him that they don't like epileptics in the States. It isn't true, but I know someone had told him that. Apart from that, I think he was looking forward to actually going to America. He was up for it: Chelsea Hotel . . . I didn't think he was 100 per cent fed up with it all. Whatever it was, I don't know, but I didn't think he'd go all the way.

The first thing I thought after he died was, it's going to be like another Jimi Hendrix. You're going to have people coming round saying, 'What was he like?' Which didn't happen as much as I thought it was going to. I was sort of 50 per cent sad and 50 per cent angry: really angry at him for being stupid and doing that, and angry at myself for not doing something.

Tony Wilson: It was a Sunday, early afternoon, and I was working as an assistant producer on *World in Action*. We were in the editing suites in the first floor at Granada, a very sunny Sunday afternoon, and the phone goes. 'It's for you, Tony'. And it's Rob. 'Hello, Rob.' And Rob just says, 'Ian's dead, he was found this morning.' So I go, 'Five minutes, Rob.' Put the phone down. Now I didn't tell the people, because obviously we were making *World in Action* for that next night, so I just said, 'You don't need me at the moment. I'll be back in fifteen, twenty minutes.'

And then I got in my car, the old Peugeot, and drove to Rob's. And one of my main memories is coming out of the house after fifteen, twenty minutes with Rob and seeing my car parked sideways in the middle of the road. When something like that happens, the way your car is and how it's parked just has no relevance whatsoever, so my one memory is the fact that my car was in the middle of the street, sideways with the door open, and was left there for thirty minutes while I was inside with Rob. So that was my memory of that afternoon.

Lindsay Reade: I was with Jeremy Kerr, lying on a hill in the sunshine in Charlesworth. Tony had gone in to work. Jez had stayed at our house for some reason. We must have gone there straight away to get away from the house. It was a beautiful sunny day, and the juxtaposition between Ian's onstage performance and his personality and a beautiful day and the most terrible news I think I'd ever heard in my entire life . . . I just couldn't believe that anything so awful could have happened.

I had this huge row with Tony on the day because I didn't think he was seeing Ian as a human being so much as this iconic pop star, which ironically is what he's become. I just felt that he needed something that he wasn't getting as a human being. I don't know what it was, I don't know if any of us could have given it to him. Well, we didn't, and we were all guilty of not giving it to him, I think.

Deborah Curtis: It might have been that he saw death as the only way out. He told me he didn't want to do *Closer*, he said he'd just wanted to do *Unknown Pleasures*, 'Transmission' and that's it. But there must have been a lot of pressure, knowing that if you didn't go to America, the rest of the band didn't go to America. He couldn't really turn around and say, 'I'm not going.' I don't want to blame anybody, but somebody should have said, 'This isn't working, something's got to happen.' He should have gone into hospital, not gone on tour.

But that's not fair to them, because Ian made sure that I wasn't in communication with the others. Because he was telling them one thing about me, and telling me something else about them. I don't think they realised he was telling so many lies. He was a very good liar, he was very convincing. He could go to a gig and say he was having a really bad time with Debbie, Debbie's moaning about this and that, and people are always trying to be tactful; nobody's going to ring me up and say, 'What are you playing at?'

Tony Wilson: Herzog was his hero, and Herzog was a concomitant factor in his suicide. He was with his parents and he didn't want to put his dad through watching this film late at night, so he went home to watch this tragic, romantic film where the hero commits suicide at the end. You know the famous last line, where there's a dead man in the cable car and the chicken is still dancing, which is why with our usual sense of fun we put the chicken's feet on the run-out of the first three sides of *Still*, then on the last side the chicken stops.

Kevin Cummins: I got a call from Rob, and all he said was, 'That silly cunt has killed himself.' Nothing else, and I knew exactly what he meant because of the way the conversation had been the previous night. He'd been saying how Ian wasn't happy about going away, that his life was in a mess and he couldn't cope with various things, and Rob was like, 'When you get to America, you'll be fine, don't worry. It's the best thing for you, you'll be away from everybody.'

Annik Honoré: I took the hovercraft back very early Sunday morning, like six o'clock or so. I took the train to Calais and then the hovercraft, where I felt really sick, although the sea was quiet, and then arrived in London, and the phone call never took place, he never rang. So I thought, 'Maybe there's a problem, I should call his parents,' because that's where he was supposed to be staying. And when I called, his father just said, 'Ian is dead,' and he put the phone down, and that was it.

So I called Rob. I was desperate to find out what it was, and Rob hadn't heard, he didn't know. They all went out the day before, and he said, 'No, they must be playing a cruel joke on you,' he said something like that, and he said, 'I'll call you back in a minute.' It seemed to last a long time, and when he called back, it was to confirm that Ian was dead. Yeah, Sunday afternoon.

To me, this suicide is somehow still an accident, because he had been drinking alcohol, and the mixture of the pills and staying up late and being tired, and probably having some arguments about the divorce with Debbie, altogether it was just too much for him to take. I realise it takes a lot of courage to hang yourself, so I don't know exactly how he managed to do that. But I don't think he planned it the day before; it was just something he did on the spur of the moment. Suddenly there was no other possibility.

Because six weeks before, he appeared very sincere in the fact that it was an accident, that he never does it again. I think it was a time also when we were not seeing each other because it was getting far too dramatic and complicated for me to be in a triangle. It's the worst thing, and I was very young and I didn't want the guilt of going out with a married man. It was getting far too complicated for me to take.

When Debbie found out, she called me and she was absolutely going out of her mind. That day I decided it was over, that I couldn't take any more and it would be more simple to separate, but I don't think that's what he wanted either. I can't say, it wasn't clear in his mind; maybe he wanted both women. The disease was the worst – I still think you don't die because of a wife and a girlfriend, for God's sake – but he was very unhappy to be sick, that's how I see it.

Bernard Sumner: We joined a group so that we could be utterly irresponsible and extend our adolescence, and we were in that frame of mind. To have done something for Ian would have taken someone with responsibility, and it was nowhere to be found, and I just think that's because of the head space we got ourselves into. Because it started so suddenly with Ian, we had this difficulty: we didn't know how severe it was, and it's easy in retrospect, but we didn't really know. It wasn't just the epilepsy either, he was in a terrible state emotionally.

In fact, when he first tried to commit suicide and took the overdose, it was a complete surprise. It was the breakdown of his relationship, accentuated by the quantity of barbiturates he was taking to subdue his epilepsy. Barbiturates make you so you're laughing one minute, crying the next. He'd had a physical breakdown, a relationship breakdown, which caused an emotional breakdown. Apart from this strange suggestibility, which I don't really think anyone else noticed, he was mentally all over the place.

If it had been me, I would have been extremely worried, but if we agreed that we were going to keep the band together but weren't going to do gigs any more, how come a month later we were going on an American tour? It wasn't right. People start getting all the wrong priorities once you start becoming successful. They don't know when to leave you alone and give you a fucking rest. You need more than one kind of sleep in this profession.

I think there's always another reason why they do it that nobody knows. There's all the public reasons, but there's another reason: that last section of a personality that no one knows about. Ian would hide those thoughts from you completely. It was a bit like, 'Oh yeah, I'm really looking forward to going to America, can't wait. Yeah, I've been out buying clothes. Yeah, we should do this song, we should do that song, it's going to be great.' That was what he was like, never mentioned his fits and was just completely positive and really looking forward to it: 'Next time we go back I think we should be doing this kind of tour, we should play these sort of clubs next time.'

There was never any indication. Obviously there was after the first time he tried, and I tried to discuss it with him then and talk him out of it, but once he'd made his mind up, he'd made his mind up. I remain convinced to this day that if someone is going to commit suicide, they're gonna do it, no matter what the fuck anyone says to them. Ian was gonna do it. According to Debbie, he'd talked about doing it years ago.

Deborah Curtis: I think he wanted to be like Jim Morrison, someone who got famous and died. Being in a band was very important, he was very single-minded about it. He'd always said that he didn't want to live into his twenties, after twenty-five. I think it was the teenage thing. Teenagers like to have something to be miserable about, don't they? But it changed. He stopped talking about it. I don't think he forgot about it. I thought he'd grow out of it. And when it got too late really, he wouldn't talk about it. You couldn't discuss it with him, you couldn't find out what was really going on.

When we were kids, lots of people were miserable. But they grew out of it. I think he enjoyed being unhappy. I think he liked to wallow in it. There were times when we were happy, but they were when we were on our own, when we went out walking or things like that. But I don't think he liked his friends to know that he was happy. You know that Ian was very charismatic, and he tended to lead people, and people liked to be part of his will, so I don't think anybody really questioned what he was doing very much. Because he was different, so many people admired him.

Bernard Sumner: I came to terms with it pretty well straight away, because it was the third one. I knew why he'd done it. Or I could put my own reason on why I thought he'd done it, why I would have done it. At the time I remember going very silent, not being able to speak very much. Just feeling very down. I think it makes you very hard. I feel now that I'm quite cold, and when I was a child I was very warm. Now I can be quite cold and detached. I can never really make close friendships, just because everything I've ever been close to has died.

It just seems a bit callous to do that towards the people that love you. If you're going to do that, you've got to think about your parents and your close ones more than yourself. It seems quite a cruel thing to do, so my heart's angry but my brain is saying, 'Don't be so judgemental.' It's hard to get in Ian's head and think, 'What did he think his future was going to be?' He must have had a bleak image of his future, because he was very, very ill, very ill, and those days weren't these days: the care for it wasn't as good as it is now.

Mark Reeder: I was completely surprised. And angry that he'd robbed us of more brilliant music. I couldn't believe it. I spoke to him at his home in Barton Street about two weeks before they were going to America. I knew he was having a bit of trouble and I said, 'When you've done these gigs in the States, come to Berlin. Just have a break.' And he said, 'Yeah, I'm gonna do that.' I know he was a bit frightened about flying, and at first I thought it might be that. But that's stupid really.

It was Monday morning when my friend Mark Farrow phoned me up and goes, 'Have you heard about Ian?' – 'What? They're going to America.' – 'No, he killed himself.' – 'Who told you that?' He said, 'Rob just phoned me.' And I was like, 'Are you mad?' I didn't believe it. Then I put the phone down, and five minutes later Rob phones and tells me. This was the worst news I'd ever heard in my life, at that moment. And it affected me so much. I was distraught, I didn't know what to do. I was devastated. Rob was trying to console me on the phone. I was in tears. He phoned me up every single day, tried to calm me down. He said that Ian had left a note. He told me everything and said, 'Don't tell anybody.' Who am I going to tell? Who would I talk to about it? This is personal business. It's got nothing to do with anybody else. I was hoping to go to the funeral, but I never managed it.

Rob told me what was in the note. It wasn't about the band at all. And it wasn't really about Debbie, either. It was just that he couldn't

deal with the situation. I think, personally, that he just didn't want
to give up on the relationship that he was having with Annik or the
relationship that he was having with Debbie. I think the decision
was, 'If I can't have one or the other, then no one is going to have
me at all.' It was the worst day.

Peter Hook: The next time I remember anything was when we
all went and sat in the Bluebell Inn, Moston Lane, and just sat
there staring at each other, until Rob presumably got involved in
the funeral arrangements and things like that. I spent most of the
time in the pub. We spent most of the time together, all of us – me,
Twinny, Terry, Barney – we'd all go and sit together, just sit in the
pub. I think we couldn't take it in really, what had happened.

I mean, one of my greatest regrets in life is that I didn't go and
see him after he was dead. I really, really do regret that, but I think
we were so young we didn't know what the bloody hell. Nobody
offered. You'd think someone would say, 'Do you want to go and
see him?' Fucking right, do I want to go and see a dead body? Do
I fuck, you know? I'm twenty-two, I'm going to the pub, fuck that.
But I really do regret not seeing him and saying goodbye now, I
really do. It was only Bernard and I that didn't go. Everybody else
went.

We went to the funeral. I mean, you just felt like you were watching a TV programme really. I remember going for something to eat
after the funeral and being really shocked when his sister screamed
at the funeral, so we didn't go to the wake, we didn't feel like we were
welcome really, I don't know why. And the next thing I remember
after that would be the inquest. Was there summat happened at
the inquest? Something really weird, his dad said something really
weird at the inquest.

I'm sure he killed himself because he couldn't handle it. I've been
through break-ups that have driven you to the brink, and if there's
nobody there to pull you back, it would be quite easy. When you
take into account what he was going through with epilepsy, mis-
tress, child, wife . . . Fucking hell, all the ingredients are there, all

the warning signs were there – cutting himself up with a knife, taking his first overdose – everything was there. You don't need to be a bleeding genius to work out that he's going to top himself sooner or later, and he did, and that was it.

Deborah Curtis: He didn't commit suicide because he had marital problems. He had marital problems because he wanted to commit suicide. I felt angry with him because he got the last word. How can you be angry with someone who's dead? They aren't there, you can't shake them, you can't smack them around the face. You're totally impotent, it's horrible. It's like putting a big sign up, saying, 'There, I've done it, and you can't do anything about it. So much for your talking.'

Tony Wilson: Certainly on the first night that we went to see Ian in the chapel of rest, my memory of that was of Alan going in first, and then Alan making us wait outside cos Ian's mum and dad were there. What Alan did – typical Erasmus, wonderful Erasmus – they'd got the collar down here, so the fucking rope marks were all here, so Alan – I don't know how he did it – had just moved the collar up so that Mr and Mrs Curtis wouldn't see the rope marks. I thought that was very sweet of Alan.

Paul Morley: Wilson actually showed me the body of Ian Curtis, which Wilson now claims he didn't do, being Wilson. I do remember it because it was so preposterous, but he said to me at the time, 'When you write the book . . .' He was planning already, and he's had his way, which we might call sweet or sour or bitter or charming or whatever. He said, 'When you write the book, you've got to have seen the body,' so it was all a bit odd for me.

Tony Wilson: Then our job – this was Lindsay's and my job – was to look after Annik, so that Annik wouldn't go to the funeral. There was all that kind of shittiness going round, so Annik didn't go to the funeral because it was my job to make sure that she got on the plane back to Brussels and there was no scene at the funeral. Certainly, looking after Annik for five or six days – I'm sure she probably doesn't remember this much – she was playing both albums back to back, non-stop, twenty-four hours a day for the entire time she stayed in the cottage. There you go.

Annik Honoré: I arrived back in London on the Sunday, and my landlady saw me absolutely devastated and so she gave me some sleeping tablets and I explained to her, and decided I will go to Manchester. And so I took a train to Manchester the day after. I think the first person I saw was Rob. He had arranged to meet me at the station or somewhere, and in the meantime he had agreed that I could visit Ian at the chapel of rest. He had discussed with Debbie that if I was to go there, then would I not go to the funeral? I could only say yes, so he took me to the chapel of rest, and Tony and Lindsay arrived. I remember Paul Morley was there too, but I don't think he came with me. I was on my own when I saw Ian, and from there they decided that the best place to go would be to Tony and Lindsay's. They were living in the countryside, in Charlesworth – from what I can remember, a very isolated place. But Lindsay kept giving me sleeping pills and stuff to calm me down because I was crying non-stop.

So it's a bit vague, but I can never thank her enough, because everybody was lost. It was extremely nice of her, and of Tony. And so I stayed there for five days, because I still had my plane ticket for when I returned to Brussels on 23 May that Tony bought, and my name said A. Curtis because he didn't know my name, Honoré, and so I came back to Brussels and Michel Duval was waiting for me at the airport.

Mark Reeder: After Ian died, Annik contacted me. I was in the middle of nowhere, in Berlin. Ian kills himself, and she had no one to turn to. No one in Manchester had any time for her. The band didn't know her: they didn't have anything to do with her, even when she was with Ian. In Rob's eyes, she was the Belgian bint, you know? They didn't know anything about her at all. I got to know Annik very well, and she became my girlfriend.

And then I realised exactly what kind of relationship she'd had with Ian. Because she was a virgin at twenty-four, and it was, 'How does that work?' I thought they'd been having this sexual relationship, and they hadn't at all. It was only about her being an intellectual sparring partner for Ian.

Paul Morley: I think in our private lives – not just with me but everyone – love lives, family, it was all disaster, but we didn't talk about it. We were very determined to locate value and purpose and greatness and art and this stuff, but we didn't really talk about our lives. You'd never really get to know anybody at all. I remember going round to Factory Records after the funeral, and they played *The Great Rock'n'Roll Swindle*, and I just remember being frozen throughout it.

I think we were all frozen at the aptness and yet the absolute stupidity that we should be doing this. It was classic putting on a brave face, doing it in a showy way and not really dealing with the emotion. That idea that Joy Division was all about emotion, but none of us ever displayed any emotion in front of each other. It was almost like we were too damned self-conscious about maintaining a ridiculous kind of degraded cool, a kind of cool that time was meant to destroy, but we still didn't really talk to each other.

Tony Wilson: Martin took it the worst in the end, leaving the family aside, who obviously suffered much more. I always think that Martin never recovered from Ian's death in many ways, because Martin had found his performer, the person through whom his art could find its way to the world. How stupid we were, the fact that we didn't see there being real problems. I can remember there was that line on the *Closer* album – 'A cry for help, a hint of anaesthesia' – that's what we thought that first attempt was. It was just like, 'Oh well, it's just that.'

Martin Hannett: It was an accident, wasn't it? Thirty-two barbs and half a bottle of scotch. I never saw the inquest. It totally did my head in, that. I was in the Townhouse with the Buzzcocks, and for some reason I wrapped the session up, rocketed back to the hotel, threw everything in the boot of my car, drove home to Manchester, got home at ten, was enjoying a coffee, and Tosh Ryan phoned and told me. That was the day after, Monday morning. It wasn't totally unexpected, because he'd tried to do it weeks earlier.

Tony Wilson: Well, there's a thousand theories. Did Ian take it all too hard, and did he blame himself? I used to think he blamed himself. I know that Bernard's point of view is that the drugs they were giving Ian for his epilepsy were profoundly taking him over the edge.

I have my own personal belief, which is that if you have a child, you love that child, and Ian loved Natalie. But you've grown out of love with your first wife and you've fallen in love with somebody else, you can't stay in the marriage but you can't leave your child, and guess what the only way out is? The only way out is to top yourself. So that's my version, but of course the only version that really counts is Ian's version, and we'll never know.

Paul Morley: I still didn't realise with Ian, even though he was writing those lyrics, even though he was having terrible trouble in his private life, even though he was collapsing onstage, even though he was obviously very ill, even though he tried it a few times before, you still didn't really, really believe that it would happen.

But yeah, that distraction he played all along – certainly towards the end – of everything being okay. Even my brief conversations with him, having very recently had my own experience with suicide, knowing the distraction and the disguises and the con tricks that the potential suicide can play on you, to the very bitter end, as if there's nothing wrong: 'I'll see you later,' and you never do.

Peter Saville: The day Tony phoned me to tell me that Ian had died, it was during that conversation that I suddenly thought of the cover we had, and I felt it necessary to point it out, and Tony was very concerned. The notions of sensationalism or exploitation were there, and I said, 'Tony, we've got a tomb on the cover of the album,' and he was like, 'Oh fuck.' The cover was done, I don't know, weeks before Ian died. It was done by the time the album was done, and it had gone to print, or at least to proofing.

They had to decide whether to go ahead with it or not, and it had been decided: the group chose it together, including Ian, it was their cover, and it's a great cover. Anyway, so he went away and he and Rob and Steve and Hooky and Bernard dealt with that. I mean, what was going through Ian's mind at the time, we don't know.

There is one song on that album which I've found upsetting for all these years. I cry when I hear 'Isolation'. I cry a little bit just thinking about it. It's far too upsetting listening to it. It's such a straightforward statement of feeling, but a far more troubled feeling than we've come to associate with people writing pop songs. People project, but obviously with 'Love Will Tear Us Apart', and ultimately with 'Isolation', Ian wasn't projecting, wasn't going somewhere and then coming back out of that place. He was obviously too long in that place.

'Isolation' is a letter from that place, from a place where there doesn't seem to be any point in going on. I mean, we all have times like that – hours, weeks, days – but most of us have the filters to protect ourselves in that mood. It is most likely a chemistry thing, and all I can imagine is that Ian got into one of those moods at that time, wrote from that mood but didn't come out of it, and the whole thing becomes extreme: the cover becomes extreme, the images strangely predictive.

It's difficult to listen to 'Isolation' knowing that somebody has written a song and killed themselves soon afterwards. The line 'Mother, please forgive me, I'm ashamed of the things I've been put through, I'm ashamed of the person I am,' it's very difficult to hear someone say that, it's very difficult to hear anyone ever say it. But in the context of somebody that you know and respected who has then committed suicide as a cumulation of those feelings, it's terrible to listen to. It's like listening to someone's suicide note.

Jon Wozencroft: It's well documented that he had tried a few weeks previously to overdose on pills. The night of his suicide doesn't add up, though, even if he had succeeded in engineering an evening where he was going to be on his own, for the first time in ages. If one accepts that Ian was a chameleon-like figure who could be various things to various people at various times, added to the fact that he was having serious personal problems, what was less clear to anyone outside his close circle was the way that he was being seriously destabilised by the treatment for epilepsy that he was on. All treatment was an experimental treatment at the time.

But he was also on the cusp of exactly what he wanted, which was to get out of Manchester, to travel and see the world, to go to America, the land of some of his heroes. And he didn't want to let anyone down.

We know that he'd drunk a bottle of whisky, we know that he was on some pretty powerful medication, we know that he was listening to Iggy Pop, we know that he'd just watched Herzog's *Stroszek*, which is an extraordinarily depressing film, but also a very powerful one, uplifting in some ways, because it doesn't come darker than that. The film would have finished by the early hours. There's a haunting scene at the end, with the auctioneer's voice selling off Stroszek's trailer home. Money worries were a big thing for Ian. Nearing dawn, evidently reaching breaking point, he wrote a letter to Deborah. Afterwards there was only a perfunctory inquest and no full coroner's investigation into the last hours or even days of his life. Deborah found him hunched over the washing machine in a foetal position, kneeling, with his hands stretched forward. It could well have been a grand mal fit.

So the fan is left with this kind of myth of Ian, the rock suicide, which I think does him an extreme disservice. I think it's a very personal tragedy. I think it's got absolutely nothing to do with the demise of people such as Jim Morrison or Janis Joplin or Kurt Cobain. I think it's incredibly sad and poignant and tragic in the closest familial sense.

Terry Mason: Everyone thinks there's some deep, dark, mystical secret, and there's not. He was a nice guy, got into a strange situation, and the only way that he could think of out at that time was to kill himself. Sorry, no secrets. Cut. I've had that, though, for years. No one would go up to Barney: 'Hey, Barney, why did Ian do the old . . .' But for me: 'Oh, you're not close enough to care, but you're close enough to know the secret.' Anyhow, there's no secret.

Paul Morley: I think suicide ultimately will find a way. Oddly, in full view of us all, he could hide himself, peculiarly, so it was the best set of circumstances for someone who will inevitably do it. He was sending us messages, very literal messages about his state. His life was in turmoil, people knew that. There were undoubtedly conversations internally about the pressure he was under. He'd tried it, and it's easy now to say, 'Well, we must have known. How come we didn't?'

But he would have found a way, either in full view of everyone and yet hidden, or later, or in America, or when it had quietened down. I think in the end the suicide has that sense of destiny, and certainly once you start to try it, you get a taste for it. My father tried it, you see, my father tried it a few times. He clearly got a taste for it, a weird glamour, I think, a weird way of becoming a murderer. All of that would have played into Ian's mind.

There is a sense of you could become something, and the weird idea that you could be a self-murderer, you could enter the territory of Dostoevsky and Kafka and you could make that grand move. My father was a fairly ordinary bloke in one sense, but there's no doubt that once you're thinking on those levels, that must play into it a little bit to make that move, to make that moment, to know, and in one sense the vastness of America coming up might have been a big contributing factor.

It's such a soap opera, such a sitcom, such a tragedy that we all try and say, 'Well, how come Wilson' – because obviously he becomes our metaphor for blame – 'how come Wilson didn't sort that one out?' But how could he have sorted it out? Or Gretton, the managers that were around that were organising the situation but didn't want to deal with the reality? That's a northern thing: we quite like the glamorous kick but we don't want to deal with the reality. We just hope that sorts itself out.

It was anarchic, wasn't it? It wasn't a conventional set-up in any area whatsoever. Everybody was making it up as they went along, artistically, musically, and that was exciting, and all of us were getting a big kick out of that, the idea that something real was happening. There's definitely a northern element about that and there's a human element as well: you don't want to get too close to people even though the whole thing was about closeness, it was about intimacy, but that didn't necessarily mean that that would transfer into the way we dealt with each other.

Tony Wilson: The great thing about rock'n'roll is, far from being bullshit and hype and everything else, it is totally, totally honest: it's all about the song. Whatever you spend on a band, if you haven't got a great song you can spend £20 million and not make a penny. If you spend nothing and the band's got a few great songs, they're going to be successful. It's about great songs, and if there wasn't 'Transmission', if there wasn't 'Love Will Tear Us Apart', if there wasn't 'Atmosphere', we wouldn't be here.

It's just great songs. Yes, it's a fabulous story: the story of the rebuilding of a city that begins with them, the story of a tragic suicide, a moral story and a cultural, academic, intellectual, aesthetic story, but at the heart of it it's only here because they wrote great songs, and great songs never die.

Martin Hannett: The interesting thing about Ian for me was that onstage he was totally possessed. It was me who said 'touched by the hand of God' to a Dutch magazine. He was one of those channels for the gestalt. A lightning conductor. He was the only one I bumped into in that period.

Paul Morley: When you ask the question, 'What's your favourite Joy Division song?' obviously you want a one-word answer, but I'm incapable of giving a one-word answer. You suddenly realise that Joy Division spins you off into quite a number of groups, as if they actually did have quite a long career.

I'd go to 'Transmission' instantly, because there was a hit single that wasn't even a hit single, but in a way was; and I'd go obviously to 'Atmosphere', because it seemed to be the iced-over lake that Ian strolled over to go to his doom, and yet is really, really exciting to listen to, you're not weighed under the horror of it; and 'Love Will Tear Us Apart', because there was another great single; and then 'Isolation'. It's very hard, because the snob that I was cannot possibly answer 'Love Will Tear Us Apart', because it's too corny.

But there is a world where that's the answer, not least because of the way that it's entered the canon and has now become possibly one of the greatest songs written in the twentieth century. It can take multiple interpretations and constantly releases meaning. You think you can't possibly re-release meaning, but it does because it was an extraordinary piece of writing: just the words, let alone the fact that somehow these young northerners managed to find a way to sonically piece together music that matched the quality of the words.

Bernard Sumner: We were making it up as we were going along, and we had a great sense of discovery in the music and in what we were doing. We were like, 'Oh look, you can do this. Hey, here's another chord, what is it?' – 'It's a D chord, isn't that fantastic? Yeah, what can we do with that?' And I think that makes it fresh. I think the closer to perfection you get, the more boring you become, and we were quite far away from perfection but we were still quite tuneful. We didn't just make a racket, we had tunes, and anyone can make a racket, but to write strong melodies is a very difficult thing.

Peter Hook: There was never any question of not carrying on, because I think we were enjoying ourselves doing what we were doing so much, there was no question of not carrying on. We didn't know how we were going to carry on, and it was very, very difficult. There was no question of it – we were having a great time, Rob was having a great time, we were all enjoying being successful musicians – so we just had to carry on, and we wanted to find a way. I don't think Ian would have wanted us to stop.

I was glad to have Ian for as long as I did have him, and I think he left something behind that still moves people now: an amazing legacy that we created very much together, which is the beauty of Joy Division. The four of us didn't know what we were doing, and the chemistry was unbelievable, but talk to one of us and we didn't know. Maybe Ian might have known, but I suppose that's something we'll never find out. But it was easy, it was easy writing those songs and playing that well, it was easy, and it only got difficult when he died.

Bernard Sumner: That was tough. Ian would give us the direction. And he was very passionate at those moments, and we really missed that when he died. Suddenly, we didn't have any eyes. We had everything else, but we couldn't see where we were going.

We'd had a taste of the good life by then. By that I don't mean loads of dosh and the rest of it; I mean we enjoyed making music and the creativity and the freedom that it gave us, and we'd all given our jobs up and couldn't go back to them. We all had responsibilities, girlfriends, and we needed somewhere to live and some way of earning money, but then it was, 'How do we follow in the shadow of a group like Joy Division, when they made such a big impact? How do we carry on?'

So I don't think there was any question that we didn't want to work together, the three of us: 'Right, well, Ian's gone, and I don't want to work with them two.' That was never the case; we always knew that we'd carry on, but it was a question of how. We weren't a contrived band, we'd done everything by instinct, we never had a plan for anything, so it was like, 'How do we reinvent ourselves?' It's not just going to happen, is it?

Stephen Morris: Why did we decide to carry on? Well, we just carried on, we never even thought, 'Should we carry on or not carry on?' We went to the funeral, we went to the wake at Palatine Road, so 'Monday, see you on Monday then,' that was it. To this day we've never really sat down and said, 'Well, we're going to do this and we're going to this and we're going to do that.' You just start and do it and hope for the best, because that's the way we are.

A Note on Sources

The great bulk of the interviews were done by Jon Savage and Grant Gee during the production of the Brown Owl Films documentary *Joy Division*, in autumn 2016. In order of appearance:

Bernard Sumner (two interviews)
Peter Hook (two interviews)
Stephen Morris
Tony Wilson (two interviews)
C. P. Lee
Peter Saville
Paul Morley
Liz Naylor
Terry Mason
Pete Shelley
Iain Gray
Alan Hempsall
Richard Boon
Kevin Cummins
Jeremy Kerr
Bob Dickinson
Richard Searling
Lesley Gilbert
Richard Kirk
Malcolm Whitehead

Jon Wozencroft
Lindsay Reade
Annik Honoré
Anton Corbijn

These are supplemented by interviews done by Jon Savage in preparation for the Joy Division article published in *Mojo*, issue 8, July 1994, for which interviewees included Bernard Sumner, Peter Hook, Stephen Morris and Gillian Gilbert, Tony Wilson and Deborah Curtis. Martin Hannett, Peter Hook and Tony Wilson were also interviewed in 1989, during the preparation of *England's Dreaming*.

Supplementary interviews with Mark Reeder, Kevin Cummins, Daniel Meadows, Jill Furmanovsky, Dave Simpson and Dylan Jones were conducted in 2018. Michael Butterworth was contacted during the research for a *Guardian* article on Ian Curtis's reading, published as 'Controlled Chaos' in May 2008.

ACKNOWLEDGEMENTS

Thanks must go first to the producers of *Joy Division*, Tom Astor and Tom Atencio of Brown Owl Films, for allowing use of their copyright material. Then to my publisher Lee Brackstone. I would also like to thank the following for their help and support during the book's preparation: Rebecca Boulton, Grant Gee, C. P. Lee, Mark Reeder, Alan Hempsall, Bob Dickinson, Lesley Gilbert, Linder Sterling, Jon Wozencroft, Mary Harron, Daniel Meadows and Dylan Jones. Thanks also to Marc Issue Robinson for tape transcription. For their friendship and support: Paul Savill, Johnny Marr, Neil Spencer, Chris Jennings, Ian Davies, Ben Thompson and Paul Fletcher.

A special mention must go to Mark Price at Joy Division Central – joydiv.org – who has been unfailingly helpful in answering enquiries, whether obvious or arcane. Please visit the site for a comprehensive overview of Joy Division's activities between 1977 and 1980.

Finally, thanks to Joy Division, who were and will always be:

Ian Curtis
Peter Hook
Stephen Morris
Bernard Sumner